THE FBI Wife

A MEMOIR

SANDRA WINDSOR

abbott press

Abbott Press books may be ordered through booksellers or by contacting:

Abbott Press
1663 Liberty Drive
Bloomington, IN 47403
www.abbottpress.com
Phone: 1 (866) 697-5310

ISBN: 978-1-4582-1985-5 (sc)
ISBN: 978-1-4582-1986-2 (hc)
ISBN: 978-1-4582-1987-9 (e)

Library of Congress Control Number: 2016900371

Print information available on the last page.

Abbott Press rev. date: 02/15/2016

Dedicated to:

Tamara, Raymond, William and Scott

Part One

I feel a change comin' on
And the fourth part of the day's already gone.
Bob Dylan

Delaware 1963

ONE

Dear Mr. Hoover

She was a faded yellow, one-story house on a huge weed filled lot backing to a busy street, not my ideal 1920's two-story with a white picket fence, but with some flowers in the vacant window boxes, paint on the peeling shutters and, yes, a bright new coat of paint on the front door, she would do. Temporarily. Once Cliff got settled in his new corporate job, we would most likely upgrade from this rental. But for now I could acknowledge her as my home.

In celebration of our recent move, I set the table for dinner, not my dream dinner because the wedding china and silver were still packed in one of the many moving cartons crowding the living room of our latest rented house. I had cleared the flimsy, scarred kitchen table pretending with its linen tablecloth to be seating for a family celebration. I looked at the final setting and liked what I saw: four place settings, two of plastic for my toddlers, candles I'd retrieved from the box with the dishes. Yes, we would have many of these family celebrations. Cliff had accepted a great job with my dad's company. We would settle. Life would be good.

I heard the car pull into the cul de sac, then the door slam and finally footsteps to my scratched and dented front door.

I watched him walk toward me and the open door, fatigue in his step, tie loosened and jacket slung over his shoulder. I smiled as I met him with my arms extended for a hug that somehow fell apart. I leaned forward for the kiss that brushed my lips.

I told myself he just needed a little time to adjust to yet another new job. After five moves in five years for two teaching/coaching jobs and a military assignment, we were back home in Newark, Delaware where for the first time in our short marriage, I could plan dinner and feel I was playing a role in a 50's June Cleaver segment where Mommy dresses each afternoon in preparation for Daddy's return from a job he loves.

Tonight, instead of a snappy greeting for the kids, he waved at them where they sat atop our unpacked boxes. I offered to take his jacket, but he held it as if it were somehow an important possession. I watched this strangeness move down the hallway where he acknowledged his day had been okay. But my self-confident, positive husband hadn't walked in the door. Someone else had.

Something was up, and it probably had something to do with me. Had I been too excited about being back in Delaware? Did he feel he'd been coerced into this new job? Something.

"Are you up for coffee?"

His "no, thanks" came slowly, almost as an afterthought, so I poured myself a cup and snuggled close beside him on the recently cleared brown plush sofa, only to feel him adjust his body sideways, making a correction, or was it a statement? With more distance between us, he moved slightly to the side to face me. His wrinkled brow suggested he'd rather avoid whatever this conversation was going to be. He opened his hands in front of him as if I would find meaning in his gesture. I sipped my coffee and adjusted my angle so as to directly face him.

"I wrote a letter to J. Edgar Hoover."

There it was: no warning, no discussion, no sharing until this announcement. Was I just an extra in this play called marriage?

"I've been thinking all day about how to say this because I knew you were going to be upset." His stare expected some reaction.

"Upset? You're right! I am upset. At least I think so. A letter?"

"Listen, honey, I know you're happy right now, but this sales job isn't going to work. It's boring and uninteresting. I can't do this the rest of my life." He turned his hands, palms up as if to say, "that's it." "Besides, it doesn't feel right working for your dad."

"You don't even know anything about this job yet." I could feel my dinner churn in my stomach as I scanned his face, the set of his mouth for indication I'd heard him wrong. "Give it time. You haven't been in it a month."

"Time in this job isn't going to change anything. This isn't the life for me. I know it. There has to be something else."

"But it is for me," I said as I moved closer to make a connection with his rigidity. "Look at me. This is the kind of life I want. We've been moving around from pillar to post for the last five years trying to find the perfect job for you. Now you tell me it isn't this one either? What else is there we haven't considered?" I willed the tears to stay in their hidden places.

"I know you like this life; you've told me that since we got here."

"What's wrong with my wanting this kind of life? We have a nice income, benefits, and you're home regularly. Is all that so bad?" I blinked at the wetness and took a breath.

"There's nothing wrong with the life. It's the job I don't want. I have to be doing something that makes a difference for people, like teaching or coaching but not those." He paused. No, he had already tried those.

"That's why I wrote the letter." He lowered his gaze with this announcement.

"I don't know what this is all about, but I'm your wife, and we have two small children. I'm sorry you're bored, but from where I'm sitting things look pretty good." I turned my head to meet his gaze, which wasn't directed toward me at all but at a distance across the chaos of our room.

He turned to stare at me directly as if he could brain dump the contents of his mind into mine. "I've always been curious about the FBI so I went to the top with my letter. I didn't really expect a reply...."

"So you wrote a letter to J. Edgar Hoover? The J. Edgar? You've always been interested? Why didn't I know any of this? Is there anything else I should know?" My hands involuntarily flew to my face. "Why didn't we even talk about this?"

I listened to my words as they tumbled unsolicited from my mouth. Did they sound as desperate as I felt? I wriggled my way to the opposite end of the couch for a change of perspective and picked up my nearly empty coffee cup for comfort. My hands needed something to do. I looked down at my fingers wrapped around the curve of the cup and turned them to feel anew the radiating warmth. I looked at this man, my partner, the one with whom I thought we would always share everything. Now, I felt solo. I saw concern in the wrinkles of his brow so familiar to me when he was under pressure.

Of all the words I might have expected that evening, these weren't even a consideration. That he wanted a divorce, that he was going back into the military, that he was....? I set my cup down and stared across my cardboard table to this stranger with the odd expression.

"Look, I should've told you, but I never expected to get an answer. Then, today I got a phone call from the Baltimore Special Agent in Charge." His chin dropped slightly before the next sentence blurted from his lips. "Mr. Hoover sent him a copy of my letter, and now they've invited me to meet with the Resident Agent in Wilmington. He also said...."

"Stop!" I raised my hand to halt any more words. Silence slithered like an ominous cloud across the box-filled warehouse of a living room. "This is insane. You think I want to be married to some G-Man or whatever they're called?" I stared at this husband turned stranger and thought of Eliot Ness, made famous in TV's *Untouchables*. Surely Ness didn't have a family; no family man would consider such a career. And why would the FBI want a man with a family?

"Look, I have an appointment to meet this agent tomorrow in Wilmington to find out more about this organization. It's just a meeting. It isn't even a remote possibility until we actually know something." He raised his hands in an action of resignation, turning his palms up as he twisted his wrists. I watched his non-verbal statement that he had to do this.

"What's happening to us?" I didn't expect an answer so I continued. "I don't want to be part of the FBI; you just need to know that. I read the papers, see the 'Wanted' posters in the post office..." My hands, too, were speaking, wrapping themselves around one another. If I focused on them, maybe I could keep the tears at bay.

It wasn't the letter itself. It wasn't even the writing and mailing it. It was the secrecy involved as if I were somehow incapable of understanding my husband's obsession for finding his passion in the workplace. I might never have known about it except for the Bureau's reply.

I stood up from the couch, walked into the tidy kitchen and refilled my coffee cup. I resisted the allure of the road behind the house. Fight or flight? My preference at the moment was to run. I knew I wouldn't. But I did seize the opportunity to grab my jacket from the closet as I bolted out the front door to some place away from the chaos my life had become.

I walked briskly around my small cul-de-sac until behind me I heard his footsteps; not a clop, not a shuffle but a firm even step confirming his assuredness.

"I'm sorry about the letter. I was wrong. I was just afraid talking about it was premature and that it was another pipe dream that wouldn't materialize. This whole FBI thing," he said, "I just didn't know how you'd take it. Or maybe I did." He reached for my hand, the one that was in my pocket, the one whose fingers curled around my Kleenex, the one whose fingers clenched more tightly. I thought of many things I wanted to say, but nothing seemed right.

That was it, wasn't it? He hadn't told me.

T W O

Another Beginning

It was just a form. That's what I told myself each afternoon as I typed content onto the endless pages of the application form. The meeting with the agent had gone well, and Cliff had come home with a fat application packet. I agreed to help him as long as we both knew I had reservations about this new career direction. Perhaps while this process was going forward, a better idea would surface, or maybe he would even decide Delaware was pretty nice and he could stay in his present job, or we could both look for teaching positions. Maybe all or none of this could happen.

Evening conversations on the brown couch became our board meetings, the chance at the end of the day to check in with each other. Seated side by side, working together, felt like a relationship renewal. It was just an application that we didn't necessarily agree on, but we were earnestly talking. Actually mailing this thing would be another matter. Of course, if Cliff were accepted, he could always say no.

Who was I kidding?

Checked, double checked, and signed, I mailed the application packet. Then one afternoon a few weeks later I saw the postman across the cul-de-sac.

"Gary, anything for me besides bills?" I extended my hand like a kid waiting for Santa's treat.

"Might be something here in this brownish envelope. Looks like government." He handed over a slim packet of envelopes. A letter from Mom, a few bills and this ugly yellowish tan oversized envelope addressed to Cliff. It could be. Yes, it could be what we'd been waiting for.

The children were napping. No one would know. Well, he would when he saw the ripped seal. No, this was addressed to Cliff. I wouldn't want him opening my mail. But then I had a vested interest in the contents of this envelope. Hadn't I typed this damned thing?

Suddenly, I didn't care who this was addressed to. The envelope and I went to the kitchen for a knife. Only momentarily did I think about putting it in the stack with the other mail. Only momentarily.

As Cliff opened the door some hours later, expecting his usual greeting, I stepped into the entryway with my outstretched hand, shakily extending the government envelope bearing the inexpert scars of a kitchen knife.

"Here it is. It isn't over. I couldn't stand to just look at it so I opened it."

Cliff's face with dark circles cradling his eyes and frown lines etching his forehead, told me this had not been a good day.

"Do I want to know what it says?" He slid his coat over the arm of the chair, extending his hand as if he feared another in this week's disappointments.

"I think so," I said, handing over the envelope. "Look, it says everything's in order. You have been selected for the training academy at Quantico."

I watched as he slipped open the un-taped flap exposing the contents, half-smiling as he read the brief notice. He shook his head in disbelief while I smiled. It felt good to see Cliff smile.

What did I want? Truthfulness and respect in our relationship from a man who loved me. This train we were about to board would be a drastic change for us, one I wasn't yet sure about.

It was settled. I knew it. We were about to become an FBI family. Training at Quantico and the interview with Hoover were all that remained. Pack up the house, contract with the movers, get airplane tickets and for two months move in with my parents in Michigan. This is where the children and I would wait.

In celebration of our summer stay with them, Dad decided to take a week off from his duties as president of Motor Wheel Corporation, and spend it with us at "The Dome," their summer home on Lake Michigan.

I could smell the warm, inviting aroma of Lake Michigan and the hot sun in the air before we actually turned onto the one-lane trail leading to a distinctively rounded igloo shaped dwelling. The driveway, newly blocked by the dunes which had shifted since Mom and Dad's last visit, brought our journey to a halt as we tumbled from the car to inspect how much sand we would need to shovel to get to the house. Tami and Ray's running, jumping and rolling down the dunes reduced the volume or at least spread the sand in new directions.

I hadn't been here for a while, long enough to have almost forgotten its effect. It wasn't the house or the fun foosball table and player piano inside. It was the sweeping vista, the caramel colored sand flat against the blue-gray water, as if to defy it to come closer on shore, then rising cliff-like straight up to a plateau where some courageous person like my dad might construct a refuge. Stretching for miles, the sand and wind danced with the lake's waves as if to remind me that nothing stays the same.

I needed to be here, to be quiet, to listen. And I did.

Hours and days passed in a rhythm luring me to the warm sand, covering my feet and swishing my hands at my sides, I watched the wind take the clouds across the water, maybe to Ontario, and felt myself attach to them, allowing their drift to take me without resistance. Now if only I could remember this feeling of releasing to these clouds. If I could carry this with me…

In the middle of one of these reveries, Dad joined me on the beach to build a sand castle with Tami and Ray. We were in need of an engineer as our structure was lacking balance and stability, slightly listing to one side.

"Hi, honey, isn't this beautiful? Mom and I should come up here more often."

"I love it here, Dad. I'm so glad the kids and I could come. I needed this time away. Besides, I get to spend time with you and Mom." My hands played over the roof of our latest sand creation, smoothing the wrinkles.

"Honey, I'm happy about your new direction. Cliff seems excited about his future with this organization. It's a good job: good pay, good benefits." Dad was my mentor and my hero. I understood his message: "this is a good opportunity; make it work."

Returning to my parents' home in Lansing, I sat in my mother's sunlit kitchen enjoying a second cup of coffee while I waited for Tami and Ray to get up. During these weeks together, Mom and I were best friends sharing this special time together. Each day brought a renewed closeness. Frequent excursions to Potter Park Zoo, Bancroft Park, a shopping excursion for the latest in fashions and maybe even a few bargains. Each day brought a memory in the making, even if it were just helping Mom tend her flower garden or prepare the evening dinner followed by grandpa's arrival from work to take the children to the carousel at the local shopping mall. I was living the June Cleaver life, and I loved it; this was the kind of life I wanted: settled, stable, shared.

Leaf raking would soon be in order as I watched a few yellow shapes cascade from above. The phone rang. This early call could be news of our assignment. This train I had hesitantly boarded was headed where?

"Well, it's a place we've never lived. We're on our way to Houston."

"Hmm… Texas." I heard a voice reply without emotion. "Well, whether we like it or not, at least it's only a year or so."

"Two other agents from my class are also being sent to Houston, so we'll already know some people there," Cliff answered reassuringly.

"That's good." It was going to be good, wasn't it?

In planning the details of the move, I learned that while the FBI professed to take care of all expenses, they really only covered Cliff's travel and the transportation of his personal belongings. Under Director Hoover, a family was superfluous. The saying was if the Bureau had wanted an agent to have a family, it would have issued him one.

Down to the last day of waiting, I watched as Cliff and our brown station wagon entered the circle drive. After three months we were together, about to actually board the train for our new life. Well, not really. We still had to make everything fit into our station wagon.

On that memorable sunny Sunday morning of our departure we tried to play normal. Pack up the few remaining clothes and toys and stuff them in a crevice somewhere amid my dad's carefully engineered packing. Cliff and Dad had designed a play space for Tami and Ray, a quasi fort behind the front seat, somewhat safe and padded in this pre-seat belt, no child restraint era.

Waiting to board my seat in the vehicle heading south, I buried my head in my mother's neck smelling her sweetness and cried unashamedly.

"I love you, Mom."

Tears streaming, I looked over at Dad. He flashed me a smile to say he knew I was going to do great. He took my hand; I knew a roll of cash would be in it. Just in case.

Part Two

Anticipation was luring us forward with expectations of a life somewhere in between what we had dreamed and what we had left behind.

Houston
1963-1964

THREE

Expectations

The road rolling before me undulated like my own emotions. One-hundred miles of silence as the tires of our brown station wagon marked the distance from my parents' Michigan home.

I looked over at my husband whose intentional focus on the stretch before him suggested he'd like to be left in that state. As Tami and Ray napped in their little cave behind me, I took off my shoes and curled up in my seat, content for the moment to be in my own reverie. Could it be that only six months had passed since Cliff had decided to pursue a career with the FBI? I closed my eyes and pictured us in our next house on Mobud Street, the one Cliff had leased upon the recommendation of another agent in the Houston office. While I hadn't yet seen my latest in a series of houses, I pictured the three bedrooms, their sizes and colors and what I might do to personalize them. I daydreamed we were settled enough to cook meals and sleep in hastily made beds, and other agent families had arrived to show us the ropes. The tires rolled on, lulling me with their soft whine. No music or jabbering, just thoughtfulness and silence I wished were interrupted by conversation.

I opened my eyes to see if I had moved backwards or forwards in my dream state. Tami and Ray were still snoozing, curled up together like two little puppies. Cliff reached over and took my hand.

"You had a little rest, but you were kind of noisy, mumbling something."

"Did I say anything interesting?"

"Something about never moving again."

"Sounds like a possible wish. I wonder when we will stop moving."

15

"Our second office should be longer, maybe up to five years. Some people even manage to stay in their second office their entire career."

"I can't imagine that'll be us," I said. "You know, I was just thinking about your time in Quantico. You haven't told me much about it except you ended up first in your class. Wanna' fill me in?" I nudged his leg with my curled up foot as if to awaken a response.

"Quantico was good; mostly law classes, firearms training and procedural stuff we'll need to know in the field." His right hand left the steering wheel as if to dismiss the whole Quantico experience.

"Hmm, what about the life for us as a family? Is it true we can't tell people who you work for? Suppose I slip and tell my neighbor friend. Could I innocently put your job in jeopardy?"

"We can tell people I work for the government or the Department of Justice. It's the Director's policy that we remain anonymous so that's the way it is." I looked at him for signs of annoyance with either me or this Bureau policy.

"How about the actual work? What do you think this assignment is going to be like? Since it's just your first office, you won't be working real cases, will you?"

Moving sideways in my seat, inching closer, I tried to read something in his posture. No clues; just a tanned, relaxed man mostly focused on a rolling road framed by farmers' fields.

"They told us this first office assignment will be mostly training and working with senior agents on various desks in order to get broad experience. I don't know about specific cases." He flipped his hand, palm up, from the steering wheel in dismissal. A hint I didn't take.

"Helping other agents do what?" I sensed I was pushing the limits with these questions.

"I don't know what I'll be helping them with, but it won't be dangerous. Listen, I'm telling you all I know, which, at this point, isn't much. And I've already told you that when agents are called in on a case, the Bureau has so much information about the case that there are no surprises. So if you're still worrying about the danger part of this, stop!"

Sure.

Maybe that's why they wore business suits and a shoulder holster instead of a uniform and visible firearm. Since he was dressed like a businessman, I could pretend he did this investigating from the comforts of an FBI office. He couldn't tell me what really went on during his day so I could draw my own conclusions, couldn't I?

In between my internal musings, I looked over to see if he were sending me any reassurances. I wasn't looking for guarantees; well, maybe I was.

Our 1,200 mile journey brought us to our new "home," a blue/gray contemporary rancher on a corner lot with a large fenced yard perfect for the kids. Cliff pulled our filthy brown station wagon into the driveway on the carport side of the house. Relieved to be out of the car and anxious to see if my new house was anything like my expectations, I walked through the carport past the laundry/mud room and into the kitchen. With its galley design, it wouldn't be a gathering place; that would have to happen in the dining room, an extension of the living room. The house wasn't large, but it had enough storage space for our empty boxes and those I would choose to leave packed up. Carefully storing our empties was important since we would have to pay for new ones on the next move if we discarded these. Besides, these were my friends, the decorated curators of all the Brownings' treasures.

I savored these minutes with my new house. A few flowers and maybe a small garden next spring would make her more beautiful.

According to our neighbors, Red Adair, the world famous oil field fire fighter, actually owned our residence. From them we soon heard many stories of Red's dangerous escapades fighting fires all over the world. We were living in Red's house, but it would soon sport a unique front door, that signature touch it needed to make the house feel like mine.

"Here it comes!" Tami's voice carried down the street as the yellow Mayflower moving van arrived only thirty minutes off schedule. I stood with the front door propped open and watched Cliff and the kids' expectations as if this very large truck contained more than what it had picked up in Delaware. This was the magical part of the move, the reuniting, reconnecting with one's life, those packaged memories that would make this our home. The expectation—that was it.

Moving day is an emotional one for any neighborhood: someone's life is changing. Today, it was ours. With our van's arrival, children of every size converged on our front lawn to check us out, chattering, introducing themselves and offering to help. Mothers of these newfound helpers soon appeared to scope out the new family, and we were on our way to becoming part of this collection of families called a neighborhood. By the end of the day we had connected names with faces and houses. Mary Ann, who lived next door, was retired, an anomaly on this kid-filled street. Brady and Carol belonged to Sylvia just three doors east of us. Over the next year we would wear a path between our house and theirs. I was happy. These were my new connections.

Unpacking was like Christmas morning. As we began to open the boxes, the house looked like a site for make-believe everything: packing paper mixed with Tonka trucks, newspaper shredded as it rolled from dolls awakening from a long nap. Would I ever restore order? Sure.

"Hey kids, wanna' do something fun? I need help. We need a color for our front door." They knew the routine from the last house. This is how we connected with each new neighborhood.

"Yea! We get to paint the door! I know what color I want, Tami cried."

Jumping up and down, they piled into the station wagon, talking as only preschoolers can about the merits of colors. Off to consider paint chips at the hardware store, not just any color, but the one just right for our first FBI front door.

"What about blue? No, maybe green." The suggestions, some wild, flowed from my two experts. They pointed and I pulled the color swatches from the racks to find just the right hue. I ruled out green as that was the door color we had selected for the last house.

"Hey, how about a happy-face color: yellow." Yes, a sunshine yellow. Not yucky yellow green or faded yellow orange. No, it needed to be "happy face" yellow. All smiles and armed with our quart of just the right paint, we headed home.

We could now tell people we lived in the house with the happy yellow front door, our statement to our new neighborhood and FBI friends.

Three other FBI families lived in our Sharpstown neighborhood. The Woodsons, who had arrived just a couple of weeks ahead of us, were the first to invite us over. Cliff and Joe were in the same carpool so Cliff had already met Joe's family. As we pulled up to their house, a replica of ours except for the exterior color, Cliff commented that I'd really like these people. *Good. I was ready for new people in my life.*

Marianne, the Woodsons' tall, gangly ten-year-old daughter, met us at the door and immediately took Tami by the hand and led her inside. Her little brother, just a year older than Ray, shyly followed behind. Moving toward the patio voices, Cliff and I were soon greeted by a man and woman about our age who met us with hugs and beer. I'm not sure what I expected an agent to look like, but here was another one, and he didn't look like Cliff.

Joe's wife, Adrian, took me by the arm and led me outside where we could both watch the kids and talk. She was tall and slim with reddish hair and a subdued air about her: not bashful but more quietly confident.

"Well, here we are," she said. I don't know how you got here, but Joe applied for the Bureau as soon as he finished law school."

"No, we didn't take that route. Cliff took the law test instead." I looked at her somewhat puzzled. "Why, as an attorney, did Joe decide to join the Bureau?" For the first time I wondered how Cliff felt about not being an attorney.

"I don't really know except he thought he would like the investigative part of the Bureau. And he makes the decisions about his employment."

"I know about that. Cliff's already talking about opportunities he might have in the future. It seems we won't be here long. At least next office we may have a longer stay."

Our afternoon with the Woodsons was lovely. I knew my friendship with Adrian would blossom. Cliff didn't need a friend; he had a job he was in love with.

"You know, we can have a terrific life with this organization," he said on the way home. "We're already bringing in twice as much money as I did with teaching. And with the Bureau pay scale we'll be looking at regular pay raises plus the benefits are outstanding: health insurance, a month of vacation per year, life insurance. Honey, this is going to be a great life for us."

I smiled.

What he shared with me specifically about his day to day was limited, but for now I felt more secure not knowing. This way I could keep up the pretense that this job was much like a corporate position.

Except for the night when Cliff was out with Joe on a lead, and I received my first call from the dispatcher. She called to tell me she had heard from Cliff by radio, and he would be late. They had run into a small problem. I was to call Adrian. What kind of a problem? Car problem? Crook problem? I asked but dispatch had no answer.

Immediately, I called Adrian, the fearless woman who believed what she heard and nothing more. Her imagination stopped with the facts. Mine didn't. I looked around my living room and saw shadows made by the drapes as looming figures and heard noises coming from the carport that couldn't be described as wind.

I was figuring out, without much help from anyone, that this would never be a nine-to-five job. It already seemed criminal activity increased at night. Seasoned wives told me the next office would be different. How different? They shrugged and suggested "just different." Cliff and I had agreed, prior to the move, that we were going to see and experience as much as possible while we were here. A warm Saturday in October was just right for a starting point.

"Hey, who wants to go to the zoo?"

"I do, Daddy," Tami said. "Me too," Ray echoed.

"Okay, let's help Mommy pack a lunch," I said. "You both need shoes and maybe a sweater." We were a family going on an outing, just like any young family.

"Here we go. Elephants first? Okay, let me look at the map. I see them, they're not very far." I looked into the excited eyes of my children and recalled my own days at Potter Park Zoo in Lansing. It was pretty small, and I remembered the scary bear cages as Cliff looked at his watch and at the map.

"Why don't you and the kids go to the elephants, and I'll catch up with you. I need to call in to the office." He nodded, and I nodded. Tami, Ray and I walked away. Checking in with the office meant locating a pay phone, placing the call and waiting for instructions, which might mean to report somewhere or nowhere. Yes, he had told me about this requirement, but it hadn't yet registered.

"Come on, Daddy," Tami said.

"In a minute. I'll catch up with you. I have to call the office."

"Brady's dad doesn't have to call," Tami whined.

"Well, Daddy has an important job so he has to call in." Secretly I wondered if we would ever be able to go anywhere without the Bureau's permission. During this phase of my training as an FBI wife, I never knew if a Saturday or Sunday would ever be free. This was part of the job.

"We're good, "Cliff said. "We have at least another two hours before I need to check in again."

I wasn't learning this routine very fast. It seemed like the kids and I were often getting stuck somewhere, feeling like an anchor my husband was dragging along. I hated this waiting beside some phone booth, trying to keep an eye on two less than patient children. By the time he finished with the office, I was ready to go home. Over time I would learn that it was less disappointing if we made plans that didn't include Daddy. That way if he could be available to his family, it was an extra special event.

FBI Wife 101 course was underway. I wasn't sure I was making superior grades, but I was still on this train with Cliff. He was laboring to demonstrate why he had been first in his class at Quantico, and I was observing and listening so as not to be an impediment to his success. I was an eavesdropper, my most important source of information. That's how I knew whom he was working with and on what kinds of cases. Forget Hoover's rule about not sharing information with the wife.

I talked with other wives, and we shared ideas of how we saw our role. A few saw the role as a passive one, disconnected. Others, like me, wanted to be part of their husbands' lives personally and professionally while retaining their own personal identities. How much of me belonged to the Bureau? Was there a danger this organization could creep in and usurp my very identity? Or would it change our relationship into a love triangle? Two months into this experience, I could really offer no definitions or predictions, but then two months isn't very long.

On one of those evenings when life as an FBI family seemed almost normal with Dad home early, nice dinner, kid play and baths in a typical routine, Cliff and I settled onto the familiar brown couch.

"So tell me, Mr. G-Man, after a couple of months, is this the job you thought it would be?" I was taking the room temperature. Should I finish unpacking all of the boxes?

"It's about what I thought it would be. I've got a lot to learn, and I'm sure by the time I get to my next assignment, I'll have more of it figured out. It probably would be easier if I were an attorney; it's really more legal stuff than anything else."

"So maybe I was right; you should have gone to law school." Maybe that was still a possibility. "I don't know about this life yet," I said. "It sounds like this office may be an anomaly. I keep hearing I'll really learn about the FBI life in the next office. The next office; is it all about the next office?"

"Yeah, I guess so. It seems like you talk to the other wives though."

"I do, but even the women who've been here a few years just speak in generalities, like don't get a divorce, don't get involved in suspect organizations, but most of all, don't embarrass the Bureau." My husband's face broke into a smile at my uttering the FBI standard.

As he rose to get a coffee refill in the kitchen, he squeezed my knee in passing, signaling he understood but didn't have answers, he was ready for a new topic, or this special connection was ending.

FOUR

Anticipation

A moment of anticipation like that time when I so desperately dreamed of a date for prom; that moment when I stood at the entrance to the church, on my father's arm, staring down the aisle at my husband to be; anticipating the arrival of my first child with all the promise and responsibility of becoming a mother. Those moments when time stood still because I was unable to take another breath, afraid if I did, the moment would vanish.

A similar moment of anticipation occurred for me November 21, 1963. Actually, it was Wednesday the 20th when I awoke early, threw on my ratty grey Delaware sweatshirt, my morning uniform, and padded to the kitchen to turn on my very smart new coffee pot. Waiting for the pot to brew and savoring the smell that only brewing coffee emits, I stood at the kitchen window staring out in a day-dreamy state. Cliff had already left for the office, and the children were not yet awake; these moments were mine to think in the quiet of the cool morning hours. Our November weather was a nice reprieve from the early fall heat.

I filled my cup with the dark roasted liquid and padded to the front door. Yes, the yellow color had been a good choice. I unlocked both locks as well as the screen door and felt my bare feet hit the cool cement. "Good morning, world." I looked down my quiet street as I sipped my coffee and thought about what I might have planned for today. Maybe a play date with Sylvia's kids, for sure a trip to the grocery store. I could work on the curtains for Tami's room. I could finish reading my new book.

My reason for this journey to the front yard was the newspaper. Unfolding its pages to first scan the front page, I read of an experience that could be mine right here. President and Mrs. Kennedy were coming to Houston. Right here in my town, which meant I could go see them as they rode down our main street. It would be a hassle to get everyone ready, load the car and head to a viewing site along with thousands of others, but the other alternative was to forget it and miss the chance to be on the same street with Jackie, the one person I admired more than any contemporary woman. No, I couldn't miss it. She had made a connection with me during her husband's 1960 campaign. She was young, beautiful, educated and a mom. I loved her smile, her style, her poise. I wanted to look and act just like her. I had even purchased two pill box hats resembling hers, and my drawer was filled with many pairs of gloves. Ladies wore hats and gloves to lunch, to tea and to church. As young women, we didn't have to guess what was fashionable and appropriate: we had a model.

Cliff had already left for work so there was no possibility of sharing my excitement with him. But Adrian would understand so I took my paper inside and dialed her number.

"Hey, friend, know who's coming to town tomorrow?"

"My God, you're up early. No, I don't know who's coming to town. I don't even know where I'll be tomorrow." It's a really good friend you can call so early in the morning.

"Adrian, Jackie's coming to Houston tomorrow. There's going to be a motorcade from the airport to the Rice Hotel in the afternoon."

"That's pretty exciting. Are you going?" I knew she was already saying she would join me.

"Sure. Pick you up about 10:30. You make the lunch, and I'll fix snacks and stuff."

When Cliff had told me of our assignment to Houston, I never considered this possibility. Maybe I had underrated the opportunities here.

For President Kennedy it was an important trip politically. He was convinced he needed to make the trip to Texas, the home of his vice president, and he especially needed Jackie to accompany him, which she was not inclined to do especially since her son Patrick had died just two months previous. In the end she relented as it was to be a short trip with stops in San Antonio, here in Houston and on the Dallas.

Their reason for the visit was immaterial to me. I had voted for Kennedy, but Jackie was the primary reason for my Democratic vote. On the campaign trail she looked directly at me, a young mom, nine years her junior, entranced by her classic sense of style and demeanor. Jackie was everything I aspired to be: I wanted to look like her, act like her, decorate like her, carry myself with her same self-assurance. If I could only be just like her, I would…

Not long after she moved into the White House, she announced to the nation that she would be redecorating the "people's house." She wasn't merely redecorating; she was restoring the house to a splendor and richness it had once enjoyed. She researched the archives and found treasures for respective rooms. When completed, in her soft-spoken, cultured voice she took us by the hand through each room via television. I watched awe-struck as she inspired me to bring my little rooms to life.

My excitement overcame me. Cliff hardly had a chance to close the door.

"She's coming! I just might get to see her. Did you know the Kennedys were coming? I read it in the paper this morning…did you know about it?" Surely he must have.

"My God, slow down. I was just going to ask if you knew about the motorcade. I know the route from the airport to the Rice Hotel if…"

I watched as he slipped off his suit coat and walked to the bedroom now surrounded by two small bodies clinging to his legs asking to be carried on his shoulders. He was strong; he could carry this family.

"I've got news too. I just found out this afternoon that I've been assigned to the FBI team working with the Secret Service on the president's visit here. Actually, I may get to meet him tomorrow. At least, I'll be close to him." He went on to explain that this was standard protocol for protection when the president traveled to a city where the FBI had a Field Office. This was the first time Cliff would be working with the Secret Service, but it wouldn't be the last time. The Brownings would be busy on Thursday the 21st. Cliff felt honored to have been assigned to the detail, and I felt part of history. I glanced over at my husband, filled with admiration and a tad bit of envy. This was a pretty glamorous job he had, and he seemed so perfect for it. Maybe I had underestimated this whole career decision.

My smile confirmed my pride. What else was the FBI involved in? I didn't know they worked to protect the President. I saw Cliff looking at me with a slight smirk on his face. Had he guessed I kind of liked this part of the job?

If nothing else of significance happened during our tour in Houston, seeing Jackie in the motorcade would be enough.

In years to come, I would be able to remind Tami and Ray of the time in Houston when we went to watch the Kennedy parade.

I rose early, gathered and fed the children, packed up our station wagon, picked up Adrian and her children and took off for the motorcade course.

"How does this look? We're a ways from the main street, but we can walk." I pulled into an available space, delighted to be as close as we were. I filled the stroller with snacks, jackets, stuffed animals and other necessary treasures for the trek.

Adrian spotted a vacant grassy space between the sidewalk and the street. We were early so we claimed our territory and laid out our blankets for a place to enjoy lunch. We would have a little wait, but having a front row seat would be worth it.

I opened the lunch bag and offered each child a sandwich. Food always tempered tension. I looked at my new friend and hoped we would always be close.

"Thanks so much for coming with me, Adrian. It's so nice to be able to share an experience like this. I wonder what other excitement we'll have while we're here."

"I don't know, but I'm always game. Joe usually doesn't like to do stuff like this and was glad not to be working this detail. He doesn't even like to go shopping or to the movies. So it's usually the kids and me."

"I don't know that Cliff doesn't like to do this stuff, but he's working all the time, trying to build a reputation. He loves this job maybe more than anything else. Ironic that he and I are both in the same place today."

I had only been to one other motorcade in my life when I was in elementary school on a field trip with my class. General Eisenhower had come to Lansing where the city was turning out to celebrate his war victories. A child of the Second World War, I could only watch this motorcade and think of the service banners I had seen each morning on my walk to school commemorating those serving or already dead in the war. Dad's best friend, Howard Alexander, had been missing in Germany. Even with his whereabouts unknown, I continued to write him letters. Now as I sat on my blanket waiting for my second motorcade, I felt grateful this was a celebration of a different sort.

Light gray clouds formed above us, not threatening rain, just a soft covering protecting us from direct sun in the sixty-degree weather. I looked around at all the people. Did they all admire Jackie the way I did? Had they bought the coffee table book, a Kennedy pictorial? When I had ordered the book, Cliff had frowned. Neither he nor my father were enamored of the Kennedys, but I had a suspicion my mother was a Jackie lover.

Tami and Ray were getting tired of the wait. Now came the questions: "What is a president? Who is Jackie? Where are they? Is Daddy here? I want to see Daddy."

"Daddy's here somewhere; we just can't see him." I, too, wondered where he was and had been scouring the parade route for him.

"Listen, I hear something."

Faintly, to my left I felt the vibration of drumbeats and the 1-2-3-4 of marching feet, or were those horse hooves? My fellow celebrants rose and pushed closer to the street's pavement. I boosted Tami to stand on the stroller's seat while I simultaneously lifted Ray into my arms, and we, too, moved closer to the pavement, the marching feet mimicking my heart rate inching closer in time to the bands' rising volume. Already, I could feel the shivers moving down my arms; goosebumps in this weather? The crowd's voices rose like a swelling wave, moving toward me, mixing with the bands' loud announcements. I stretched taller, begging my eyes to see more than they could capture. I was ready.

Voices, hands waving, feet stomping, all to the beat of the next band. Cheers arose as the electricity roared down the line of bystanders, first faintly then louder until in front of us, the headlights of the lead car. Oh-this was really it. The Kennedys were coming. Ray was heavy in my arms and screaming in my ear following the lead of the people on either side of us. Tami's enthusiasm extended to clapping, baby-girl-like clapping. Shifting my weight and stretching to the left, I saw another set of lights preceded by men in dark suits: Secret Service. Maybe Cliff was here with me.

Hosting these lights inching toward us was the long off-white hood of the convertible limo the government had flown in from Washington. I yelled, "I love you, Jackie." Tears were inching their way down my cheeks, but no one seemed to notice. They were glued to the two before us, our President and First Lady, the closest we had to American royalty. I strained my eyes to capture all I could memorize as the limo stretched before us. I grabbed my children's hands and raised them, along with my own, in a broad wave stretching skyward. I looked at Tami and Ray wishing for a brain dump into their tiny memories so they would not lose this moment. I could feel the emotion welling from my chest into my throat triggering soft tears of pride and admiration. What if I had decided not to come today?

"Wait, slow down, stop," my inner voice pleaded. "I want to see you better. Do you look the same as your pictures? Jackie, what are you wearing? Oh, an off-white belted dress and that brimmed black hat perched on the back of your head making a statement of its own. Yes, you are stunning. What color are your shoes? Never mind, I'm sure they're perfect. I'm so glad you're riding in a convertible, one that matches your dress, so I can really see you. And your flowers, yellow roses instead of red. That's interesting."

In slow motion I memorized the scene before me, the confident faces and sincere smiles promising us our future was secure; everything would be all right. They both waved, making eye contact as the limo moved slowly past as if they, too, were reluctant to have this end. I moved my body to the right, straining until I could no longer see the taillights. Soon they would arrive at the Rice Hotel where they would be received by hundreds more admirers.

As I slowly packed up the kids and prepared to return to the car, I wondered what it must be like to be the First Family. Did any part of their lives resemble mine? Jackie was a government wife, like me; she had small children, like me; she loved fashion and the arts, like me; she was educated like me; and as I had hoped, she had a connection to her house, for her the White House. Was she ever afraid; did she see impending danger or only promise on the horizon?

Tired and hungry we were ready for Daddy's arrival home. As he removed his shoulder holster, I looked with pride and admiration at this strong, handsome man who was my husband. I loved him at these moments when I felt we truly did connect on some level.

"Well, how is my Jackie lover? Did you go to the motorcade?" He smiled at the reference to my favorite person.

"Yes. It was so great. I loved it. Thousands of other Kennedy lovers and me." I felt my hands rising, falling, extending in exuberant gestures. "Oh, I almost forgot," I said. "You were there too. I looked for you, but you must have been working another part of the route. How was it to be working with the Secret Service?"

"It was interesting, different from what I expected. I think working Bureau cases will be a better fit for me, though."

Cliff's travels to find his professional course had been trying, but he was convinced he had found it. I looked at him with one child in each arm and smiled. He returned the smile with one more teaser.

"It's pretty exciting to be right in the middle of history, isn't it? I'm betting we'll have lots more moments like this."

FIVE

Innocence Gone

Beware, nothing is safe forever, not even one's ideals. There are those moments when all we hold sacred is shattered by forces foreign to our understanding. We dig deep into our souls to discover the why of the moment, feeling more vulnerable than we have ever felt.

I awoke that Friday, November 22, 1963, with renewed optimism after my Thursday encounter with Camelot. Cliff had already left for work by the time the children and I awoke. No rush for us this morning. Over Rice Krispies we talked about what might be fun on a sunny, warm Friday with weather just right for exploring outside.

"Mommy, let's go to the zoo," Tami suggested. Ray echoed his sister.

"Okay. Why not?" This was always their choice, so gather up the doll, stuffed animal and the blankie and head out.

There are those days that are memorable for no really big reason. This particular Friday morning at the zoo with my two children was one of those. No demands, just my children. I pushed the empty stroller from exhibit to exhibit while Tami and Ray ran from one animal sighting to the next as we chattered about their favorite animal stories like *Babar, The Saggy, Baggy Elephant* and *Curious George.* Yesterday's motorcade had been an outing for me. Today's zoo trip was an outing for them. I loved my children, and I loved being their mom. Today I felt relaxed in myself and my environment. Maybe I was beginning to settle into the FBI routine. Cliff's schedule hadn't been too bad—so far he hadn't often been called out at night. And I was becoming comfortable with my house and my friends.

Was it possible I'd been wrong in my fears about this FBI decision? Too early to really tell though.

Happy, sticky and slightly sleepy, Tami and Ray climbed into the back seat for the return trip home, already arguing about who was to sit on which side and who was infringing on whose territory. Some music was in order, maybe something sing-a-long to keep them awake until we got home. I was already looking forward to their afternoon naptime, my special time. My new Book-of-the Month Club selection, *The Group* by Mary McCarthy, had arrived yesterday and was teasing me with its cover. This afternoon while the children napped, I would crack those pages, curl up on my comfy couch and dissolve into another world.

My favorite radio station filled the car with the Beach Boys' "Surfing USA," a happy upbeat song and we all sang along. Our loud discordant voices rang out as a finale to our unspoiled morning, only to be interrupted by a somber voice saying, "We interrupt this program for a special announcement."

"Hey, we were singing that song," I said. "Don't interrupt us." The kids laughed as I grabbed the volume knob to hear what must be an important announcement.

"Mommy, turn the music on."

"I can't, honey. They're telling us something. Just a minute, let me listen."

"Three shots were fired at President Kennedy's motorcade today in downtown Dallas."

Innocent faces looked up at me in the rear view mirror as I fought the reality of the news interruption. Fear and a terrible loss gripped my arms and hands as I looked at the cars around me. They must all be hearing what I was hearing. I must have screamed because Tami started to cry.

"It can't be. I just saw them yesterday," I whispered to myself.

"Mommy, what happened?" Tami's sad little face looked up into the mirror. Ray stood rigidly against the back seat as if unable to move. His mother was afraid.

"Honey, Mommy's okay." I looked at the traffic around me; it was as if the world had stopped. Mine had. Just yesterday I was the happiest young woman in Houston. Now, in a vapor, the promise was gone. Or was it? Maybe there were just shots.

The voice continued, "Shortly after 12:30 p.m., President John F. Kennedy was shot in Dallas' Dealey Plaza. Governor John Connelly has also been shot. No word yet on the President's condition." And that was it? Two men shot? What about Jackie?

I looked at my speedometer and realized I was holding up traffic in the center lane. I tried to loosen my fingers enough to safely turn into the slow lane. If only I could turn yesterday's beautiful memories with the Kennedys into today's reality. Yesterday Jackie and the President had waved at me, their smiles convincing me there was a place called Camelot. Yesterday was gone.

Concentrate on driving. Pretend you didn't hear the news, at least until you get home. It could be a huge mistake. The news isn't always right. And just because someone was shot at doesn't mean he's been shot and killed.

I needed to just get home where I could learn this announcement was all a mistake. Just like the 1938 radio enactment of H.G. Wells' "War of the Worlds" that sent people screaming from their homes in fear of attack by Martians who had reportedly landed in New England. It wasn't true, but people had believed it. This could be the same scenario. It had happened before.

Mulling these possibilities to myself, I gripped the steering wheel, demanding the car to stay the course.

Where was Cliff? Oh God, where was he? Yesterday he had worked the Presidential detail; yesterday he, too, could have been in the line of fire. Is he now on his way to Dallas? Maybe he's left a message at home. Maybe the dispatcher will call.

"We'll leave the radio off. There won't be any music for a while, kids. Besides, I'd better pay attention to my driving." Two bewildered faces nodded.

I could see our door as I rounded the corner onto our street. Today its yellow smiley face looked like an anachronism. I swung into the carport, grabbed the snack bag and stroller from the trunk and quickly ushered the children inside. The television's blank face invited me to confirm or deny the news out of Dallas. I resisted. There would be time once Tami and Ray were down for naps.

"How about a snack and a story before naps?" At almost three and a half, Tami wasn't convinced she needed a nap any longer, but I had a rule that we all rested in the afternoon. She didn't have to sleep; in fact, she could look through her books if she wanted to. Ray was still too young to argue.

Driven, almost robotically toward the TV, my fingers trembled as I pushed the "on" button and adjusted the volume to low. I softly padded around the rectangular coffee table as if trying to avoid rousing a tragedy.

There it was: an update. What I had heard on the radio hadn't been mis-reporting. Shortly after 1:00 p.m. CST it was official: the President was dead, the First Lady was covered in blood, the Governor was injured, and a great deal of other speculation as to who had done this unbelievable act and why....

I stared at the screen willing the announcers to say something was going to be okay. But the sour taste moving up into my throat told me this was the only news they had. I swallowed repeatedly to force my fear into that place where it needed to hide. My teary eyes blurred as I recalled the optimism of yesterday's motorcade with the hopeful music and Jackie so beautiful in her off-white dress. What couldn't happen in the US just did.

As I folded into the couch, numbness moved down my arms and legs. Is numbness a form of denial or a protection against something too painful to deal with? Like when my mother called me at the University of Delaware to tell me my grandpa was dead, the man I loved more than any other man in my life. Tom Shoulars was gentle and slim, with soft brown hair and brown eyes that sparkled with an inviting smile that said he loved me. I remember taking Mom's call and feeling all the energy in my body turn off. I flew to Michigan for the funeral and returned to school remembering nothing. I wasn't ready for him to leave my life. Now I felt that stupor-like state return. I wasn't ready for the Kennedys to leave my life either.

While being at the pulse of the country had felt wonderful at yesterday's motorcade, today it felt like being too close to the open fire and feeling the heat singe your arms. All gone, all promise extinguished by gunfire. I wasn't yet at why; I was still at what.

Where was Cliff? I needed to talk to him, to hear his voice. Surely, being on the inside, he would know something. At least he wasn't in Dallas. Or was he? As if in response, the ringing phone jangled me from my state of disbelief, and I hurried to the kitchen to catch it on the third ring.

"I've just got a minute. All hell's breaking loose. Are you okay?" I heard the tension and adrenalin rush in Cliff's staccato phrasing.

"No. How could I be okay? Where are you? Are you okay? I've been so worried."

"I'm fine. No casualties on the Bureau side. Don't worry about me."

Worry was my middle name; it was what kept me on the edge always examining options.

"Can you tell me anything? Or is it all secret? Who would do this?" Was this my voice I heard, the one disconnected as if someone had pushed the "no emotion" button?

"Honey, I don't know much yet except the Bureau is working every conceivable lead in Dallas. Look, it's going to be okay. We're going to find this person." His words were hesitant.

"No, it won't be okay. Kennedy's dead, and it won't ever be the same."

As my words tumbled out, I recognized I had connected with the heart of my sadness. There are times in your life that are benchmarks or milestones, when you refer to the time either before or after them. Like when you graduated, when you married, when your first child was born. These become mile markers in your life. Events happened before or after these. This day would become one of these for me.

"Well, at least you're here. Who knows who else is targeted and will be killed. Whoever shot Kennedy could be shooting FBI agents. I'm just not sure…"

"Look, I'm on my way home. They're sending me to Dallas. Can you pack me a bag?" His request blurted over the phone lines; if he hesitated it would be too hard to say.

"An overnight bag?" Barely able to breathe, I waited for his response.

"No, I could be gone longer than that. I don't know how an investigation like this works." And who would? This was the first assassination since the Secret Service was formed. Cliff was a first office agent. Why would they be sending him? My sadness wanted answers that I couldn't have right now.

As I hung up, I stoically walked to the bedroom and pulled the suit bag from the closet top shelf. I grasped its handle and threw it on the bed. Packing was mindless as I went through drawers and hangers to select a working wardrobe for an assassination investigation. This couldn't be happening.

I thought about how I'd tell the kids Daddy would be leaving for a while. Cliff had been away before for training, but that was different. Now it would be the three of us. I would need to figure out how to establish a new normal without him. It was unlikely this would be the last out-of-town assignment in his career.

An hour or so later Cliff pulled the Bureau car into the driveway and burst through the laundry room door on a mission. His bag was waiting, as were the three of us. "*I can't cry,*" I told myself. "*I want to, but I can't.*"

"Where you going, Daddy?" Their little faces with the sad frowns said it all. Suitcases for Daddy had to mean something sad.

"Daddy has to go to Dallas to work for a while, but I'll call you on the phone."

"What do you know?" I whispered.

"They've arrested a suspect. Actually, they arrested him for killing a Dallas police officer named Tippit, but now they think he may be connected to the assassination. I really won't know much more until I get to Dallas. I'll call you when I can."

"I love you. I'm scared. Please be careful." I grabbed his sleeve as if to hold him here.

Cliff held me and whispered, "It's time for you to be strong. I'll be home soon."

"I love you," we called out.

We watched him pick up his bag and walk to the car, a car with a sputtering radio and lights reminding me he wasn't going off to work in some high-rise building. As he pulled the gray government car away, I took my children's hands and walked back inside. I knew he believed this was where he belonged, in the middle of one of the most important cases the FBI had ever handled.

Back in the house, the blank TV screen stared at me as I set the table for dinner. I poured the children's milk twice which they thought was funny. I stumbled through the remainder of the day knowing that it was more important than ever for us to have a routine. Just twenty-four hours ago we had all been seated around the table talking about the Kennedy motorcade.

As darkness descended, I felt a chill as if something had changed in my home; something positive had left. Moving from window to window to draw the curtains ever tighter against the darkness, ensuring that each door was locked and double locked, I walked from room to room. I was the sentry who would insulate my little family from the outside world.

I'm alone; the house is quiet as if she knows I need it this way, I whispered to no one. Not even the air conditioner needed to run. I poured myself a glass of wine. I turned on the TV, thinking the noise would help blot out the events of the day. I had held my tears in check because of the children; now they could flow freely. I crossed my legs Indian style, almost in a pose, and allowed my body to react to my shock and grief. What about Jackie? What would her life become?

I didn't expect to hear from Cliff until later so I allowed my tension filled body to ease into my enveloping brown couch. I looked around the quiet room with its furniture we had so carefully selected on our tight budget and how we had taken this sofa, the rocking chair and the print fabric my mother had given me for drapes and turned it into a warm, safe, inviting room. Now I sat in this room alone, needing to feel I was safe. Would I ever learn to roll with the danger in this job, the irregular hours and the god-awful isolation?

I took a longer than normal sip from my wine glass and settled back to learn Johnson, in a rush to succession, had been sworn in as our 36th president with Jackie at his side still wearing her blood splattered pink suit and matching hat, so perfect just hours ago. The suit that now said, "This is what you did to me." The plane with Johnson, Jackie and President Kennedy had left for D.C. She had come to Texas to support her husband; now she was returning without him. She would soon have to explain to her children why their father was gone and wouldn't be back, and tomorrow I would have to tell my children something. In the years to follow I would remember this night, and I would find myself like Jackie in the middle of a tragedy trying to explain.

When my tears ebbed, I refilled my glass, this time to induce sleep. I listened to the silence around me, so warm in its embrace. The numbness was returning, a blessed state as I speculated on my husband's role in this now unfolding investigation. When Cliff had first shown an interest in this career, my main concern had been his safety. I did not have a compelling urge to be a young widow.

Walking into our bedroom filled with the special items that made this room uniquely ours, I gravitated to the large mirror anchored over the manly cherry double dresser. Glancing sideways as I approached, I saw the profile of a young, dark haired woman looking taller and stronger than her five feet three inches. The reflection in the mirror resembled mine except for the smeared mascara and little color where makeup had been. I looked into her gray-green eyes for signs of recognition. If she were to build a life with her husband within the FBI culture, she would need to toughen up.

Morning brought the brilliant sun trying to pierce the heavy handmade drapes tightly drawn against the outside world. Saturday morning, November 23, had arrived despite yesterday's tragedy. My routine was intact as I padded out the yellow front door whose hue matched the morning brilliance. The morning paper was closer to the door today as if the deliverer had thrown it with more intensity. I unrolled it as I walked back inside. Among the information I already had, I read that there had been four telephone calls threatening the President's life Thursday while he visited Houston. He could've been shot while we were watching the motorcade.

The news reported Americans had gone into hibernation. On Friday Broadway was dark, the stock exchange had closed at 2:07 p.m. EST, and churches were filled to overflowing first with prayers for Kennedy's recovery and then for his soul. The souls of many of us were dark. Cliff was finally able to call from Dallas on Saturday evening.

"Hi honey, sorry I haven't been able to call, but I wanted to let you know I'm okay, just really busy."

"If you can just check in, I won't worry so much."

"I'll try. Tomorrow they're going to move Lee Harvey Oswald, the suspected assassin, to the Dallas County Jail. I've been assigned to that detail so I probably won't be able to call until after that."

"Do I need to worry about you? This guy has already killed the President."

"Remember what I've told you over and over. The FBI is always prepared. I'll be fine. Gotta go. Talk to you tomorrow.

"Love you."

A prisoner transfer, not just an ordinary prisoner but a presidential assassin. How safe could that be? Maybe Oswald had friends. And why my husband? Probably because he had volunteered to be in the thick of the action while I'd be worrying that I'd end up like Jackie. My initial rejection of the whole FBI career idea was probably right. It was right. It was wrong. It was what?

I'm not sure why I wasn't in church, but on Sunday while the world was waiting for the details of the Kennedy funeral services, the networks switched to the now familiar over-crowded corridor in the basement of the Dallas Police Department where I could see the figure of Oswald, who looked like an ordinary prisoner, accompanied by two plainclothes policemen, one at each side. Without warning, out of the corner of the screen, I saw a man's back, and then shots rang out. Shots, more shots as Oswald slumped amid screams of, "He's been shot! He's been shot!" How had I happened to have this damn TV on at this moment? I folded into the couch fearing to learn more. I was going to be a widow, wasn't I? High profile people were dropping like flies. Where was the bullet with Cliff's name on it? And how safe were we, his family? Pandemonium unfolded as Oswald left by ambulance, and a man by the name of Jack Ruby was taken into custody by agents, one of whom I later learned was Cliff. My body jerked forward for a better look at the faces and bodies surrounding Oswald and Ruby. Was he there? Could I see him? Was he safe? This Alfred Hitchcock moment sent shudders from my shoulders into my hands. I reached for the volume control; perhaps they were saying something I shouldn't miss. I heard no more shots as they carried Ruby off in handcuffs and Oswald off on a gurney.

A President shot and killed, a Dallas police officer killed, a governor wounded and now the suspected assassin shot and killed. All of this carnage in two days. Cliff called as he had promised.

"Sorry I couldn't call earlier. You probably already know what happened with the transfer. I've been busy interviewing Ruby, and I'll probably be tied up on this for a while." His voice was belabored and fatigued, and he talked like he was speaking to the press rather than his wife.

"It's me you're talking to. Remember me? Your wife with two children?" Is this what I was to become, this person on the other end of the phone listening to a dictation from a current case?

"Sorry, honey, it's just been so tense here. How are you? Is everything okay there?" If it weren't, then what?

I needed to talk, to ask questions, to look into his eyes for reassurance that this was still a good career choice for us. This kind of talking wasn't going to happen over the phone.

"I know you can't tell me anything, but will we ever have a chance to talk about all that's gone on?" I didn't need details; I needed promise.

"I'm not sure how much I'll be able to tell you, but we can talk."

Talking would be a start.

"I love you."

"Love you too. Don't know yet when I'll be home. We've got a lot of leads to track down, and the Director has ordered us to issue a statement as soon as possible. Hoover believes the public needs assurance Oswald was the lone assassin."

"Was he?"

Silence.

I watched preparations for the state funeral and grieved along with the nation. Jackie was a mother with two small children, Caroline six and John three; I was a mother of two small children three and two. Today on his 3rd birthday John would salute the casket of his dead father with the seriousness of a seasoned soldier. Ray, on his twenty-third birthday would memorialize his father. I couldn't know that then. I could only fear as I stood watching Jackie define for me what grief looks like, a black statue of strength and mourning, a model for the unthinkable. In my own grief in the years to come, I would revisit that image, knowing she had walked before me and survived.

SIX

Can We Talk?

The Thanksgiving holiday came and went; the days dragged without Cliff, but soon the children and I were looking forward to Christmas. Colorful catalogs came and were dog-eared within the week—oh just look at all those toys. I carried on, pretending everything was okay, moving forward in the holiday planning. Maybe Cliff would be home for Christmas. Maybe Santa would come. Maybe there would be no more investigations. And maybe we could be a family delighting in the holiday season.

This year would be my first Christmas away from my parents and sister. Following Mom's tradition, I baked cookies from her favorite recipes, wrapped presents, mailed Christmas cards and decorated the house. Sylvia, my best friend and neighbor asked her husband, Tom, to help me put up the Christmas tree to house the long, colorful chains and cut-out snowflakes the kids and I had made. Somehow the traditions we were building as a family seemed more important this year. I needed to bring color into this house, bright lights to help wipe the grayness away. I decorated, waiting for friends and family who would not be coming this year. Pangs of emptiness filled my stomach with an ache that bore no relation to food.

"Growing up is sure not what it's cracked up to be," I thought." This wasn't the deal I made—alone with two little children at Christmas. Why couldn't Mom and Dad be here? I needed them. They had apologized but said they were still busy settling into their new house in California. I cried for their absence. Wallowing wasn't attractive so I saved it for my journal.

A slim possibility still existed that Cliff could be home for Santa and the festivities, but my holiday plans called for his absence: Christmas Eve church services, opening one package from under the tree, threatening the children with Santa's arrival in order to get them to bed, and finally retrieving Santa's packages from respective closets. It would be sad, but I would have to make it okay for Tami and Ray. Next year maybe they would have their dad home, and I would know once again what it was like to have a husband.

Ready for Santa's arrival, I settled into my favorite spot with a glass of wine and my thoughts, which were interrupted by noises coming from the carport. That's all I needed, some goof deciding my house would be a good target for a Christmas Eve burglary. Where had I put my Louisville Slugger, my preferred weapon of defense? I heard more sounds, almost familiar, like the trunk of a car closing. I stood in my narrow galley kitchen facing its only door, knowing I hadn't the energy for a break-in. I looked ahead and watched the knob turn to allow the door to open inward revealing my absentee husband extending a dozen roses in my direction. Daddy was home, and all was right with the world, at least in our world.

He was home, at least for now, and we could finally talk. What a backlog there was. 1963 had been a year of change with a move, a summer separation, Cliff's new career with the FBI, and most recently, the Dallas assassination separation. Except for a few snatched minutes on our road trip to Houston, we hadn't really talked. My list of topics that "must be addressed" was growing. A quiet New Year's Eve seemed the time. A few snacks, maybe a glass of wine and good conversation would be a romantic way to usher in 1964.

"I'm so glad you're home. The kids and I missed you." My purpose wasn't to make him feel bad—or was it? Sometimes I didn't know my own intentions.

"Dallas was hard. I barely had time to think of anyone or anything other than the job. There's so much to know, and if you goof up, the whole case may fail. I've been working leads sixteen hours a day, then falling into bed." He seemed preoccupied with his statement. He was sitting beside me, but where was he really?

"It was hard here because I didn't know if you were safe. People were getting killed all around you. And I rarely heard from you. Is this the way it's always going to be?" I looked over to see his reaction. I was aiming for open discussion, but my emotions seemed to be getting in the way. Start again. Listen to him. Don't interrupt and don't whine.

"Look, I don't know how it's always going to be. This is my first office, and an assassination isn't a run-of-the-mill event. I keep telling you not to worry. What's with this?" His wrinkled brow and piercing eyes communicated his displeasure.

"What's with this is I don't want to end up like Jackie Kennedy, a young widow with two small children." I could feel the tears beginning to well in their hiding places despite willing this crying stuff wouldn't happen.

"I can tell you this. You'll be well provided for. In fact, with all the insurance, you'd be better off financially without me." His smile was not reassuring.

"That's just it; I don't want a life without you. It's not money I want, it's you." I snuggled closer to be held within the arm that extended over the back of the sofa.

"Let's talk about something else. What would you think about a vacation this summer, a real trip, maybe to see your parents in California? For the first time, I get a paid vacation. That's got to make up for something." What would it make up for? His absence? Okay, I'll take it.

"What's up with you?" I asked a few nights later. "You look so serious. Are we transferred? Are you having second thoughts about this job? What?" Cliff wasn't that hard to read; something was coming.

I sat up a little straighter, put down the mail I was reading and looked directly at him.

"No, none of that. I just wanted you to know I have to meet someone later tonight. He's a potential informant for a car ring we're working. It's kind of funny because when I asked him how I would recognize him in the bar where we're meeting, he laughed and said, "No worries, I'll recognize you when you come in."

"So, you're going to meet this guy. Is someone going with you? I mean, you don't know this person. And you said he might be an informant for you?"

"Right. The Bureau uses informants to solve cases. These people usually form a relationship with a particular agent. It's rather symbiotic, I guess." His brow had wrinkled slightly as he carefully chose his words.

"Can I ask you something about this informant stuff? Why do these people give you information? They must be getting something out of it. Do you pay them?" Always a bit suspicious, I wanted to understand what my husband's relationship with these people was going to be.

"I'm told these people who turn information are very loyal to the agents they work with, and once they settle into a working relationship, they're reluctant to share with another agent. They don't do it for the money; their motivation is something else."

"Why do I need to know about these people?"

"When I'm not home you might get calls because I hear these people are often reluctant to go through the dispatcher. You would just need to take a message for me."

"Well, you don't have one of these yet, so I'm not going to worry."

"Right. After my meeting tonight I'll let you know if we have our first informant."

Our first informant? When did I become the other agent in this household?

Cliff had his meeting with a man known as Henry in the designated bar. When he arrived home, he had a smile on his face, which told me the meeting must have been successful.

"Well, Henry was right. I parked the Bureau car and walked into the all-black bar. He had no problem recognizing me." He laughed again in the retelling. I joined him in the chuckle. I would take humor wherever I could find it.

Summer rolled around with its incredible Texas heat. Thank God for the pool. We lived in swimsuits and flip-flops that summer. Our routine was almost normal; I hardly would have known we were different from any other family. Cliff made a couple short trips to Dallas, but he was working in Houston for the most part since the Warren Commission had taken responsibility for investigating the assassination. I wasn't sure what this meant for me, but new roles and rules were mine to learn.

Summer vacation. Yeah! A first for our family. We set off in the faithful brown station wagon for Los Angeles to see Grandma and Grandpa who had their own pool. Dad had taken a job as president of Rohr Industries, and Mom finally had them settled into their new home.

As our trusty car rolled west, voices exploded from the back seat asking, "Are we still in Texas?" followed by, "How much farther to Grandma's?" An interminable trip over brown hills, dried river valleys, and vast deserts finally found us rolling down the last big hill into Los Angeles. Disneyland, Knott's Berry Farm, Sea World and oh so many wonderful attractions awaited us! I soon felt renewed and even fantasized that my marriage to Cliff could approach that "happily ever after" feeling. My perceptive mom had a spectacular idea.

"Why don't you and Cliff take a couple of days for yourselves and go north along the coast or east into the mountains, and Dad and I can have some fun with our grandchildren." It was obvious from the way she presented this plan that she had given it much thought and had cleared it with my dad.

"Do you mean it? Oh, gosh, that would be wonderful. We haven't had any time off together since before the kids were born. We could really use some re-connection." How do moms just know these things? I hugged my mom tightly and told her I loved her.

Cliff and I made our plans, kissed the children good-bye and left for blue sky, mountain vistas, and dramatic coastlines. Enjoying grown-up conversation, we were ready to let the world go by for two days. Not even the dictatorial Bureau could intervene. Well, in truth, the FBI could find us if it wanted to as agents were required to file a vacation itinerary with the office, just in case.

Cliff looked over at me as he drove. "Did you think we'd have this time together? I didn't." It was an opening.

"No, this was Mom's surprise. I can't believe she's doing this." My mother was a perfectionist whose house resembled a layout in *House Beautiful*. Now, it was inhabited by two messy toddlers who would be creating forts with velvet sofa pillows and leaving pint-sized sticky handprints on doors, windows and tables as if leaving a trail for Grandma to follow.

"I've been so wrapped up in my job that I've been counting the days until this vacation. I really needed to get away." He reached across the seat for my hand.

"For sure it's been a trying year in many ways."

"I've really missed you. How about a little wine, a nice dinner and lots of romance?" I smiled, particularly at the prospect of romance, an element recently missing.

"I want these two days to be about you and me," he said. "That's all. At times I feel I'm losing you. No time for us for over a year, not since I joined this crazy organization."

"Crazy is a fairly good descriptor."

"Remember when we met at Delaware, on the steps of Kent Hall? Seems a long time ago, doesn't it? I knew that minute I wanted to spend my life with you." He let his gaze wander from the road to assess my reaction. Was he losing me?

"Eight years is a long time ago. We were so young and romantic. I wouldn't give those times up for anything. But, this job is what you wanted, isn't it? We've both made sacrifices to make this happen, and it's probably not going to be easy going forward." I listened to my cautious words.

"I love this work. I can't think of anything I'd rather be doing. It's even more exciting than I thought it'd be. But how are you with it?" He turned his head slightly in my direction. This was the first time he had asked.

"I don't think I've had enough time to know what it's really going to be like. Everything you're involved in is so secretive, I feel like I'm married to two people: the Cliff I'm with today and the man who lives in our house sometimes but isn't really there." I peeked to my left to confirm which man I was really with today.

"Enough about job, kids and all the rest," as he reached across the seat to tenderly hold my small hand, my left one, cradling my white gold wedding band. I squeezed his strong, warm fingers in return.

We drove to a quiet spot along the coast to a small inn whose name Cliff had gotten from an LA agent. Its outside façade was unpretentious, welcoming and warm. We walked into an intimate setting overlooking a rocky coast whose waves sounded melodic tones through the open windows. A deck lured us outside to a breeze promising renewal. We stood there, holding hands and promising to make things work between us. We'd probably never re-capture the euphoria of falling in love, but our relationship could become stable and strong, couldn't it?

Two days passed quickly providing much needed renewal for the coming year. Grandma and Grandpa were smiling and just a bit weary. Tami and Ray were jumping up and down, talking at the same time. It was apparent they had done fine without us.

Vacation was over and we were ready to make our trek back to Houston. Dad felt sorry for us with no car air conditioning so he presented a solution. Dad always had a solution. As an inventor, he had developed a unique water-filled tank that fit in the window of the car. The movement of the vehicle against the water in the tank brought a nice cool mist into the car's compartment. Just a bit of a problem though—when one pulled the string to expose the water to the air outside, regulating the flow of the mist was erratic. So, periodically, those seated closest to the contraption got soaked. Tami and Ray thought this hilarious and argued over who should have seating privileges. It was so hot that the wetness was welcome. Good intentions on the part of Dad and lots of laughs for us.

Part Three

Ready isn't perfect; it's an anticipation, an
expectation that things will go as planned.

1964-1969

SEVEN

Just Different

Jacksonville would be different because I was different.

Like many families in this unsettled era of the mid '60s, I was becoming more aware of differences surrounding us. We were an FBI family, and although I wasn't yet sure what that meant, I already knew our life was different from that of our non-FBI friends. Where and how we lived was a reflection of our experiences. My neighbors and non-Bureau friends hadn't seen the Houston motorcade, nor had their husbands been involved in the assassination investigation. Our experiences in Texas had changed us. Years later, when I was asked what the real story was with the Kennedy assassination or what was the inside scoop on Dr. King, I'd look at my friends, smile and drag my fingers across my lips.

As we drove across the Florida panhandle I experienced a landscape different from what I had expected. I had been to Florida three times before: once as a teenager with my parents on vacation, once on my honeymoon and once again with my parents as a mom-to-be. Clearly, Jacksonville wasn't the Florida of Miami or Tampa with their palm trees, green golf courses and warm winter temperatures. More like southern Georgia with its flat landscape, cool, humid air and Spanish moss hanging from every tree. Mysterious, sort of Faulkneresque. I would reserve comment, though, until I had seen more. Right now I silently worked on accepting what was different from my expectations. Perhaps the winters didn't always feel this cold; perhaps the skies weren't always so gray; perhaps spring came early here frosting the trees with green canopies.

"Hey, look at this great bridge, kids," I said. "That's the St. Johns river." Actually, the river looked more like those in the north, ambling and confident as it rolled through the landscape.

"Yeah, this might be where we'll have our boat," Cliff offered.

"But where's the beach?" Tami wanted to know. And so did I; I could see it on our map, but it was going to be a bit of a drive from Cliff's office.

"Honey, the beach is a little ways," I said, "but since the moving van won't be here for a couple of days, how about taking a trip out there tomorrow? What do you think, Daddy?" It wasn't yet swimming weather, but we could definitely scrounge for shells and other sea treasures. We'd pick up some lunch items on the way and plan for a cold weather picnic.

"Sounds like a plan," Cliff said. "First, though, we need to find a house." I agreed on the priority.

Since Jacksonville isn't warm in December, we had carefully selected a motel with an indoor pool. While Cliff was checking in at the office Tami, Ray and I enjoyed splashing and dog paddling around the shallow end. Both children, now four and three, had learned enough about swimming in Houston to give me some level of confidence. They jumped from the side into my arms, one at a time. Their energy was boundless; mine was not.

"Okay, you've tired me out. Let's go see if Daddy's back." It seemed we were always waiting for Daddy to come back from somewhere.

Our timing was perfect. From the window I could see Cliff sprinting up the steps and into the doorway beaming and talking non-stop.

"You're going to love it! These people are all so helpful. Look, I have names of realty companies, and they tell me the market is genuinely depressed with more vacant properties than people to rent or buy them." His enthusiasm was almost contagious as he shed his jacket to share the housing information with me.

"That part sounds good. So where are these properties? Any place we'd want to live?" Less expensive housing would help as we were still trying to recover financially from past moves.

"If we're able to find a house before the van gets here, we won't have to put our furniture in storage," he said. This was also good news since the Bureau only paid part of the cost associated with storage.

Cliff settled into the one desk in our standard-issue motel room and dialed the realtor he and I had selected from the agents' list and scheduled a meeting with him. After some discussion, we decided it might be better to rent rather than be stuck trying to unload a house if we were transferred before the market turned around. Although we could be here as long as five years, it wasn't a certainty. Under Bureau transfer policy, we'd need to pay any costs related to any sale. So that was settled. We'd rent.

Our realtor piled us into his car for a tour of possible areas. University Park met our criteria: settled family area, close to town and office, good schools and by the looks of the toys in the yards, plenty of kids. A cute but unkempt red brick rancher at 3953 Meek Drive seemed to have our name on it. This three-bedroom, two-bath ranch was owned by FHA so they were happy to have us sign a rental agreement for $125 per month/no lease required.

This sad, little red-brick house needed a family, and now she had one. While Cliff examined the exterior, I walked the interior with decorating in mind and Tami and Ray ran and chased each other in the overgrown backyard. I prayed it was too cold for snakes.

Since we now had the house lined up, Tami, Ray and I stood in the street, looking at her carefully to see what might cheer her up a bit. She needed more than a colorful front door; a new lawn and some flowers would help. But we'd start with the door to give her a little pride. Standing before her, as we had our other houses, we asked her for a color preference. What would make her feel most regal and proud? "Blue," she said. And the right shade would work well with her red brick.

So, according to tradition, Tami, Ray and I were off to bring home the requisite blue samples. The first selection was just right, a nice nautical blue. At the same time we decided we would buy the paint to spruce up her white shutters and railings. We were on a course to make our little house look sassy and alive.

We were almost settled, although the swing set assembly was still calling as were the kids as they relentlessly begged their dad to put it together. Late one evening Cliff and I decided this was the time for that project. We put the kids to bed and were in the backyard working on matching up pieces when a strong, distinctive odor wafted over the fence.

"Phew, what's that smell?" I asked as I covered my nostrils and mouth with my gloved hand.

"Smells like somebody broke a bottle of mash." Cliff didn't miss a beat in attaching the next leg piece.

"A bottle of mash? What's that? God, it smells like a brewery." My nose was stinging, and I started to sneeze.

"Well it is, sort of. We might have a bootleg operation going on behind the fence." He actually smiled at the thought.

"A bootleg operation? Like Al Capone in the '20s? I didn't think they even made that stuff anymore. Who in the world would buy it?" I looked toward the back fence and imagined men standing before their stills, perhaps sampling a product. But here it was in my backyard. I smiled in return. How was it I'd ended up with these interesting neighbors? I didn't know, but it was almost like a romantic fantasy where a couple moves into a neighborhood and finds they have bought into a different way of seeing things. I was going to like living across the fence from these people.

"Yea, it's sort of like Al Capone. It's illegal to produce booze for sale because of the tax issues, but it still goes on. My relatives on Dad's side were Tennessee moonshiners; at least they had a still to produce liquor for their own use."

Startled by this new piece of information, I dropped the piece I was working on and moved closer to the fence. A whole new story was developing here.

"Are your relatives still in the business?" He told me once that he had gone to Tennessee one summer while he was in high school, but he'd never mentioned this part to me.

"I don't know; they might be. When I went down to Red Boiling Springs that summer after my junior year, my uncle Plez showed me around, meaning he took me to their still. I was sixteen and thought it was kind of cool." Cliff smiled and clapped his hands with the recall. "See, there's more you didn't know about me."

What I did know is that his growing up had been trying. His father left the family saying he was joining the army to get away from all of them. His mother, too, threatened to leave when she walked to the bus stop and told the two children that she couldn't stand it any more. They had stood at the bus stop, waiting and crying until their grandmother became worried and rescued them.

"I'm thinking there's plenty more I don't know. But about this mash. Do these things break regularly?" The burning in my nose had risen to my head, settling into a large sized headache.

"Not sure, but I don't think it's anything to worry about. I'll check this out with Alcohol, Tobacco and Firearms in the morning. I'll bet our neighbors have been running this operation for years." Cliff didn't seem concerned, and my curiosity was piqued, but not for long.

"Well, I talked to ATF, and they chuckled when I mentioned our backyard experience. They know these people well. It's a family operation dating back to the '20s."

"It's a black community, isn't it?"

"Yup. I'm sure they're good people. It's not likely we'll see much of them though. Remember we're still in the south."

"I like that they're here."

In the evenings I often sat in my family room whose sliding door faced my back fence neighbors. On occasion I'd observe cars with no lights driving into and out of the property. On other occasions I'd see fires, which Cliff said were most likely set by ATF agents to destroy the stills. I decided it must be a dance of sorts. First, build a still. Second, ATF burns it. Third, rebuild the still. All would be quiet for a time, then activity would resume. Curiously, I observed the comings and goings, at times with longing for the days of Gatsby. Silently, I cheered them on for their entrepreneurial vigor in spite of the law. I never met any of them, but I felt them in the shadows of the night. I was an outside observer looking in through an opaque window, allowing me to see only the shadows and outlines of persons. They and I shared secret observations in closed communities.

We soon did, however, have a face-to-face encounter of sorts over the back fence with a little black boy, too shy to come into our yard but curious enough to peek through the chain link. Ray was curious and asked if he could come over to play. We invited him, but he didn't come.

Having now lived in Georgia and Texas, I had seen unequal treatment first hand. Perhaps that's why my heart was soft for the moonshine operation in my backyard so different from my white middle-class University Park neighborhood populated by professionals and one other Bureau family,

Doris and Fred Ferris. Doris called on me even before I had the house settled. I answered the door in my grubby sweats hoping if she ever saw me again she wouldn't recognize me.

"Hi Sandy. I'm Doris, Fred's wife from the office. I live just a couple of blocks from here." If she were Fred's wife, was I Cliff's wife?

I opened the screen door to allow her to squeeze into the entryway still stacked with boxes. "Please come in. You can see we aren't yet settled, but I'm sure you're familiar with this moving routine."

"It's been a long while since we've moved. Fred's an accountant, and we came here to our second office seventeen years ago and stayed." Her smile suggested that this could also happen to us. Would I want to stay in Jacksonville? Way too early to know.

"Anyway, I just wanted to stop by, introduce myself and welcome you to the neighborhood and to the office as well. You're probably familiar with the Agent Wives organization. Ours meets monthly; it's a luncheon, and we usually have a speaker. I also wanted to ask if you play bridge. We have a small FBI wives group that plays every two weeks, and we're looking for an eighth member. Alice's husband was just transferred."

I answered with my best smile. "Yes, I love to play if it's not too serious." I had played bridge every place I had lived where I could find a social game. Yes, I would play any time, any place. This group of FBI women would inform my life in many ways, only a few related to the tasks associated with being a Bureau wife. From them I learned to listen rather than talk, to never share any FBI information with anyone, not even another wife, to agree with your husband even when you disagree.

EIGHT

On the March

As a young girl, way before I'd discovered the moonshiners, my family, including my Grandpa Shoulars, decided a trip to North Carolina to visit his sisters would be a good idea. We got out the map and located Spring Hope, our destination and home of my great-aunt Lillian and great-uncle Jim.

It was a long drive from Michigan to this sleepy but stately southern town. Our fatigue and dustiness must have been evident as we pulled into the circle drive, stopping our cars in front of the wide steps leading to the largest front porch I'd ever seen. It was exactly how I imagined a plantation porch would look: thick impressive columns spaced several feet apart as if proclaiming substance while at the same time supporting a slanting roof protecting its visitors from summer's stifling heat and occasional pouring rain. As I stepped lady-like from the car's back seat, I imagined I was playing a role in a plantation movie. I smoothed my wrinkled polka dot dress and pretended I was the heroine seated in one of those colorful rocking chairs with their plump flowered cushions sipping something seductive. This was the largest, most beautiful house I had ever seen, nothing like any house in Lansing. These people must be very rich.

Aunt Lillian descended the once stately stairs toward us, extending her arms to my mom and grandpa and then more tentatively reaching out to shake Dad's hand and to pat my sister and me on the head. Against the backdrop of her grand home, she looked like a photograph in an historical novel. Dressed in a blue afternoon dress suitable for greeting visitors, she welcomed us to her home, taking us into the parlor where we were introduced to Hetty, the housemaid and Tom, the yard man. I remember looking at these two black people wondering how they fit into this household. Did they live here too? Were they left over from slavery? I had learned about that in school.

A few questions were answered when Aunt Lillian followed up with instructions: breakfast at 8:00; dinner, the main meal, at 1:00; afternoon quiet time; tea on the porch at 4:00 and supper sandwiches at 6:00. If we had questions or needed anything, we were to ask Hetty, and she would take care of us.

True to schedule, we assembled in the dining room the next morning for breakfast. It was the largest table I had ever seen, and Aunt Lillian told us where we should sit. Thankfully, she put me beside my mother. I looked around this large wallpapered room with a breakfast table set properly for guests: white cloth napkins, matching tablecloth and our breakfast served on lovely light blue china. I was playing a movie role. Hetty had done well. Curiously, though, aside a healthy serving of scrambled eggs and bacon lay a mound of white stuff resembling bumpy mashed potatoes. What was this stuff? I looked at my plate and then at Mom. Her look told me to eat everything. I started with what was familiar and left the whiteness for last. I cautiously placed my fork prongs into the mass, which by now was sufficiently cooled to be lumps. My mouth opened to the first lump. I tasted nothing, but I felt the uncomfortable texture on my tongue. I wanted it out. Could I spit it into my napkin? No. Everyone was watching. For the week we were there, I tried claiming a breakfast stomach ache which brought some other horrible substance to my mouth. I gave in and ate the grits, certain I would die from this morning blob.

I later learned there was another black maid, the woman who made the bed, emptied the trash and cleaned the house. My mother was three when her parents moved from North Carolina to Michigan so this lifestyle was foreign to her. Aunt Lillian explained to her that by making the bed she was taking work away from Mary.

It didn't seem right. It wasn't the way my mom and dad lived. I heard all the explanations: Jim's family had once been wealthy and owned much of Spring Hope, but they lost almost all of it in the depression. They were accustomed to hired help, and they would maintain this lifestyle even when they no longer had the resources.

I returned home from the North Carolina visit with a new set of observations and questions. Now almost twenty years later we were revisiting issues of civil rights, this time with protests, marches, sit-ins, freedom riders, and killings. Years hence I would be able to trace my strong beliefs regarding equal rights to this very early experience. My years within the FBI circle would only strengthen those beliefs.

A few weeks into my new life in Jacksonville, my social life was expanding. I met Ann through church; she and I had children the same ages. And Sheila, who had a two-year-old boy, lived next door. Her husband taught at Jacksonville University. My other neighbors were peripheral friends, people I played bridge with, saw in church or arranged play dates with. This was my outside family, outside the FBI. Even though I worked at keeping Cliff's vocation a mystery, it wasn't long before they caught on. Our kids played together, and finally I didn't care if they knew.

My inside family was my FBI wives bridge group, wives of men who had been in the Bureau several years and who had made peace with its demands. Margaret was the leader of our group as she was the boss's wife although she worked very hard at being one of us. Her husband, Bob, had been an agent for over twenty years, and they had been transferred at least a half dozen times. A mother of four, three of whom were grown, she had not forgotten the challenges of raising children in a law enforcement environment. I didn't have Jackie any longer as a model, but I had Margaret as a different type of example. I would look at her with her dark shoulder length hair, manicured nails and understated but fashionable dress and wonder how she had worked through the challenges and the isolation which I was learning were part of the unpredictability of each day.

As close as I felt to these seven women, I was always a little guarded not just with this group but also with my non-Bureau friends. Something told me to keep the discussion away from Bureau issues. So, where did I take my concerns about this new life? To Cliff? No, he misinterpreted my concerns as criticism. Mom? No, she thought I must be living a very glamorous life. Adrian was too far away; besides she had her own issues, and judging from her letters, their marriage was teetering. I confided in my journal, but that was really only myself talking to myself.

My primary task at the moment was to create a home from this house. I flattened and stacked my empty boxes. Storage space was limited so once again I left the silver, china and crystal packed until I could save enough money for a hutch. As I hauled these now graffitied manila cartons to the storage closet, I cherished the memories I had stored in each. Unfolding the ladder, I climbed to the new shelf Cliff had built to accommodate these flattened friends of mine, our final step in the unpacking. I smiled as I stacked them.

I knew where they were in case I needed them.

Cliff, too, was finding his place in a new setting where he was developing a network, one composed of police officers, other agents and criminals. Initially he was assigned to the UFAP (Unlawful Flight to Avoid Prosecution) desk, which meant he chased fugitives, those men whose faces graced the post office posters. This fugitive work was dependent on close contact with a strong informant base. While I was a little nervous about what this would mean for the family, I tried to stay positive. From our conversations in Houston I knew I would eventually be taking messages from these people. I wasn't sure I was comfortable with this intrusive role, but…

In the midst of my ruminations the phone jangled for my attention. This wouldn't yet be one of those informant calls; we didn't have any informants yet.

"Hi, hon. Listen, the SAC just called on the radio to say I'm being sent to Alabama."

"Does this have anything to do with all the civil rights issues there?" I wanted to ask why he was always called but refrained.

"Yea, it does. President Johnson is sending a federal team to protect the safety of those planning to march with Dr. King from Selma to Montgomery. Plus, there's still the issue of the missing civil rights workers."

I listened carefully for the emotion in his voice, and I heard enthusiasm and excitement for being selected for another historic investigation. I had earlier watched violent images of beatings flash across the TV screen. Selma didn't look to be a safe place for a white federal agent.

"This is kind of like Dallas, a major case, isn't it? I just wish you weren't going." Sure, I was proud of him; I knew he was becoming a very good agent, but it wasn't the agent part I had married.

"Apparently this is how this job works. Anyway, we're leaving right away so I'll need to pick up a bag. Can you help me out again?"

"Sure. Packing is something I'm becoming good at."

The drill was this: he'd come home, pick up the bag, give us all hugs and kisses and promise to be home soon. Soon is a variable concept. The kids would pout or act out, and I would try to explain why Daddy's job was so important. More important than us? Yes, it felt that way at times.

I had worried when Cliff was in Dallas, but at least they had the assassin by the time he rolled into town. This was different: the news reports suggested that in Alabama both blacks and whites felt they had much to lose. Children had been killed in a church bombing and three civil rights workers, two white and one black, were missing. What were the chances they'd be found alive? And how would Cliff and his fellow agents be seen by blacks or whites? As support or part of the problem? Martin Luther King was still trying the keep the movement non-violent, but many of the protesters were beginning to feel they would never make progress this way.

At the same time I thought of my extended family in North Carolina. Did Aunt Lillian still have "colored help"? I could still see Hetty serving us breakfast on the grand sweeping porch and wondered how a country could become so splintered. Had I as a child romanticized the racial situation in Spring Hope? In my lifetime I hoped I would see a healing; perhaps Cliff would be able to play a role in that.

I watched the Bureau car roll out of the driveway as I waved and remembered our recent beach date. The sea was beautiful that day; because it was still winter, crowds were missing. I loved the sounds of birds calling or conversing, the clouds a little grayer than I would have liked and the temperature teasing us with the onset of spring. It was a lovely morning.

"Hey, let's see how many shells we can find for the kids," Cliff said. This outing was my idea, a morning plus lunch with just my husband.

"Sure, they're excited about their growing shell collection." As he leaned over, I gave him a gentle nudge into the water. Then I laughed and ran, knowing he would chase me and catch me.

"Okay, you want to play rough? I'll show you rough," as he grabbed my middle and hoisted me on his shoulder and ran toward the water threatening to throw me in.

"Don't. I didn't bring any extra clothes. I'll race you though to the next dune." I took off as he put me down. Breathless at the capture point, we fell into the sand in each other's arms.

"You know I love you, don't you?" He asked. I shook my head and leaned into his strong body.

"I love it when it's like this, just the two of us, no distractions."

That was two weeks ago.

Each night I waited for his call from Selma.

"Hi. How was your day? Are the kids doing okay? This is a mess here; I'm not sure this is solvable. When you're in the middle, it's easier to see how desperate each side feels." His speech was slow and labored.

I listened. Did he really want to know the heat pump had broken leaving us shivering or that the balance in the checking was running low?

"We're doing okay. The kids are driving me crazy with questions about where you are and why you had to go there so we had a geography lesson with the atlas. Now they can find you on the map."

"Yes, well it's Alabama, and it's a crisis situation. The hours are endless and both sides hate us. The blacks are suspicious because we're outsiders. They're reluctant to talk to us for fear of retribution by the Klan or other white townspeople. Whites see us as intruders, outsiders, troublemakers. I've never felt so disliked by so many people."

"What about the local law enforcement? Aren't they allies?"

"No, that's another problem since so many of them are Klan members."

I listened to Cliff's frustration in his nightly calls and tried to find something positive to say besides, "I love you and miss you. Come home—I hate sleeping alone."

Glued to the television each evening, I felt myself identifying with the leaders of the civil rights movement as well as the white housewives, students, nuns, ministers and just plain workers who had traveled to Selma to correct a wrong. I could make a difference only within my little family and social circle. I was on the outside looking in and the inside looking out.

That being said, I told myself I should consider some activities independent of the Bureau: more hobbies, an outside job, volunteering for a cause, an affair? No, not that.

Cliff's six-week absence passed slowly. History had confirmed that any time a crisis erupted he could be sent on assignment. From a family standpoint, it was challenging. None of my close friends with children were FBI so Tami and Ray felt different about not having a father around. I was a single mom before I knew the label existed.

If I needed to be both mother and father, I would make our home a shelter, a safe place to play and cry and talk, really talk. We needed some Browning traditions. For starters, I decided dinnertime would be family discussion time. Each of us, including the children, could bring any issue to the table: civil rights or being civil to one another might be starters. Over the years no issue would be off limits. Some of these repartees were funny, deadly serious, or argumentative, but they were ours in our little corner of the world.

Meantime, in Selma, the other corner of our world, it was almost over. March 25, 1965, Martin Luther King led 25,000 people, including Cliff, from Selma to Montgomery and handed a petition to Governor George Wallace: "I say to you this afternoon that I would rather die on the highway of Alabama than make a butchery of my conscience." Prophetic in a way neither he nor Cliff could yet know.

Cliff called with his version of the march.

"Honey, while I'm not necessarily an admirer of Dr. King, I have to say he's a leader. I've seen him in action with all kinds of groups here. He's a brilliant man." Cliff said. His voice sounded lighter, more peaceful. I could hear his pride.

"What an incredible experience personally meeting and working with these people. Dr. King means so much to so many people."

"He's much different than I'd been led to believe. You know, or maybe you don't, Mr. Hoover despises Dr. King and resisted sending agents here." He hesitated as he took in my silence. Should he tell me any more? "Apparently, the Director has been collecting information on King and his associates and has some pretty damaging files on him, especially his affairs with white women."

Silence.

"Wait, you told me this earlier, and I told you I don't want to know this kind of stuff. It's not the affairs that bother me but the fact that Hoover has files. Does he collect this kind of info on a lot of people? People like his agents or those he doesn't like for personal reasons?"

"Forget what I said. I shouldn't have shared any of this with you. It's just that I don't really have anyone to talk to either."

This wasn't the first time Cliff had felt compelled to share with me. He had told me in Houston before the motorcade that the Director had files on Jack Kennedy that would destroy any illusions I had about the President's leadership. I asked him then not to tell me any of that "secret" stuff. I could figure things out on my own. Now, here it was again, those damned Hoover files.

There was a second call very late that same evening

"Hi, hon, I won't take long. I just had to call." His voice sounded low and disturbed.

"What's wrong? Are you okay?" Oh God, I knew this was dangerous.

"I'm fine. Well, I'm not, really. This evening as I was driving back to Selma from Montgomery, I saw a car off the road, barely visible in the ditch. It hadn't been there earlier in the day. It looked like someone might need help so I pulled off the road and went down the incline to check it out." He paused like he needed to take a breath and cleared his throat.

"It was too late to help. Inside was a white woman I recognized as one of the civil rights volunteers." He paused.

"Was she okay?"

"No, she was dead. Apparently, she'd been driving black marchers back to Selma when she was run off the road and killed."

"Oh no. How horrible. How can you do this job?"

"It's not always like this. Sometimes we get to do good things like get dangerous people off the streets."

"And sometimes you see the worst. This is horrible. I'm so sorry. I wish you were home." He didn't seem to hear me. Instead he needed me to hear him.

"When I saw what I had, I called dispatch with the license number. The woman is Viola Liuzzo, a volunteer and mother of five from Detroit." Cliff's voice, low and halting, carried a message of doubt.

"Another family destroyed by senseless violence. Please come home, Cliff."

Words, that's all I had. I couldn't hold his hand or wrap my arms around him. I couldn't make it better for him or for me.

Later in the investigation, Cliff learned a car had pulled up beside Viola and fired directly into the driver's side window killing her instantly. Arrests of Klan members followed, one of whom was an FBI informant. It was perhaps that piece of news, that informant piece, which hit me the hardest. Criminals turn in other criminals to solve crimes for which they are paid, get off easier on other crimes and continue to prey on the rest of us? It was individuals like these who would be calling the house? They would know where we lived and who our children were. This was not the kind of reassurance I needed.

Hanging up the phone and trying to recover from this assault, I walked into the kitchen. I needed a glass of wine because I wanted the dark red color to be for something other than someone's death. For the second time in two FBI assignments, I felt tied to the families who suffered assassinations. Tears crept down the inner crevices of my face, around my nose and into my mouth as I remembered Jackie standing forlornly with her two small children. Now another family would face the terrible grief associated with losing a wife and mother to a cause.

When Cliff returned from Selma some weeks later, he was different. Initially, we sat up late at night while he recounted the violence he'd seen in Alabama.

"God, Sheriff's deputies chased blacks in cars, on horseback and on foot. One officer had trained his 'mean-assed' horse to attack blacks by chasing them and biting them on the head or wherever the horse could reach. I saw the Klan chase blacks into Brown's Chapel and threaten them with fire or worse."

"How could people do this to one another?" I shivered.

"I don't know. The whites are scared. They're fighting for their way of life. In many of those southern towns they're out-numbered so if the blacks ever get the real right to vote, the whites believe they'll be driven out of office."

I wondered how I would have reacted in such a Selma situation and how I now felt about the conflict he was describing. Would I have been brave enough to stand with these people fighting for their rights? Or would I have been terrorized like many of the townspeople? Seeing a situation on TV and actually being in the middle of a conflict are very different. Until an individual is personally involved in any situation, she really doesn't know how she would react or feel.

He was home. That's all that mattered. Over a lazy Saturday morning pancake breakfast when the children had found something interesting in the backyard, I poured us another cup of coffee.

"I'm so glad you're home. Stay here for a while, huh?"

"I should be here although one never knows. I go when the Bureau says 'go'."

"I know. I've been thinking about this whole civil rights battle. I want to get involved maybe with voter registration or …"

Cliff's raised his hands in a halting gesture.

"Look, I know how you feel, but you can't get involved in any organization that's not on the Bureau approved list. And I doubt any of these civil rights organizations are. Your involvement could ruin me." My hands involuntarily slapped the table in an expression of disbelief causing Cliff to rise and take his plate to the sink.

"What? Are you saying I can't even help out a cause that's important to me unless it's Bureau approved? And where is this approved Bureau list? And does this mean Mr. Hoover has a file on me and you and other people who are trying to make a difference?" My voice increased in volume, and I didn't care who heard me shouting from this place that was becoming a prison.

"I should never have told you about Hoover's files. Forget I ever said anything."

"Forget you ever said anything about anything? Get me a copy of this approved list of organizations. That is, if there is such a list."

NINE

Encroachment

The ugly St. Augustine grass was greening and didn't look quite so spindly this morning. Bulbs were surprising me with green stalks as they erupted in the weed filled flower gardens. Those beds would need my attention soon. This backyard sure needed some trees and a whole lot more flowers. While I needed to surround myself with some outside color, our budget was already tight. My thoughts wandered as I refilled our coffee cups.

Since Cliff's return from Alabama our evening talks had opened to include more sharing of his job challenges and accomplishments. I was seeing how the seductiveness of this job could be entrapping. Cliff came alive when he talked to me about his exploits: his dark brown eyes turned almost black, his speech became animated, his hands moved in exaggeration. I watched this transformation in our recent conversations. This wasn't a job; this was a mission.

At first I felt privileged to be on the inside, to know things other people didn't know. Although it had a sense of power associated with it, I felt I was walking a tightrope. I needed to watch for clues that I was overstepping my boundaries by asking Cliff too many questions or of accidentally spilling some tidbit of information I had gleaned in living with him.

"Nice morning, huh? I'm so glad to have you home. I missed you. It feels like we've been apart as much as we've been together this past year. I want you to stay right here with us for a while." I reached over and gave his hand a big squeeze. He looked at me with that seductive, dimpled smile and wink.

"It's great to be home. I missed you, too. Hey, the house is coming along. I like what you've done so far." It felt like we were getting reacquainted when Cliff noticed my little decorating touches, like new towels or pillows.

"Can I ask you about the information you share with me?"

"Look, I really shouldn't be telling you anything. The Bureau wants info to stay inside, you know. You can't ever repeat the things I tell you." Cliff's smiling face turned to a scowl.

"Does that mean I'm outside living inside?" I waited, not really expecting an answer. There was no doubting the seriousness of his statement; I must forget what he told me, but I was soon going to need a bucket for these pieces of information I wasn't supposed to have, a secret cache only available to me. He must follow the Bureau line, and I must follow my own moral compass.

My FBI training continued. Cliff was home, and his caseload now revolved around fugitives, those who had fled from justice through prison escapes and parole violations. Enter my relationship with informants. I soon learned his motivation for building an informant base was tied to his performance rating which was statistically driven not only by the number of cases he opened and closed but also by the number of informants and their leads. Recommendations for in-grade advancement or merit increases were based on a complicated algorhythm. So it made sense for me to help him by taking an informant's message when he wasn't home. I was sort of like the other agent.

"Are you going to let me know when one of these informants might call? And how am I supposed to react?" After learning that one of the FBI's informants had been in the car with Viola Liuzo's killers, I was less than positive about this experience.

"I'll always tell you who my informants are and who might call. Not all of them will. Just take the message and tell them I'll get back with them." I wondered if I really wanted to know who these people were. Just take the message?

"Why will these people call you here? Aren't they supposed to go through the dispatcher?"

"Some of these people just don't like to talk to the dispatcher."

"I can understand that. Even when I call looking for you, they make me feel I'm intruding, that I shouldn't be wasting their time. I'm only a wife; why am I calling?"

"Any time you need me, tell them to find me."

"Okay, but I must tell you up front I don't like this whole informant piece. I don't even believe in the concept; you use criminals to trap other criminals? It makes me feel exposed and vulnerable. And I sure don't want the kids taking these calls. One more question: do these people know where we live?"

"No, that information is always protected. Don't worry; you'll see it's going to be fine."

Not feeling any more secure, I nodded in agreement.

Enter Alice, a bartender at a combination biker tavern and pool hall. Cliff told me she had worked at this particular bar for a number of years and knew the Jacksonville underground well. This wasn't an establishment for respectable persons, which made it a safe haven for fugitives and criminal entrepreneurs.

Some time after Cliff had developed Alice as one of his most productive informants, I drove by her establishment. I needed to see it to put a place with this voice and imagine her as the real person I had created.

The bar's triangular corner location was made prominent by its suggestive billboards, peeling beer signs and a large neon sign announcing steaks for $2.99 and the next band that would be playing. Its faded green shabbiness caused my shoulders to shiver as I maneuvered my station wagon to be face to face with Alice's workplace, a mysterious world. Plenty of cars whizzed by making my presence almost undetectable. As I pulled around the corner, I imagined her tending to customers and addressing most of them by name, inquiring as to their recent activity and what information might be relevant to Cliff. Who knew when the next face on a "Wanted" poster would appear in her bar, and she would call me with information for Cliff.

Such was the evening when we were entertaining two non-FBI families for dinner. After answering the phone, Tami, our astute five-year-old, entered the dining room to announce, "Dad, Hairy Legs Alice is on the phone. She says it's important." Silence crept into the room. On a previous occasion, when Cliff was jokingly describing Alice to me, he had referred to her as "Hairy Legs Alice." He was great for making up nicknames, private ones. Little people have big ears, and Tami was no exception.

"That's Alice Rogers, and she's an important person for Daddy to talk to," I said quietly. No one snickered, but I did see a couple of our friends suppress smiles. Cliff rose from his chair to take the call in the bedroom, leaving me to offer some sort of explanation.

"Her name is really Henrietta Alice, not Hairy Legs Alice. Tami must have heard it wrong." My friends looked at me, not knowing whether to laugh or dismiss the whole situation. They left and as Cliff and I were cleaning up, I suggested to him that I was uncomfortable with the kids' exposure to these callers.

"Well, tell them not to answer the phone. These people are going to call here."

"That's your solution? A five-year-old with phone restrictions?" I twisted around to look at him, shaking my head in disbelief. "No, that's not the answer, but I'm going to talk to her about these creepy people calling for you. I think it would help if you didn't bandy about these informants' names. She's a five-year-old; she's going to repeat what she hears."

"Look, I'll try to get these people to direct more of their calls through the dispatcher." I nodded.

"Good. I don't especially like talking to these people either, but I can handle it." At that moment the platter I was drying slipped from my hands, splattering shards all over the kitchen. Cliff 's startled expression told me he wasn't sure this was an accident.

These intrusive calls continued despite my trepidations. My daughter was answering the phone and speaking to the people in her dad's world. These weren't nice people. Now they knew Cliff had a daughter. He said they didn't know where we lived, but I wasn't convinced.

Alice remained a valuable contact even when Cliff was moved to the bank robbery squad, which now required a new specialty, a bank robbery informant. His name was Red; at least that's what he said. I don't know if I ever knew his last name. His relationship with Cliff began with the bank robbery assignment although providing information specific to banks was only one of his talents. He knew lots of people in high places and in low places. When I took his calls, he would give me his information such as an address and hang up. Often he didn't even identify himself, which was fine because his soft slurred tone was distinctive. One night when he called about 11:00, I overheard Cliff agree to go to an address where Red told Cliff he would most likely find a certain group of robbers counting their money.

I heard him go into our room to change his clothes for another late night.

"Looks like you have a lead," I said. "How do you know this isn't a setup? You don't really know this Red, do you?" My hands grasped one another behind my back for security.

"This looks good. Bob and I should be making an arrest. Bank robbers aren't very smart." He smiled at what he considered a joke. And there were lots of bank robber jokes like the one about the robber writing his demand on the back of his own deposit slip.

"Honey, I should be home soon; I don't think this is going to take very long."

This time he was right. Cliff picked up Bob, his partner, and they made the arrest. Red knew a lot about criminal activity in Jacksonville. But sometimes having information doesn't insure success. On another such night, Cliff didn't come home early, and I received a call from the dispatcher.

"Mrs. Browning, this is dispatch. Your husband asked me to call to tell you he's in the emergency room at Baptist Hospital, but there's nothing to worry about."

Not worry? I worried about whether the kids' socks matched. "What happened? Do you have any more information?" My overactive imagination was in full bloom: he'd been shot, was on life support. A little information is worse than none.

"He said it's just a few stitches. He'll call just as soon as they've finished."

Maybe I should get a sitter and drive to the hospital. No, it's too late. I could get them up and pile everyone in the car. No, I'll wait a little longer. Minutes passed like hours while I waited for a call.

"Hi hon, did the dispatcher call you?" He sounded fine, no cracking voice or faintness that I could detect. "It's nothing, really. The guy was a lousy shot. He did wreck my suit though, and they had to cut the leg open to stitch me up."

"What do you mean he was a lousy shot? Are you telling me you are now a shooting victim? You've been telling me all along this is a safe job. Safe it isn't. Shall I come get you?" Now the volume in my voice had escalated several decibels.

"No, Bob is here waiting for me. I'm going to have to submit a requisition for a new suit though, although I doubt the Bureau will cover it." At least it was only a suit we had to worry about.

He was right: his injuries were minor, and the suit was ruined. He came in the carport door limping a little, carrying his ruined suit pants and dressed in scrubs the hospital had loaned him.

"You don't look too great. Sit down. Let me see the damage. This really isn't a minor event, you know." I took his clothes from him and guided him to the kitchen chair.

"I told you it's nothing. See, just a few stitches," as he pulled down the scrubs to reveal the bandaged upper thigh.

"Sorry, it's not nothing. Normal people don't walk in after being shot'"

"Actually, I think I tore it open scaling the barbed wire fence."

I had heard wrong? So which story was it?

And, no, the Bureau would not cover the cost of the suit even though it happened in the line of duty. Mr. Hoover was a frugal man.

Since Fridays were bank robbery days, the day when banks had the most money. Cliff and Bob's schedule consisted of chasing robbers on Friday night and working the investigation through Saturday or even into Sunday while the leads were hot. Initially, I thought if Cliff worked the weekend he would get time off during the week. Not the way the Bureau worked.

Cliff's days were long, often into the night. These were the hardest and loneliest times. Is this what those wives meant by the second office being different? On those days when he did arrive home in time for dinner, Tami, Ray and I followed him hungrily from the door down the hall to the bedroom, each competing for his attention, talking non-stop louder and louder. Each of us had much to tell Daddy. As long as everything at home was intact and no one had required stitches that day, he didn't need to know the details. But I needed to share those with someone.

Squeezing in evening talk time was hard given the many phone interruptions. Sometimes I wished we could go outside, to the far side of the fence, close to the moonshiners, where we couldn't hear its ring. On one of those quieter evenings, Cliff's expressions told me he wanted to talk to me about something that perhaps I didn't want to hear.

"Sandy, you're probably going to resist, but you should know how to protect yourself and the kids here at home."

"Protect myself? I'll call someone if I have a problem. Aren't you supposed to be available? I live with a person who protects people." Now my wrinkled brow matched his.

"Yes, but I'd feel better knowing you could protect yourself without me. I think you should know how to shoot my .38 Snubby, just in case." His .38 had recently become available due to a bizarre progression of events.

My parents, on a recent visit, asked us if we would go to the local gun store with them. Go to a gun store? They didn't even own a gun. Thinking this was for my dad, we piled in the car, and Cliff drove to a place I'd never seen, in a part of town I'd never happen into unless I were lost. The building's dusty light brick couldn't quite hide the latest graffiti marks. Its large front windows, shielded by bars, could have formerly been a pawnshop or a strip joint. A uniformed security person stood unsmiling at the door. Cliff flashed his badge, and we filed into an arsenal crowded with weapons of destruction in every shape and size, some locked in cases, others standing in racks like sentries. I wasn't sure my children should even be seeing this, but Ray acted as if he had found nirvana as his dad was attempting to answer his rapid-fire questions. Mom and I, on the other hand, definitely didn't belong here. She, in her fashionable dress and matching high heels and purse, stood out among the NRA attire of the day.

"Dad, what kind of gun are you looking for?" Cliff was proud to be able to showcase his expertise.

"Oh, he isn't looking for a gun, Cliff," Mom said. "It's for you. I want to buy you an early birthday present. If you're going to be in this dangerous job, you should have the very best protection." Her seriousness caused Cliff and me to stop mid-aisle, my face registering absolute disbelief. My mother didn't buy guns for anyone. Her weapon of choice was a Louisville Slugger. I was playing some bit part in an insane comedy.

"Mom, I have a government issue .38 which is more than adequate. The Bureau equips us well." Cliff was stumbling for words; he was shopping for a gun with my mother, a woman driven by what's chic and fashionable. Weapons didn't really fall into either of these categories.

"I just want you to be armed with the best. I have my daughter and grandchildren to think of, so if you were to buy the very best one of these for your job, what would it be?" She waved her hand toward the lineup of devastating weapons. She was serious; it was the first time I had seen her concern for my safety. I also knew her well enough to know she had given this situation a great deal of thought. "Let's find someone to help us."

Dad and I trailed along behind this unlikely duo.

"Well, gosh, if I were able to buy a new revolver, it would be a .357 Magnum, but Mom…"

"Okay, why don't you show us some of those," Mom stated confidently to the salesman who had appeared from behind one of the many counters. I knew she didn't know one caliber from another.

The salesperson explained to Cliff and Mom the merits of the various models. Satisfied all his questions had been answered, Mom proudly wrote the check for this blue-black Smith and Wesson .357 Magnum, one more gun in our growing armory. Cliff and Mom were the two proudest people that store had seen in a while. I looked at Dad; he smiled that knowing smile of his as if to say, "Maybe you don't really know your mother."

So now we had an extra .38 that had my name on it. Just in case.

Just in case of what? For the most part I was careful to lock doors, check the windows, keep the drapes closed at night, and we were thinking about getting a dog. Maybe I was feeling more comfortable in my home and neighborhood than I should have. Maybe there was something I was overlooking.

"If this gun is in the house," said Cliff, "you should know how to use it, how to protect yourself and the kids."

"Well, take it out of the house, or you can leave it here safely tucked away from the kids in a hard-to-find place, but if you're suggesting I actually fire it, the answer is 'no.'" I hoped the firm set of my jaw convinced him I wasn't going to go to any firing range to practice for something I wasn't going to do. End of discussion.

Without belaboring the dialogue and to satisfy his own concerns, Cliff loaded this small, but supposedly effective, hand gun, which he now referred to as mine, with a scattershot load that was sure to hit someone if I just pointed it and pulled the trigger. I didn't argue; if it made him feel better to have it loaded, just in case, okay. Pretty sure I would never need this instrument, I carefully lifted this cold piece of steel from Cliff's hand, afraid I might set it off in the process of stowing it under my sweats in the bureau drawer. I shuddered and shook my hands to remove any residue.

A few weeks after this conversation, my resolve was tested. Reading in our pleasantly furnished bedroom late one night, I waited for Cliff to get home. The house was unusually quiet: no rain hitting the downspouts, no cars on the street, just me, waiting, then listening to a scratching develop to my right against the outside wall or was it against the window? I couldn't tell. Thinking it may have been a cat known to favor the tree just outside the window causing the branches to hit the glass, I cautiously inserted my fingers behind the edge of the blind and peered through the crack, where I saw, not a tree branch, but fingers scratching. I inhaled and stifled a scream for fear I would wake the children. Quietly, with my hand over my mouth insuring no sound erupted, I crept from the bed toward the bureau drawer where I had stowed the pistol that I said I would never use. I pulled the drawer open and felt for metal under the folded sweats. What I felt was cold and smooth. What if I shot someone or myself? I wrapped the fingers of my right hand around what felt like the grip and lifted it toward me. I pointed it downward and raised my shaking body from the floor. I looked down at this evil looking blue-black piece of steel now cold and heavy in my hand. I moved, trembling, into the hallway. Who could I possibly scare other than myself? Despite my objections at the time, Cliff had told me that if I stood in the hallway and aimed straight ahead I would hit the person as he tried to enter through the carport door. Assuming I could pull the trigger. I crouched on the floor and dialed the dispatcher to relay a message to Cliff that someone, possibly a burglar, was trying to get into the house. Later I would ask myself why I hadn't just called the police. I thought I lived with the police.

I planted myself in the hallway just past the children's rooms, willing the shaking and tears to subside, not standing but hunkering in my bare feet and pajamas. I looked at my children's closed bedroom doors and resolved to do what I thought I couldn't. Poised and set with tears streaming down my face and my firearm at the ready, I waited and waited and waited.

Endless moments later I heard movement in the carport just as Cliff had predicted in our earlier conversation; if someone were to try to break in, it would be through the carport, dark and sheltered from street view. Who was out there? Could he see me through the frosted jalousie door? Did he know how terrified I was? Now I knew I couldn't shoot him.

"Please hurry! Please send someone to help me." I willed my prayers to anyone listening. The ringing phone blared through the now deafening silence. I crawled back to the bedroom and picked it up to stop the screaming.

"Honey, I'm on my way home. Are you okay?"

"No, I'm not okay. Where are the police? Hurry! He's in the carport. I can hear him." I stood motionless and ready, ready for something, anything. Could my husband protect us, or did he only work cases for other people? My ice cold hands shook, not from the weight of my .38 Snubby but from the raw fear now compromising any rational action. I could shoot him; I couldn't shoot him.

After what felt interminable, I saw lights through the carport door flash into the driveway. The jalousied door opened. I was frozen into place. Shoot? Don't shoot? Oh no, is this what it's going to be like? One of Cliff's informants, a suspect in a case, just some unwelcome visitor waltzing by? Not the latter, for sure. In my mind it was all related to Cliff's job.

I heard a voice call to me from the door. "Honey, put the gun down." I pointed the barrel down toward the floor and inched it down the side of my leg toward the floor as if any jerk or unplanned movement would cause it to fire. When Cliff saw the gun lying on the hallway floor, he walked toward me with arms outstretched. He held my shaking body close.

"I love you. Don't be afraid. It's okay. I drove through the neighborhood but didn't see any strange cars or even anyone prowling around," he announced. "Whoever it was is gone." He held me until the shaking stopped and I could talk without sobbing.

"Was it one of your informants? Will he be back the next time he sees my light on and the car missing? I don't think I'm safe; I don't feel safe." I shuddered as I blurted, "I know this is related to your job. Other people don't live like this."

"Honey, attempted break-ins occur every day. I'm sure it doesn't have anything to do with my job. I just want you to be prepared in case I'm not home…."

"In case? You're never home. Every time you're gone will I be sitting up with my gun that I'm too afraid to shoot anyway?" I took a small step back from his body so I could look at him and see what his eyes were telling me. "And how can you be sure this person wasn't one of your disturbed informants? I don't want to live this way."

"I know you're scared, but you handled yourself just right, just the way we talked about. Besides, as I said, this could happen to anyone." He was smiling; he was smiling as if I deserved some reward.

"It didn't. It happened to me."

We could argue this for the rest of the night, but in my mind it all had to do with his job: he wasn't home, someone tried to break in, and for me the two were related.

Several hours later I lay face-up, imagining the shadows dancing on the ceiling and walls to be angels of protection encircling my little family. The ticking clock reminded me it would soon be morning, and I would relive this nightmare. I slipped my slippers onto my cool feet and made my way to the kitchen. Maybe I needed to add some security to this little house. Deadbolt locks for the two exterior doors and solid drapes over the sheers in the living room as well as security bars for the two sliding doors would be starters. I sipped my tea and reflected.

In living this life it wasn't going to be easy to maintain a glass half-full attitude. Fear for our safety was only part of it. Now two plus years in Jacksonville, I felt the insidious encroachment of the Bureau, like a sophisticated mold growing, eroding my own sense of person. How was I going to become me while fending off the assaults of living in the FBI shadow?

T E N

Two Roads and a Detour

Robert Frost suggested possibility when he wrote, "Two roads diverged in a yellow wood…and I took the road less traveled." At this point in our journey Cliff and I were exploring parallel roads: his straight FBI road with few deviations from the prescribed and my road, wandering, exploring, daydreaming and still under construction. I liked it better when we were on the same road.

Like when we attended the annual FBI picnic and firearms demonstration. It was family, all FBI families together. I felt then like I belonged to something larger than our own little neighborhood world. Or when it seemed the whole world converged on our backyard trampoline. Cliff had insisted this would be great fun for the kids. Whenever he had a few minutes he would gather with Tami, Ray and friends to learn new tricks.

"How did you know how to do all these things?" I asked.

"CYA. Every day after school I'd walk there to see Father Tim who taught me everything I know about sports. He got me into basketball, then into gymnastics and finally into weights when I got a little older. He turned my life around."

Over the years Cliff had shared very little with me about his childhood except that he was an angry adolescent and his coaches and athletics at the Catholic Youth Organization had saved him.

For the past year I had been thinking I needed a direction of my own, one distinct from the FBI tentacles I felt were beginning to strangle me. I found it in the course of searching for a kindergarten program for Tami and pre-school for Ray. As I enrolled the kids, Betsy Craft, the director, encouraged me to volunteer once or twice a week, which I was eager to do. Tami, Ray and I would go to school together. At the end of the school year, Betsy approached me with a proposition.

"Sandy, as you know, Marilyn won't be back in the fall so I'm going to need to hire a teacher for the four-year-old class. I was wondering if you had any interest. You've done a really good job helping us out so I thought I'd ask you first." Her sincerity made me feel I was already part of the team.

"Thanks Betsy, I'm definitely interested. Can I have a day or two to talk to my family?" What did I need to think through? It was perfect. Although, I was trained as a high school teacher, I already knew I could work with little kids, and I loved the part of going to school with my own children.

Driving home I relished my enthusiasm. This would be my world, one separate from Cliff's.

"You look all chipper. What's happening?" Cliff asked as he walked in the door. I was almost dancing as I followed him down the hall to change his clothes.

"Okay, what is it? I haven't seen you this bubbly for a while. Must be something pretty exciting."

"It is. I have a job! This morning Betsy offered me the four-year-old position. She likes what I've been doing as a volunteer; now she wants me as a regular staff member. It's only part-time in the mornings. What do you think?" I rattled on without taking a breath or allowing an interruption.

"Hmm, a job, huh? You seem pretty excited. I don't know about teaching every day though. You know how my schedule is. I won't be able to help. You would be taking this on your own." My expression must have relayed my disappointment.

"I won't need your help; it's four mornings a week, and you don't have to remind me about the demands of your very important job. I'm not asking permission; I just wanted an endorsement. I know what I'm taking on, and I'm going to do it." Somewhere I needed to draw a line between my role as FBI wife and myself as an individual.

Cliff's shrug in concession told me this was my baby.

The following morning I signed a contract with Betsy, my very first teaching commitment. I liked the way I felt as I left her office. I looked around the building, peeking in the other classrooms filled with wonderful, happy artwork. One of these rooms would be mine: the four-year-old room. I would paper it with projects, messy, artful pictures and create a warm, stimulating environment for the children entrusted to me. I was going to love this job, every minute of it. As I left the building I felt taller even in my flat "little kid" shoes.

Changes were underway for Cliff as well. He was assigned to a new desk: white slavery, the crime of transporting women across state lines for immoral purposes. Something called the Mann Act. White or black, it was still slavery of sorts. It seemed to me Cliff and I were sliding deeper down the social order. This was a scarier group of people than the bank robbers. I asked him to please leave me out of this part of his life. I didn't want to hear the stories about his arrests, the beatings and murder of participants or the horrible abuse of women. Even the phone calls were creepy; if they were women, their voices were desperate as if only Cliff were going to be able to help them. Cliff took these calls in stride. Violence and degradation had become part of his world.

But Brian was a different story. The first time this new informant called for Cliff, I answered and thought I must be speaking with a radio personality. His deep resonant voice captured my imagination, velvet with beautiful enunciation. He must be tall, handsome and probably well-dressed. "Have Cliff call me when he gets in; he's got my number."

Over the next year he would often call when Cliff was out on a case, usually around 9:00 p.m. I would take Brian's message. Then we would just chat. He seemed to be a sensitive, caring man. I wondered why he was an informant. Asking him would have been improper. He told me he lived in Alabama where I imagined him residing in a lovely home, maybe with a wife.

One evening when I gave Cliff Brian's message, I added that I thought he was a sincerely nice man and that, ironically, I looked forward to my conversations with him, almost as a friend. I smiled as I described my latest conversation with him.

"Wait a minute. He's an informant. He's not a friend." He looked at me quizzically and then almost sternly.

"Cliff, he's not like the others. That's all I'm saying. He's kind and thoughtful. He always asks how I am. Can't he be a nice informant? Seems to me if I'm the at-home agent, then I can like or dislike these people."

"I suppose, and yes, Brian comes across as a kind person. You just need to remember that what he does for a living is criminal."

One evening a few months later, Cliff quietly entered through the carport door, earlier than usual, with a downcast expression on his face.

"What's the matter?" I asked. "You look terrible. Must have had a bad day."

"I am terrible. I lost an informant today." Immediately, I figured someone had been arrested; this occurred on a rather frequent basis.

"Who is it? Anybody I know?" Instead of moving down the hall to change his clothes, he leaned against the kitchen counter next to the washer and dryer where I stopped folding the clothes and looked at him. He stared at me with an expression of sadness.

"It's someone you know well. I got the call this afternoon, and I've dreaded telling you." He moved closer to me as if to soften what he was about to say. "Brian was murdered last night. I wouldn't have told you, but I knew you would wonder why he stopped calling."

Unbelieving, I looked up at Cliff through teary eyes. "How can this be? I just talked to him. Who would've wanted him dead? Have they caught the murderer?"

Cliff looked at me with a perplexed look as if I had just asked him about a case in the newspaper that involved "regular" people. What did I know about my husband's other life?

"We don't know much except he was meeting with known traffickers in a small town in Alabama. Brian was involved with some very big names in white slavery; he must have gotten crosswise with someone. Life is cheap in that world." A certain callousness had become part of Cliff's job conversations. Maybe that was a way of protecting himself from feeling.

This time I turned full face, speaking louder and more forcefully, each word selected from an anger base. "So this is what happens to your informants? They work with the FBI and end up dead? I can see a wanted poster now: 'Help Wanted: people who like to talk; reward, a coffin.'"

"Sandy, the Bureau didn't kill him. These people are connected to people who operate outside the law, and sometimes they end up dead."

Throwing the rest of the clothes to be folded into a basket, I turned to release more pent up emotion.

"Just like that – dead. Well, line up another one. Except they're real people to me. Cliff, I don't want to do this anymore." There I had said it; I wanted off his road. But I knew these people would still call, and sometimes I would care about them.

On another level Cliff's FBI world barged into my personal space. Undercover work was a fact in the investigative life of tracking down white slave violators, at times requiring agents to pose as customers for prostitutes. Despite my objections, I was learning more about this side of law enforcement than I had ever cared to know.

On such raids Cliff would typically work from late afternoon through the night and into the next morning. Usually he would drag in around 9:00 for breakfast and after a brief rest report to the office in the afternoon. Not an ideal schedule. The pay-off was an occasional Saturday breakfast together while the children played, a relaxed time when we were able to catch up on family stuff. No Bureau talk at this table, at least not intentionally.

"How about coffee this morning? Have you had breakfast?" His drawn face told me he could use a cup. He nodded with little conviction, loosened his tie and took off his wrinkled suit jacket that looked like it had been slept in. His face was haggard, and he smelled of stale cigarette smoke and unwashed bodies.

"I'll grab the paper," he said as he rose from his seat.

"You're not very talkative. You look terrible. And you don't smell so great. Something wrong?"

Silence meant something was definitely wrong.

"No, I'm just tired. Give me a few minutes to wind down with my coffee. It was a pretty disturbing sting operation."

No, he wasn't just tired. I knew Cliff well, and the way he was acting wasn't like him. I looked down as I refilled his cup. His hand was wrapped around the edge of the paper revealing a white, untanned place where his wedding ring should have been. My face, on fire, betrayed my anger. My stomach's knot tightened. The one that twisted with a warning that something was more than amiss.

"Wait. Aren't you missing something? Where's your wedding band?" I looked at my quivering hand still grasping the coffee carafe like it was my lifeline to somewhere. I momentarily resisted the urge to heave the pot at the nearest object. Home invasion is what this was, that creepy encroachment I'd been fighting since day one.

"I was going to tell you this morning, but I was really hoping I'd find it before I came home. It's not what you think." The intensity of his look made me want to believe what was coming next.

"How do you know what I really think? Tell me what happened, and I'll tell you if you're right." I replaced the carafe onto the warming tray of the coffee pot and moved to my usual chair opposite my husband forcing eye contact as a gauge for his honesty. So far, we had been able to make this job work because we trusted one another.

"Sometimes, in these raids it's better if I don't appear to be married. So I took my ring off before last night's raid. It was for the undercover part…"

"Oh, so now in this job you decide when and where you're going to be married? Like, for this damned case I'll be married, but when I go to this hotel, it's better if I don't look married? That's how it works?" This time the filth had oozed in well past our front door creating a slime I wasn't sure I could eradicate.

"I know you're upset. So am I. I never intended this to happen." His hangdog look wasn't convincing.

"You took off your wedding band and left it where? The part about taking it off I get. But where is it now?"

"I don't know. I've looked everywhere. I thought I put it in my coat pocket, but maybe I left it at the motel. I've gone through all my pockets, searched the car…" His shoulders slumped, and his eyes diverted to his coffee cup as he tried to explain to me an indefensible situation.

"This is just terrific. Did you go back to the motel? Or was it not that important to you in the first place?" Whether I was playing fair or not got lost in my ire and disappointment. Likely someone else was now wearing my husband's ring, the one that symbolized a bond between us.

"I guess I know how much it meant to you." I stammered in disbelief. "You know what," I tearfully continued. "I'm sick of this. The Bureau's taking more and more of my life, and now this. What else will they take, your life?"

If I needed convincing, this detour confirmed I must no longer fool myself into thinking this was a regular job and that we were a regular family. No, he didn't work in some downtown hi-rise like other fathers and husbands. He was an FBI agent, and what he did was dangerous and ugly.

ELEVEN

Pretending

Pretending can be costly. I was eleven when I was first assaulted by pneumonia in an age before wonder drugs. I lost two months of sixth grade. As I matured, allergies and asthma became part of my respiratory battle: cold or virus leads to congestion, which leads to bronchitis, which leads to pneumonia. Moving from one climate to another had helped in the past as the allergens differed in each place. Now my "honeymoon" period in Florida was over. My symptoms reappeared with a vengeance. Doctors prescribed antihistamines, antibiotics, inhalers, allergy shots and many other drugs to control the almost constant infections. As a last resort and with urgency, my medical team recommended a steroid regimen.

Cliff and I seated ourselves at a long table in Dr. Weaver's conference room. I admired the cherry finish on the table and the professionally decorated, comfortable room. If you were delivering unpleasant news, better to do it in pleasing surroundings.

"Dr. Weaver began, "As you both know, we have tried many approaches to Sandy's almost continuous respiratory infections but only with short-term results. While this isn't a new problem, the climate here has exacerbated her condition." I liked Dr. Weaver because he called the situation like he saw it.

"She's definitely tried a lot of approaches," Cliff said. "So what do we do now?" He was looking at Dr. Weaver and dismissing my presence.

I looked at these two men who appeared to be talking about one who was absent from this conversation.

"Wait, I'm not invisible here. I'm the person we're all talking about." I looked toward the doctor spreading my hands upward on the table, demanding.

"Bottom line, it's not a good idea for her to stay here," the doctor continued. "Her body is reacting violently to the high mold content here. Eventually, she will have to move." I turned to look at Cliff. I had heard a gentler recommendation in an earlier visit, but I needed Cliff to hear it directly from the doctor.

Isn't there something else to try? I think she mentioned some kind of steroid regimen. We both have jobs here; our kids are in school here." Cliff stared intently at the doctor as if to will him to offer another alternative.

"Yes, I've mentioned to Sandy that we could put her on what we call a maintenance dose of cortisone. It's a last result situation not without unpleasant side effects."

Cliff looked from me to the doctor. "What are these side effects?"

"Usually joint pain, weight gain, immune suppression and swelling in the face to create a moon shape, distinctive with users of steroids. She may or may not feel these effects. There is another danger, and that's associated with discontinuing the drugs. There can be serious consequences if a patient abruptly stops the drugs. They must be phased out over a substantial period of time." I had already heard this list; I interrupted.

"Doctor, I've been on short doses, and they definitely work, but this sounds like a life sentence until I leave Florida." I looked at Cliff. His lack of response suggested it was going to be my decision.

"It's like this. You have three options: one, continue as you are and manage the infections as they come; two, relocate to a climate significantly different from Florida; stay here and go on the cortisone maintenance program until your next transfer when you can discuss with your doctor how to go off the program." He looked at both of us with a serious expression demanding a response. We nodded.

It was an uncomfortable ending to a consultation on an issue neither of us wanted to confront. We left the office with Cliff suggesting we go for lunch to talk about the situation. It was a little early for the noon crowd so we had a nice window table to ourselves. From my upholstered chair I looked out onto the street imagining all those professional people who would soon be swarming from the neighboring, polished buildings for lunch. I was growing to like it here. We had friends, I had a job, the relationship was working, not perfectly, but working. In the past Cliff's jobs had driven the need to move; now I was the one who needed to relocate. Funny how life turns issues upside down.

"Well, what do you think I should do? I've been on so many drugs. I don't know about this steroid thing. I try really hard to stay well, but my body doesn't like Florida. Would a transfer even be possible?"

"I don't know. I did some checking before our appointment today. The Bureau does have a provision for a medical transfer," Cliff said. "I could submit paperwork requesting a relocation for medical reasons along with your medical records and your doctor's location recommendation. The Bureau considers the request and makes a decision." His hands remained folded in front of him like they held the answer.

"And then what? What's the downside?"

"If they decide to grant such a transfer, then we would be in that office for the remainder of my career. This would be a serious step and would end any future promotions for me. I'm not saying that's the most important thing – you are, but it's probably something we want to consider."

"I get it. If I ask you to go for the medical, then I'm the one who killed your career." I looked at him; I knew such a decision would end our relationship. It had become more and more apparent that he was in two marriages, one to me and one to the FBI. This wasn't a job decision.

It was a mission decision.

"The way things are moving with your career path, all the commendations and pay raises, I'd guess we won't be here too much longer anyway. We've been here almost four years; so shouldn't you be up for transfer soon? And you've let people know you're aiming for a leadership position. So maybe I go on the steroid program and wait it out." I sounded like a sales pitch to myself.

"Are you really okay with that? It's your call. If you think we have to go for the medical, I'll listen." His expression told me to say "yes." So I did.

This could have been our decision, but he had made it mine.

I had time, and time is what I needed right now. I drove from the restaurant to one of the marinas on the St. John's River and parked my car close to the walkway. I needed to walk beside the water, to feel life in a different form. I looked down at the wide murky expanse swirling almost undetectably, moving forward as if it knew its destination. Surely this massive force encountered obstacles, some to be negotiated, some to be avoided, some to be met headlong. I walked for the better part of an hour watching and listening and thinking of my life force. I had met an obstacle, a rather complicated one. I could continue to make sacrifices for my husband's career, this time at the expense of my own health, or I could make a decision that might provide another patch to a relationship with a widening divide. As I neared the car, I could feel drops rolling down my cheeks.

T W E L V E

Promise

Five years in the Bureau, ten years in a marriage, two children and a third expected in October signified a crossing of sorts from the innocence and naïve errors of my twenties to the quasi maturity of thirty. I would celebrate this milestone in August with some sense of accomplishment: successfully raising two children thus far, holding a marriage together which threatened at times to unravel, acclimating myself to some of the challenges of being an FBI family, and excelling in my first teaching job. Not a bad base to build on.

On a Friday in mid-August Cliff asked me to meet him at the nicest hotel in Jacksonville for an early dinner celebrating our tenth wedding anniversary. He would drive from work, and I would find my way from the obstetrician's office. Pulling into the valet entrance and feeling uniquely special despite my pregnant state, the attendant met me with deference, took my car keys and escorted me to the lobby where we were to meet. Something like a clandestine affair.

Settling myself into one of the plush couches, from which I wondered if I would ever want to extricate myself, I looked around at the elegance: the rich tones of hand woven carpets, walls papered in what looked to be silk coverings in a shade of palest aqua, chandeliers glistening with glass tear drops, and music ever so softly caressing my ears. This felt like a perfect place to re-center myself. I felt my body relax into the soft buttery colored cushions and imagined myself living in this lifestyle. I had read that in times past women of means lived in luxurious hotels like this in major cities. I could see myself descending the elegant stairs for afternoon tea served on silver trays accompanied by dainty open-faced sandwiches.

I was pleased I had arrived early. Having this private time was a gift to myself. I felt my tension melt into the restorative atmosphere.

"I see you made it with no trouble. Did I choose the right place?" Cliff's smile told me he had given this some thought and had decided accurately that I would appreciate celebrating our anniversary here.

"It's beautiful. I guess I really don't know very much about Jacksonville, at least not this part of town. I could stay here. What a perfect place for a rendezvous." I waved my hand to direct his attention to the room's décor. "Have you been here often?"

"No, not often. There are a few nice spots like this in town. I guess I should get you out more."

"Yes, you should. This is just my style." I smiled.

"Are you ready for dinner?" He held out his hand to assist my rise from the enveloping cushion, put his arms around me and kissed me just like a scene from a romance novel.

Our table was special, overlooking the city and the St. Johns River. Linen tablecloths, crystal stemware, candles and a beautiful bouquet of red roses whose card had been carefully crafted, created a celebratory ambience. Cliff and the waiter attended to my comfort, pulling the chair out for me, respectfully handing me the soft napkin and placing the substantial menu at the side of my gold rimmed plate.

Ten years can be a lifetime, and our decade long journey together could never be described as routine. On that August afternoon, when Cliff and I had exchanged promises to each other to be faithful, to love one another and to stick it out together, we never could have imagined the scope of our experiences. Through trials, we had somehow figured out how to forge enough positives to keep it together. Ten years merited celebration. The next ten years promised what? Perhaps more closeness and renewed effort to keep our marriage out of the divorce court. I would do almost anything to avoid that. Almost anything.

I leaned forward, thanked him for the lovely roses and card and said I had a bit of news from the doctor.

"You may be getting the most wonderful birthday present this year." I smiled and intertwined my fingers to suggest a surprise.

"My birthday's in October," he said. "It's only August. We should be talking about your birthday." For sure. The most special day in the year for me was a few days away.

"Nope. Dr. Johnson says that this baby will most likely be born close to your birthday. Wouldn't that be special if you shared birthdays with this child?" I'm sure my eyes sparkled with the news.

"This news calls for an additional toast." We raised our wine glasses in celebration. It had not yet been determined that women should not imbibe when pregnant.

"This is wonderful," I almost whispered. "I'd like to do this more often. Have these special private times with you. No phones, no dispatcher, no informants. I don't think you know how special these times are for me." He lowered his gaze to the table for just a second. When he looked up, I continued.

"I did something for this anniversary that comes with many conflicting emotions. Please read the card first and then open the package." I had fought with myself over this gift. Should I, shouldn't I? In the end I decided to do something that symbolized my renewed promise.

Cliff reached for the card, read the hand-written thoughts and looked up at me with watery eyes. He was always able to hold tears in check. He just didn't cry; I cried enough for both of us. He looked up at me as if he knew what he would find in the small box: a shiny gold wedding band. He removed it from the box and slid it onto his finger.

"It's even nicer than the last one," he quipped. "How did you know the size?" He had gained some control of his emotions.

"Easy, I found your old college ring in your dresser box. Yes, this one's nicer; actually, I hope it represents even more than the old one." I reached across the table to finger the gold ring, twisting it as if to say this is where it should stay.

Our waiter was sensitive to our occasion and almost invisibly served us. We finished dessert, and I leaned back in my chair and sighed.

"Don't get too comfortable," Cliff said. "I have something I've been patiently waiting to give you. You deserve much more than just a dinner."

"I hope it's not something to eat. I feel like I'm about to explode." He smiled as he handed me a long thin box wrapped in gold foil and with it a card.

Carefully removing the foil, I opened the velvet-lined box from one of Jacksonville's priciest jewelers. I gasped in delight as I lifted a beautiful 14K gold charm bracelet adorned with a ruby encrusted gold heart-shaped charm etched with our anniversary date on the back. I had mentioned in a moment of crisis sometime earlier in the year that I should have a bracelet memorializing the key events in my life. I had said it facetiously to mean a life lived with so many peaks and valleys, so many calls for changes.

I looked at my 10th anniversary gift with tears welling. It had been a trying yet stimulating journey with this man seated across from me. I observed his gaze as he waited for my reaction to his gift.

"Now I can play catch-up with the charms," he said. "You should have one for each child and one for each place we've lived." I nodded. Cliff wasn't normally big on emotional gifts or scenes. His actions told me this evening was about me.

"That would be wonderful. I'd almost have a full bracelet, wouldn't I?" We both smiled as Cliff reached across the table for the box, taking my hand and hanging on.

"It belongs on your wrist, don't you think," he asked. I did think so.

With our gifts, we had each made a statement to one another. We weren't ready to give up, not yet. Promise lay ahead in the birth of our third child, my improving health, and an unknown transfer to a place presenting us with another new start.

When I had learned I was pregnant, Cliff and I discussed whether we should move to a larger house, but the possibility of a transfer still loomed. I was now feeling better, probably a combination of steroids and hormonal changes. Ultimately, after looking around at some larger homes to rent and considering the hassles and expense of a move, we decided to hunker down in our existing space. I had resigned from my teaching job and focused on pampering myself and preparing a space for this child.

October 16, William Thomas Browning joined our family. He was a beautiful baby and already seemed ready for his world. Joking with me as we drove to the hospital, Cliff asked if I might wait one more day so this child could be born on his birthday. No response was necessary. Cliff's pride was especially evident when he presented to me a congratulatory hand-written note from Mr. Hoover, whose presence always seemed to be lurking. Cliff had met him once as part of his exit from training at Quantico and described him as this short, round man with the demeanor of an emperor. I would save personal Hoover notes for posterity.

Recovering in my hospital room filled with flowers and a promise from my mother to arrive the next day to help out for a couple of weeks, I reached for Cliff's hand as he sat on the edge of my bed. *Oh, if I could only have more of these moments.*

"I love you," he said. "Since our special dinner I've been thinking a lot about us and our years together, and I've decided we're pretty special."

"You and me? Special is good; I like to be special."

"Yup. I just think we're quite a team." He smiled at me in his special loving way.

That there was a disconnect in the way we saw the events of the past ten years wasn't a secret. Cliff saw our relationship as sound. I saw it as needing nurture and care, which can only happen when two people are available to work on it. Love doesn't just flower; it must be fertilized, watered and tended. Weeds and old issues need to be excised. We needed special moments like these when we could replant and harvest what remained of our love for one another.

Promise comes with expectations, and the Bureau was about to deal us a two-edged sword.

"Hi, honey. Look, I'm on my way home. I need to talk to you about something." When Cliff said he was coming home in the middle of the day, it was never to deliver good news.

"Okay, but I'm not feeling particularly well, and I just put Billy down, so be quiet when you come in." I had been vomiting all morning; must be the flu or something. I wasn't interested in some serious discussion like whether we should sell the boat that I hadn't particularly wanted in the first place or if he were to be sent on another deployment.

He walked into the bedroom where I was lying down next to Billy and placed kisses on both of us. "How do you feel? Can I get you anything?" I shook my head "no."

"What brings you home in the middle of the day?" His expression told me this wasn't a "cheer me up" visit.

"Listen, you know we've been expecting news of a transfer. Well, this morning I got the news. It isn't what we've talked about or planned for, but we can definitely make it work. Actually, it could be a great opportunity. At least, it will be a change of climate for you." He paused and reached for my hand. "I've been told I need to be in New York in thirty days."

There was no way to deliver this news thoughtfully, and he knew I would not take it well. I looked up into his face unbelieving. Tears trickled into my mouth as I sat up on the edge of the bed, slipped on my flip-flops and headed for the living room.

"I can't go there, not to New York. I have a new baby, I'm sick, and we have two kids in school." This was my short list. Right now my stomach kept me close to the bathroom. "Move? To New York? No, it isn't possible. Tell the all-important Bureau we can't go there. Surely, there's a way to appeal this." My list could go on, but I looked up to see an expression of dismay, so I stopped talking.

"Honey, I know how disappointed you are. I was hoping our next stop would be a really great city, maybe on the west coast close to your family. I'm sorry. I thought about this all the way home."

"What exactly did you think about? Look, I've moved, lived through separations, home break-ins, shootings, suffered ill health, and for all this sacrifice I get to move my family to New York City where your work will be even more dangerous, the kids will have to adjust to new schools, we will need to live miles from the city, and I'll probably be alone more than ever. Sounds like something to think about alright." My hands were shaking as I reached into the refrigerator for Billy's bottle.

"I know all about the sacrifices, but I still have this transfer to deal with," he said. "My thought is that I'll probably just have to go on ahead, get settled and find us a place to live. It'll be okay. We've done this before." Not exactly this. He didn't have the whole picture.

"Oh, so you'll just do that. How convenient. I can stay here and hold everything together, is that right? And what if I tell you I'm not going?" I could feel my ailing stomach tightening against this news. I had expected a transfer, a regular one where we packed, called the movers and left together, excited about the new destination and its promise, possibly our last move. I knew from other wives about the FBI life in New York, the Bureau's largest and busiest office, the office from which many of the organization's most notorious cases originated. With Cliff's dedication, he would never be home.

"Can you turn it down? Would this be a good time to request a medical?" I asked. There had to be a way. Although we had talked about transfers, we hadn't talked about a separation and a difficult assignment in New York.

"No, I can't turn it down, and it's too late to request a medical. Why don't you go back and lie down with Billy. I have to get back to the office anyway. We can talk about this when you feel better."

"When I feel better? When will that be?" I suspected the cause of my morning illness, but that discussion could wait.

He rose to leave, escaping from the latest conflict.

"Isn't it convenient that the office needs you? Maybe I need you too."

"Look, I know you're upset. Let me take care of a couple of things, then I'll be back home for the day and we can talk some more about our options." I watched him leave.

Options? Option 1: refuse to go; Option 2: fight the transfer; Option 3: pack up once again and follow.

Right now I had a crying baby. A bottle and a walk were in order. I wrapped a light blanket around him in the stroller and set off down the street, anger propelling us at a brisk pace as I pondered this new development in my life. Breathing rapidly and still queasy, I slowed to enjoy the warmth of early spring, the most enjoyable season in Jacksonville. The lawns of St. Augustine grass were greening from their brown winter look. Daffodils and tulips were showing off their colors next to pink and white azaleas, my favorite southern plant. Even the Spanish moss was a little greener. Life was re-emerging in my neighborhood.

As I walked I asked myself if I could muster the energy to pull off this latest "opportunity." I knew that Mr. Hoover had recently announced a war on organized crime. One specific family, the Gambinos, was high on his list for extinction. This meant more agents were needed in New York, the mobs' headquarters. Cliff had been recognized for his work in Houston and Jacksonville so he must have looked like an especially attractive target. Young, talented and experienced.

It was said within the Bureau that the best agents are sent to New York. So if one performed well in his second office, he might next be assigned there. What a reward! On the down side, it was usually considered a permanent assignment with little or no possibility for transfer. Spend the rest of Cliff's career in New York? No. I would have to find a way out. When Cliff returned a few hours later, he said, "let's talk about this transfer and the viable options we have."

I looked him in the eye and softly stated, "I don't see my name on this transfer. I'm not going." That was Option 1, a bold statement and an emotional bluff.

"I can't get out of this unless I quit, and this doesn't seem like a very good time to do that. I understand you're disappointed, but maybe it won't be so bad." I could see he was forcing a small smile.

"I don't see you much in this office; with a long commute added, you'll become even more estranged from your family." I held my baby and posed another option. "You could consider other employment opportunities. You have a great resume. And, in case you haven't noticed, I'm not necessarily enthralled with this job of yours."

"Are we back to that? I like my job. I don't want a different one even if I could find one."

"But it is an option. You could take some vacation time now and start a search. If you have to go to New York for a while until you find something else, we could stay here. That could work." I observed the firmness in his jaw as a signal this option wasn't one he was willing to consider.

"Look, I love my job. You don't know—it might not be so bad. I know this isn't what we wanted, but it could be better for your health, and being close to New York could be a good experience for the kids." Always trying to spin it so I would be thinking about the kids.

"No, you've got it wrong. I've spoken to enough wives to know that a transfer to New York is hell; they end up leaving their husbands because they aren't ever around anyway."

"Despite what either one of us wants, in thirty days I need to report to my new assignment in Manhattan. That's not much time for us to get ready for a move, separation and other challenges."

"No, it isn't, and this time, since it's your transfer, you can handle the details." Regardless of what I said, it all meant I would be here in Jacksonville, holding the household together and preparing for the move.

Someone had to pack, contact the movers, say good-byes. That would be me.

"Sandy, give this a chance. I'll handle as many of the details as I can. Look, we've been assigned to two decent cities. Surely, we can make it in New York."

"We've had our challenges even in these two cities. And this move is scarier. Now I get to answer calls from members of these organized crime families? You'll tell me no, but I know how it works. Great, we move from white slavery and bank robberies to organized crime."

"I'm just asking you to give this transfer a chance. It's more high profile work that I love; in ways it's a promotion."

I looked up to capture his attention. My unflinching gaze worked. It was my turn. "Since this seems to be the time for announcements, I, too, have one. I'm pretty sure I'm pregnant which means we're going to have a fourth child around the end of the year." What were these tears running down my face?

His shocked expression told me this possibility had never entered his planning.

"Oh, honey, that's wonderful. Boy, these two are going to be very close together; first a surprise with Billy and now a shock with this one. Maybe I can get a delay for New York."

"A delay would be good, but I don't think the Bureau cares if we're having a baby. Of course, you can certainly ask."

Our short discussion ended with a plan to request a delay in moving to NY. Both of us knew this would be denied, which it was. Some days later with the clock ticking, we agreed that Cliff should report to his new assignment on the designated date. I would wait in Jacksonville while he settled in and found us a place to live.

Weeks turned into days as we tried to pack as much into family time as possible. When we would be reunited was an unknown. As he walked out the door, a common occurrence in our household, I turned my face into my baby's softness asking someone, somewhere, anywhere for strength. How was I going to do this? I wanted to run from this situation, but four people were now dependent on me.

In the ensuing days I dragged my exhausted body from room to room to reassure myself I was still connected to reality. Now, with another baby on the way, I could only try to adapt and somehow create a sanctuary, a little corner to shelter me. Who could I talk to? No one. Mom would sympathize and tell me everything would turn out okay. Would it?

But suppose I couldn't pull it together and make it work this time. Flight or fight? Fleeing was my preference; fighting was my only option.

Part Four

Derailing isn't detouring; it's knowing the train you're on is off the track.
Crashing isn't sliding slowly downward; it's
plunging toward bottomless blackness.

New Jersey
1969-1970

THIRTEEN

8 Standish Lane

A rational person might say, "Okay we're moving; I need a plan for scheduling the packing, lining up the movers, planning the travel and making sure it all flows nicely." What does a pregnant woman on steroids with a five-month-old and a second and third grader do? She cries. Then she starts making lists. One for the actual move and one for personal survival, which might list such actions as: pack a bag, gas up the car, hold her children and pray for sanity.

After the list and after putting Billy down for his nap, I wandered into the garage storage closet where my friends, the boxes, had remained in wait for the past four-and-a-half years. I had delayed the packing process for this move as long as possible in an attempt to persuade myself we were not actually making this move. If I didn't remove the boxes from their secure hiding places, then it wasn't happening. At last, facing the inevitable, I moved the yard stuff and toys around until I had a path to the upper shelf holding my manila friends. I looked up as if to ask if they were ready. Then, hoisting myself halfway up the ladder, I began pulling them down by grabbing an edge, dragging them toward me and letting them slide from the shelf. They half crumpled to the floor like marionettes without strings. They felt damp from Florida's inhospitable humidity, but I assured them and myself they would be okay. I then hauled them into the family room a few at a time and spread them out to dry. Tami and Ray would love this setup when they got home from school. There's just something magical about empty boxes.

When Cliff had called the previous night from New York, our stilted conversation sounded as if we were each speaking to a sales solicitor, a stranger gathering information.

"How are you feeling? Have you been back to the doctor?"

"I'm okay. Which doctor? I have several, you know. If it's my OB, he says everything looks fine, and this baby should arrive sometime in early December. He did remind me to take it easy as my body really hasn't recovered from the last pregnancy. That's kind of a joke, isn't it? I'm supposed to take it easy in the midst of this maelstrom?"

"That's good news. You've always said you liked having a baby in the house at Christmas. How's the packing coming?" He tentatively moved to this new subject.

"I got the boxes out today, so that's a start. I'll begin the actual sorting and packing soon, but this time I'm not going to be able to do this whole move myself. You have vacation time so it makes sense for you to line up the movers, schedule the extra packing, and plan our travel. Since you're the one finding us a house, you'll have the schedule."

"I'll do what I can from here, but you know how this job is."

"Please don't use this job excuse any more. Look, this is your transfer." I knew I was in competition with his other wife, the FBI, and he was currently with her in New York. He had found temporary quarters in Queens. Surprisingly, now that he was gone, I felt no real urgency for this move, so each day I worked on enjoying my new son and watching Tami and Ray blossom.

Spring, the prettiest season in Jacksonville, would soon be coming to a close. When I came here I said I wanted to plant shrubs and bulbs and maybe even a tree, which I could enjoy during my stay here. Now, as I walked around the yard I still saw raggedy St. Augustine grass but framing the yard were flower beds with blooming azaleas and spent remains of tulips and daffodils. Our cute little red brick house now projected a welcoming presence from the street; inside her fashionably painted walls were clean and comforting; her floors supported our weight with a shine. She and I had accomplished this decorative nesting together. All of our work didn't block the encroachment of the Bureau, but we had created a sanctuary of sorts. With move number nine in eleven years, I would soon have a new challenge. Cliff was drawing closer on the housing front.

"Hi, honey. Just wanted to let you know I'm making progress here in finding a house."

"You know, I'm okay here; there's no urgency on my part to move. In fact, you could just leave us here."

"No, not an option. I would sure rather be there though. This is crazy. The office here didn't know I was coming. Can you believe that?"

"If that's the case, why don't you come home? Tell them to send someone else up there in your place." So like the Bureau, one hand not knowing what the other was doing.

"I'd like to do that. They really don't have anything for me to do right now, so I've been out with realtors." I could sense his eagerness to press on from the last piece of information.

"Wait. You said they have nothing for you to do there? Then they can send you where there is something for you to do. Right here."

"I know how you feel, honey, but that's the way it is. This is a huge office, and it's terribly disorganized. I don't even think they know who works here on these various desks. When I showed up, they suggested I take care of our housing situation so that's what I've been doing." He continued as if a silence would only confirm our separation. "It's a tough market here. I've looked at rentals in a couple of locations, and that's out: too junky and too expensive. I just have to keep looking. I looked on Long Island yesterday, but it's too far, and I'd be totally dependent on the train, which is another expense. Tomorrow I'm going to New Jersey. An agent I met at Quantico lives in Jersey. I think I'll look him up."

I had no response to all this. I listened but wasn't very sympathetic to his dilemma. It was as if he were talking about a different family.

But then the call came.

"Well, I finally found something that's large enough and that we can afford. It's in northern New Jersey in a lake community, wooded and private. The school is within walking distance. I think it'll work."

"The community sounds okay," I said. "What about the house?"

"I'll send you some pictures. It's a Cape Cod on two lots filled with hardwood trees. It was built in the twenties, your favorite era. It has four bedrooms, two up and two down and two baths. I thought Tami and Ray might like to have their own apartment upstairs and maybe the two babies could share a nursery downstairs."

"It sounds workable, but what does it look like? How about the kitchen, garage, fireplace?" Was he trying too hard to sell this?

"The kitchen's been remodeled, not the greatest job, but I think it's workable, and it has a two-car garage. I'll airmail you the pictures so you'll have them in a few days."

"Okay." The photos should tell me more.

"Hopefully, you'll like it. I think we can fit into the house, and the neighborhood is great with three lakes and rolling, wooded property. In some ways you may find it resembles northern Michigan." His voice exuded the confidence he knew I needed to hear. "Oh, and did I mention it has a great screened porch where we will probably live in the summer."

"Okay, let me look at the pictures, then we'll make a decision. By the way, how far is it to the office?" I took a breath.

"It's thirty-three miles, about a two hour commute by bus."

"Which means four hours of the day for you on the road plus the long hours of the job. This translates to many hours alone for me. And what about the times you're on call or called in on a case?" None of this was new with this job, but in this office the hardships would be exaggerated.

The pictures arrived as scheduled. I carefully opened the padded manila envelope holding my breath for fear of finding either possibility or disappointment. There she was in my hand, the picture of what would most likely be the newest member of my family.

Her blue-gray face stared at me suggesting that with some attention she could become beautiful. It was apparent she had been built to be a two-bedroom lake cottage, a retreat from the city for a family long gone. Then someone had come along and added what looked like a family room and then a two-car garage. An owner who wanted to add to her charm had shielded her from the unpaved street with a white picket fence. I looked at this photo and asked what was bringing us together. Not Cliff's job. No, something else.

The interior pictures were harder to decipher as to the layout; I could see the house was empty and ready for us. If Cliff decided she should be our next house, I wouldn't argue. I asked Cliff to visit the school and take some pictures of the neighborhood and the school and send them.

I showed the photos to Tami and Ray, but their concerns were with leaving their friends and school; their next house brought little interest.

This was their first move changing schools, and when Cliff had told them of his transfer, they had reacted normally. Tami went into her room and closed the door; Ray bounded out the door shouting he wasn't going to move. At least we had gotten to the end of the school year, so they would start third and fourth grades in their new community. The more positive I could stay, the easier for them.

We made an offer on 8 Standish Lane in the Fayson Lakes community, and it was accepted. It would be too difficult for me to make the trip to see it, so I told Cliff to send me the papers. We set a closing date 30 days hence. Now it was time for me and the dried out boxes to reunite. They would need to be tough to make one more move.

As I worked, I pulled the few packed boxes, mostly those items I'd not unpacked since Delaware, from extraneous closets to see if their contents must now be left behind. Scrapbooks, memorabilia, papers, birthday cards, love letters from before our marriage. No, reseal them and stack them for the move. While some memorabilia had no monetary value, these treasures all added up to our lives, a testament that we had actually lived.

FBI policy allowed five business days for the move. Cliff would close on the house and come to Florida to assist me with the final moving duties. Jacksonville had been the longest stay of our marriage. Tami and Ray had started school here; Billy had been born here; we had established ourselves in a church and in our immediate community; I had friends, and I had even taken a job. I would miss my neighbors, my bridge partners and my teaching colleagues. I wouldn't miss the Spanish moss laden with bugs, the poisonous snakes, the unrelenting humidity, my allergies and illnesses and Cliff's long hours—even though that probably wouldn't change. After a month-long series of good-bye parties and promises to stay in touch, I prepared myself for the next "opportunity."

Packed up, loaded and ready to move. Cliff was putting his best foot forward; even he could see the sadness on our faces. "Okay, everybody, here we go on a big adventure. We've looked at the map, and Ray you're in charge of our route."

It was the beginning of summer but not yet sweltering hot so our serpentine drive up the east coast, interrupted by stops for picnics at local parks, began pleasantly, a journey broken up by overnights in Holiday Inns with pools. On the third day we neared our destination, the nation's largest city. Roads were no longer rural two-lanes but rather six and eight lane slabs of oil slicked, dirty gray concrete populated by slithering shapes of vehicles that looked like they had connected themselves to a track mindlessly pushing them in a determined direction. We were no exception as Cliff deftly maneuvered our trusty brown "house on wheels" to our designated motel on the New Jersey Turnpike, not a four-star accommodation by any stretch, but it did have a pool, and after a grubby day in transit, we all opted for a dip.

After a noisy, restless night in cramped quarters, I emerged from the bathroom to a near musical litany: "Seventy-seven, seventy-eight… eighty-nine, ninety-four….Mom, I've never seen so many trucks. I'll soon be up to one hundred."

Tami was curled up with a book, and the baby had decided on a snooze: a good choice.

"Please, Ray, shhh. Yes, there's a lot of trucks." What a perfect vantage point for a young boy fascinated with any vehicle on wheels.

"Mom, where's Dad? I'm bored," he continued. "There's nothing to do in this place." Oh my, this could be a long day. I didn't want to be in this godforsaken place either.

Where was Dad? I often asked that question myself. This time I had an answer. "He's out looking for our furniture. It seems it's missing."

"Missing?" both he and Tami chimed together. "You mean all our stuff is gone?"

Yes, they had heard right. Lost in one of the hundreds of warehouses surrounding New York City. From one warehouse to the next, Cliff demanded to know the locale of our shipment. Finally, he got a break when a warehouse worker decided he didn't want to fool with this irate FBI agent. Our treasured boxes and furniture were located and scheduled for delivery in a "couple of days or so."

Who in their right mind would steal from the FBI? Later I would learn there was a market for anything that could be stolen from a truck, apparently even my precious boxes.

"Let's get out of here and go see our new house," Cliff said.

"Ya, let's get out of here. This is boring." Ray spoke for all of us.

As we loaded up the car for the thirty-three mile drive into New Jersey, I told myself that this house was going to work; I would make it work. I had to. Four and a half people were depending on me.

"Dad, how far are we going? Tami asked. "This is way out in the country." Things were not looking up. We were all sick of living in the car. At least once we got to the house we could pretend we were on a camping trip while we waited for our furniture.

"Yah, it is sort of in the country, but you're going to love it. Three lakes, hills, a swimming pool, and you can walk to school. I think we should get a rowboat. And in the winter you can ice skate on East Lake, the one closest to our house."

Ray was no longer navigating as Cliff was familiar with the route westward. Once off the main road, our landscape turned wooded and rural with the full foliage of early summer. I had to admit it was much prettier than Jacksonville. Hardwoods, evergreens, flowering shrubs decorated the rolling hills of our roadway. I felt invited into this bower of privacy from which I would view the changing seasons.

Cliff made several turns down narrow paved lanes to an even narrower gravel path, coming to a stop in front of the house in the pictures: 8 Standish Lane, a 1920s story-and-a-half home with upstairs dormers, a screened porch. And a white picket fence.

She looked sad, her demeanor matching mine. Who had left her? What was her story? How many young mothers just like me had pulled into this driveway with expectations things would work out?

So far, so good. I hadn't cried yet today. Tami and Ray were already out of the car bounding around the yard looking for those special places kids always find in a new house. Our new home's double lot was filled with hardwood trees, which would become a golden wonderland come September. My mind's picture resembled a New England watercolor with colors so intense they radiated from the canvas.

Cliff reached over to take Billy from my arms. He was wet, hungry and disgusted with this whole undertaking. Even Tami, his favorite person, couldn't convince him it was going to be okay.

With his remaining arm, Cliff enfolded me with a gentle hug that seemed to say, "Please say it's okay."

So I did.

"I like the outside," I said. "This extra lot will be great fun for the kids, and we can put the swing set and tower in the backyard where the gravel is. I wonder who lived here before."

Possibilities.

"It's great, Mom," Ray cheered. "Look at this huge yard. Let's walk to the lake. Can we get a boat, Dad?" I looked at his excited face, trying to make everything okay.

"Sounds like a good plan. But let's see the rest of the house first."

Now for the inside. Cliff and I met the kids at the front door where I suggested to Tami and Ray that our new house deserved a bright, positive color for her door, which Cliff opened, allowing the kids to race on ahead. I followed Cliff into a vestibule, kind of a '20s foyer and made a left turn into the living room just as a guest would.

I looked around feeling breath leave my body and tears start to well. I stood speechless staring at this ample living room before me, completely paneled in knotty pine, which hadn't been visible in the pictures. My shocked expression must have said everything but told Cliff nothing.

"Look, I did the best I could. It hasn't been any picnic being up here trying to make decisions about where we should live without your input." I looked at his crestfallen face. Who was struggling the most?

"I wasn't exactly on a picnic in Florida," I said.

"I'm sorry. Tell me what's wrong, and we'll figure out how to fix it."

"This whole house is knotty pine paneling. I hate knotty pine. What am I going to do with this?" My over-burdened heart sank as my eyes took in a living room, dining room and hall all covered in a yellow-orange wood scattered with brown knots of various sizes and slices that looked like someone had tried to split respective boards. A fireplace stood centered between two bookcases on one wall, it, too, asking for relief. I looked at each wall sizing up the scope of the problem.

"I kind of like it," Cliff said. "Can't you live with it for a while?"

"No, I can't live with this. We have to do something."

I knew he had done his best, given our finances and situation, and wanted me to be pleased. "Pleased" wasn't in me at the moment. The rest of the house was dark and old with small rooms, but they were painted and could easily be repainted. I had worked minor miracles with other residences, but this was daunting, and I was pregnant and not particularly easy to please.

The kids were running from room to room exclaiming over what they had found.

"Mom, this house has a basement. It's really neat down there," Ray yelled.

"Mom, you'll like the upstairs," Tami called. "There's two bedrooms: one for me and one for Ray, and we have our own bathroom. I think it used to be an attic." Tami was talking so fast I hardly understood her.

My silence resonated throughout the old house. Even the baby picked up on my disappointment. A bottle would fix him up. Would that it were so easy for me.

"What can we do to fix this?" Cliff asked as we stood surrounded by our problem or I should say, my problem.

"We could paint this wood. The rest I think I can fix. Can you take a few vacation days to get this done? We can camp out here in sleeping bags until the movers bring our stuff. While we wait, we can paint." I truly thought I might feel better once the wood had a new coat, something like a light cream.

"All of it?"

My look confirmed the plan.

"Okay, let's go get the paint and get started. Tami and Ray, you can help me, and Mom and Billy can supervise." Cliff and I quickly calculated how many gallons we would need, and we were off on our first New Jersey venture.

We trooped into the paint store on a mission to create a home from a lonely shell. As we selected the color and type of paint to cover the pine, my eyes focused on a strip of bright colors. Yes, that's what we needed most of all, a bright red front door. One that said, "Welcome. A lively family lives here." A slight glimmer of hope was emerging. I could have a relationship with this small but stately old woman my husband had chosen. She and I would work things out. She could speak to me of other times and other families.

"I need two quarts of this bright red," I said as I handed the paint strip to the clerk.

"What do you plan to do with this? It's awfully bright," he said as he looked at me strangely. Apparently, he didn't sell much red paint.

"I'm painting my front door." My voice exuded confidence.

"Let me show you some softer exterior colors," he suggested. Never mess with a pregnant woman when she knows what she wants.

"No, this is what I want. Leave the other colors where they are. This one is perfect!" My loud response caused the chauvinistic clerk to slink toward the cash register.

Cliff looked at me questioningly. I reassured him with a smile, the first smile he'd seen in a few days. "Billy and I will be painting the front door." We would. From his stroller by the shaded front door, he could watch Mommy change the personality of her house from a complacent blue-gray door to one stating this was a house where strong people lived with red blood racing in their veins.

The furniture delivery was delayed which was okay because we were busy with our painting project. Cliff painted ceilings and walls, and I painted the woodwork. Tami and Ray played and met the neighborhood kids and brought home casseroles and cookies for our survival.

We finished just in time.

Moving day number nine. Cliff and I had worked day and night, side by side for the first time in too long. We were always at our best when we were tackling a project. This time he wasn't allowing the Bureau to steal his time, making me feel more special than I had in a while. As the summer wore on we would tackle the upstairs where Tami already had plans. The house was taking shape, feeling a bit more like my nesting place than a temporary way station. We set up the nursery to accommodate another baby; we stained the kitchen cabinets and Cliff put in a new floor. Ray and Tami's quarters upstairs were like something out of Peter Pan, a delightful space divided in half with nooks and crannies for each. A magical space for what I prayed would be a magical time in their lives.

I looked around my nearly settled rooms and proclaimed, "This is good." It was more than good. I smiled to myself as I rocked Billy in my fresh, light filled living room with its quaint fireplace. Alone with my thoughts, this would be my space on those long nights when I would wait for the lights of Cliff's mini commuter car to turn in the driveway.

FOURTEEN

Derailing

When I boarded this FBI train with Cliff in 1963, I thought I could keep my part of the train on track. I knew we might hit traffic, floods, rock slides or even avalanches, but as Cliff reminded me during those times, we were an incredible team. But incredible takes you only so far.

Settling into the New York metropolitan area proved to be as difficult as I had feared. Most of our neighbors were from the northeast with family close by. The couple next door, expecting their first baby, was in the midst of remodeling their newly acquired fix-it home. Cliff and Bob felled trees in the adjoining backyards while Susan and I conferred on decorating our old houses. Both husbands worked in Manhattan so we shared common concerns and challenges. Although I was several years older than Susan, we could make a friendship work. In addition, Donna, one of my other neighbors with a teenage daughter, invited me to play bridge with her group. Thank God for small favors. It was just a small group, four of us, but it was a connection for me. Bridge was becoming my bridge.

We had no Bureau neighbors or even anyone who worked for the government so our family was somewhat of an anomaly. We were probably an anomaly anyway without Cliff's undisclosed occupation.

In August, prior to the start of school, Mom called to invite us to visit them at their new house on Crystal Lake in northern Michigan. A timely invitation. They had recently returned to Michigan from California with Dad thinking he wanted to retire. Here they had built a house right on the water with a dock, boat and everything fun. I regaled the kids with stories about Crystal Lake, Big Bear Sand Dunes and the huge freighters docked in Frankfort on Lake Michigan.

"What do you think? Can you get some time off," I asked Cliff. "I really want to go. I know we just got here, but I already could use a reprieve from this place." I sounded pleading even to myself.

"I'll put my leave slip in. I can probably get the time off. But you never know with this organization. Better wait to tell the kids until I'm sure." He looked at me with this warning look I often got when he wanted to remind me of his primary responsibility, the demands being made by his other wife.

"Okay. I'll wait to tell them, but this is probably time to tell you I'm going to Crystal Lake with or without you." I turned and walked from the room in order to take a deep breath of reassurance.

Without a heavy workload yet, Cliff was able to take two weeks off. We loaded up the car and off we went for a welcome respite from the rigors of moving and settling. Our 850 mile drive to Michigan felt like a traditional family vacation: kids arguing over seating, the baby wet, hungry and tired, me having to pee every couple of hours and Cliff impatient with all of us.

Looking like waifs, we pulled into the driveway of a lovely lakefront home, which with its roof line clerestory windows, looked like it had its eyes open just waiting for us. I knew from Mom's description that this would be no cottage. We were met with hugs and kisses, and Mom immediately reached for Billy whom she'd not seen since his birth. I looked at her with my youngest child in her arms and forced a smile. Tami, Ray and Cliff had found Grandpa, the deck and the boat.

"Honey, how are you? Gosh, you hardly look pregnant," Mom said. "Are you feeling okay?" That's one of those questions we often ask when the response is obvious. Her concern was written across her face when she opened her door. My smiles needed to be bigger and more reassuring if I were to lessen her worry.

"I'm feeling a little better; this getting away feels like heaven. The move was hard, but we're pretty well settled." I knew she was really asking if I were happy, if Cliff were providing the support I needed, if I were really doing okay. I was biting my lip, clenching my fists to remind myself to stay in control. I was an adult; I could handle stuff. What I couldn't handle right now was any criticism of Cliff. He was my husband. I was his wife carrying our fourth child. It was not the time to encumber my mother with my marriage difficulties.

"Well, if you run into any problems here, I've lined up an obstetrician for you. I just want you to rest while you're here. Billy and I need to get reacquainted, and Dad plans to be busy with Tami and Ray. Hey, let me show you my house." I looked at my mother trying so hard to make it all right for me.

Each morning, I awoke, fixed Billy a bottle and walked with him to the deck to see the sun leisurely rising over the lake and raining its summer warmth onto the two of us. Ray was usually next to join us, exploding with noisy plans for his day with Grandpa. Once the two of them even got up at 4:00 a.m. to meet the fish on their schedule. I have to add, my dad was not a fisherman, but their time together wasn't about fish anyway. Then Tami would wander out, usually with a book in her hand. I could hear Mom in the kitchen brewing coffee and preparing breakfast, maybe huckleberry pancakes. Post breakfast, everyone took off for wherever, leaving Mom, Billy and me to relish the restorative lake sounds, smell the slightly fishy water and watch the birds diving for food.

"Morning, Mom. Isn't this just perfect? I hate the thought of leaving tomorrow." I looked over at her and wrinkled my nose. She reached to take Billy from me. He squealed and smiled.

"Honey, you don't have to leave. You and the kids can stay a while longer. Don't they have a few weeks until school?" She gestured toward the calm lake as she spoke. "Dad and I could put you on a plane in another week or so."

"I'd love to stay forever, Mom. That's the real truth." I could feel the knot forming in that familiar place and the tears welling behind my lashes. I'd better not say any more or she would know. Know what? How lonely I was? How I wish I weren't part of this ridiculous FBI life?

"You can stay. I just want you to know that."

"It's hard right now, Mom."

"I know, and I want to do more to help you."

It had to end. We had to leave. I couldn't stay. I told myself Cliff had to go to work, Tami and Ray had to go to school, and I needed to return to New Jersey. For what? I cried for my loss and the overwhelming need I felt for my parents' support. I cried, feeling the loneliness of returning to a place where my marriage was derailing.

Autumn was approaching; I could feel it. Clouds drifted higher in the sky now less hazy, more blue, and air tinged with a note of crispness requiring a light jacket in the mornings. I loved the change of seasons which I'd not experienced since Delaware. I could feel it. The change as school started, leaving me dedicated time with my youngest child. Each morning we would begin our day with a walk to the grade school with Tami and Ray, and each afternoon we would close it the same way. Like bookmarks to my day. It was early autumn, the colors brightening the space that once long ago had been filled by a couple's dreams.

Day by day I walked with Billy through our large hardwood trees looking for new signs of color: today yellow, tomorrow red or orange. In what seemed overnight our whole extra lot was ablaze with fall's color, the color only hardwoods have. Soon the leaves would fall, but for now it was my Technicolor explosion. Soon, enough painted leaves had accumulated that we needed to start raking our bounty into huge piles resembling igloos just right for jumping into and through. Now in my last trimester, I watched my children play and smiled. On one special Saturday Cliff joined them in their play, raking, re-raking and jumping. Two great kids enjoying their dad on one of those rare weekend days he was home.

Some things were the same about Cliff's job here; other things were different. On the plus side, I didn't know as much about what was going on because Cliff wasn't home enough to share much. Also, I didn't want to know about the mafia and his war on crime. It was bad enough that I got informant calls that I didn't want to answer. When the nights grew long and the phone rang, I reluctantly picked up the receiver, fearing this was a call from someone very dangerous with a message for Cliff. These messages, unlike those from the Jacksonville informants, were cryptic, and I often had to ask them to repeat so I had it right. I worried about how much these people knew about us, about me and the children and where we lived. My 1920s house wasn't very secure; anyone could get in without a lot of difficulty. In Florida I'd already had one attempted break-in, but these people weren't like that bumbler. These people were professionals. They were organized like a corporation with a hierarchy designed for efficiency in dealing with problems like snitches or law enforcement that weren't cooperating. The Bonanno, Gambino and Colombo crime families were real. They were the reasons Cliff had been sent here.

In addition, I had my own set of challenges: a flooded basement, a washer that overburdened the septic system, two children trying to adapt to a new school, a one-year-old trying to walk, a pregnant body which had not been cooperative this time around.

In the quiet of the long evenings alone, my 20s house entertained me with her creaks and groans interspersed with silence, a backdrop to my latest read. Had another young mom sat in this room waiting like I was now?

Sometimes she lifted the darkness in my spirit, but not completely. My projects with her were coming to an end. The house had taken shape, feeling more like my refuge rather than a temporary way station. The nursery was waiting for our fourth child. I liked it. I had painted the babies' room a light cerulean blue with white trim on its doors, moldings and the trim surrounding its four windows. Light filled this special room for two special babies.

While I didn't yet know if this baby would be a boy or girl, I was speculating it might be a boy. This fourth pregnancy had been difficult from the onset. My body, depleted from my third pregnancy and from fighting the Florida infections, couldn't resist incoming bacteria. I tried to explain to my doctor that I felt tired, depressed and demoralized, but he claimed the frailty was just a by-product of the pregnancy. Was there a correlation between my fatigue and depression and the steroid regime prescribed for my asthma? Months later in the midst of another medical crisis, I asked the same question, and the doctor confirmed that the steroid program would have exacerbated the post-partum depression. There was a name for the depression? And did it matter that I just quit rather than weaning myself off this poison gradually?

Needing celebration, Tami and I decided that Billy should have a special first birthday celebration on the weekend when Dad might be home. We decided that after naps would be a good time. She would bake Billy a cake, and Ray would help me pick out some presents.

The cake was ready and the presents were wrapped and in place. Tami lit the candles and walked into the dining area. Billy reached toward the cake, clapping his hands. Holding the cake a safe distance, Tami and Ray helped him blow out the shimmering lights. We all clapped and sang "Happy Birthday." Billy proceeded to dig both hands into his piece of cake and tried to fit it all into his mouth. We laughed and cheered him on. I looked at him and smiled for the first time in a while. I needed this family celebration as a small reminder that something as seemingly normal as a first birthday could bring us together as a family.

A few weeks later on a relatively quiet Sunday evening in early November, I looked at Cliff with important questions on my mind.

"I think we need to talk about plans for this baby." I was beginning to be concerned about his distance from home.

"Okay, what are your worries?"

"What if I go into labor while you're at work in the city? You might not make it home in time. Should I form a back-up plan with a neighbor? I guess I could call an ambulance."

"Sandy, you'll be fine. You worry too much. I'll be right here with you when this baby is born, and I'll take time off to look after the kids. Don't worry. Besides, we've got another month to work it all out." He wasn't worried, so should I be?

I looked across the shadowed room to see Cliff's head bent forward fighting sleep. When would he be home and awake long enough to get anything resolved? Tonight's conversation was over. When I looked inside myself I didn't know I'd be fine. I was tired, and I was about to bring a new life into my nearly dysfunctional world.

I wanted to believe him when he said he would take care of us, but my past experience raised doubt. How many times had I trudged off to get the kids sewn up or to see what was causing the 104-degree fever? No way to contact him except through an inept dispatcher who treated my calls as an interruption. By the time he replied, often hours later, all was under some semblance of control. Now with the responsibility for four children, just when I needed to be at my strongest, I was feeling more fragile than I had ever felt before in my life.

Sunday, November 9, 1969, we all went next door for dinner with our friends. Returning home a tad later than usual, I lay awake musing about life's twists and turns. Cliff's measured breaths were rhythmic. I curled up next to him, as close as my protruding belly would allow and began to drift off. Shortly, I was awakened by sharp pains, familiar sharp pains. It wasn't time for this baby. I was only eight months pregnant. I had another month to go. "Please, not now, I'm not ready. This baby and I need time." Not to be denied, the pains struck more frequently.

"Cliff, wake up. I'm in labor. Wake up." He rolled toward me in that kind of daze where waking comes in waves.

"What's wrong? Did you just nudge me awake?" He sat up in the bed beside me.

"I'm in labor, and the pains are close. We'd better get ready to go." I rose from my place beside him and lumbered to the bathroom for a quick shower.

"Are you sure? This baby isn't due for another month."

"Yes and yes. I've done this before, remember?" I stepped into the welcoming warmth of the shower begging this baby to wait just a while longer. I needed more time.

"Where's your bag? Is the house sitter's number in the kitchen? I'll warm the car up." I blocked out his rambling, trusting we would get to the hospital in time with everything we needed.

"I'll take care of my bag. You take care of everything else. The most critical is the sitter, but I've put her on notice." Everybody in my life needed to be on notice.

Up, dressed, suitcased, sitter at the door, we headed for Pompton Plains Hospital. I was still timing my contractions as I signed into Emergency. In the early hours of the morning, a hospital is an eerie place, and it appeared almost deserted on this particular November morning. Finally, a nurse ushered me back to an exam room.

"What can we do for you, honey? Let's get your vitals." At least she was calm and relaxed.

"I'm eight months pregnant, and my labor pains are close together. I think you'd better call Labor and Delivery." I thought I spoke forcefully but apparently not so.

"If this is your first baby, sometimes this happens. You think you're in labor, but it's false. And, just looking at you, you couldn't be eight months."

"Well, look again. True, I haven't gained much weight, seven pounds at my last check-up, but…" Another pain hit, fostering my exasperation with this nurse. "This is my fourth child; I ought to know if I'm in labor or not. Please, call the delivery people. Now!"

She moved.

On a cold, snowy, bleak Monday, November 10, Scott Andrew Browning joined our family. Not quite six pounds, he entered our lives screaming. He must have felt just like I did, overwhelmed. I held his tiny body in my arms, told him I loved him and that everything would be okay. Would that I spoke the truth.

My hospital roommate had just delivered her sixth child so we had a few stories in common. When the nurse asked us how long we would be staying, we asked what was the maximum stay allowed under our insurance.

"Your maximum is five days."

"Then five days it is," we both chimed.

I badly needed the rest. It would have to be Cliff's turn at home. He found it hard to visit me in the hospital, but that was okay. I enjoyed the time with my newborn son. My five-day stay felt like a sojourn to the spa, and my roomie and I pretended that's just what it was.

Cliff, who was more than busy trying to keep the household running, had a few observations. "Maybe we should try to find someone to help us out with the cleaning and laundry for a while." This suggestion was offered with a bouquet of red roses.

"That's a great idea. Why don't you find someone?" I was pretty sure this would never happen, and it didn't. As soon as I got home he would be back to his other wife, the FBI, where he didn't have to worry about clean clothes, unloading the dishwasher or preparing formula.

Mom wasn't home to greet us as she had been incapacitated with the shingles, but something else was—a full blown invasion of strep throat. All of us, except for our new family member, contracted the painful infection, necessitating individual masks to protect our delicate newborn who didn't yet seem to want to be part of this family. I didn't blame him; it wasn't a very welcoming household at the moment. Yes, there was the strep, but there was also Cliff's schedule since he had been promoted to a desk on the graveyard shift.

In order that Billy get some sleep in the nursery, I put Scott in his carriage in our bedroom, but he had severe colic and wouldn't be comforted by anything for long. I would later learn this isn't uncommon for preemies. So the picture is this: one screaming newborn, one wailing toddler because Scott is crying, Tami who's trying to help, Ray who is trying to escape and has the best chance as his room is the farthest from this mayhem.

To add to the list of adjustments, Cliff's promotion to relief supervisor on the graveyard shift meant he now left around 10:00 p.m., worked all night, returned in the morning around 10:00 a.m., to eat breakfast and head to bed. Trying to keep a one-year-old and a newborn quiet so he could sleep was impossible. About the time Tami and Ray returned from school, Cliff was getting up to have dinner with us. Once up, I would dash out the door to the grocery store, which was now the highlight of my day, a trip I couldn't manage with two babies.

In the midst of this madness, I began to question my ability to handle my growing family with little or no help. I looked in the mirror, just as I had in Houston, asking, *"Who is this person staring back at me? I see wrinkles of worry between her eyes and a mouth downturned where smiles once rested. Where is her confidence? Why can't she handle this better? And what is the 'this'? Is it the fear that she could be alone with four children? Is it that the love is seeping out of this relationship like an indefinable drip?"*

One morning before school I asked Ray to carry a load of laundry to the basement. I heard him open the door and then yell: "Mom, Mom, come here."

It wasn't the call I needed at 7:00 a.m. I secured the babies and walked to the basement door, looked down the stairway and saw what Ray had seen, a basement filled with several inches of water. I could smell its staleness from the top step, a swampy smell.

"How'd this happen, Mom? How do we get it out?" His reaction was a combination of surprise and curiosity. A flooded basement had never really occurred to him. This was the first of many homeowner lessons he would learn.

"I'm not sure, but close the door. Don't go down there. We've had rain lately. Maybe the gutters are clogged." This was the only explanation that came to mind. "Don't worry, we'll get it fixed. Just leave the clothes here by the door." I wanted to cry, but, of late, even the tears seemed to be drying up.

Cliff walked in later in the morning. "Hi, hon, how are things? Did the baby sleep last night?"

"No. It'll probably be a while. But we have another problem: a flooded basement."

"Have you called anyone?"

"No."

As the days blurred into weeks, I asked how things could get any worse. Billy, my poor one-year-old was begging for my attention. I looked into his beautiful brown eyes that were pleading for an answer. I had no time for anyone; I was neglecting everyone, especially myself. Most days I wasn't even eating. Coffee for breakfast, bites of whatever I'd fixed for the kids and wine to make it all better after Cliff had left and the kids had gone to bed. For how long could I manage this way? God forbid that anything else would descend on us. But life isn't like that.

We had a horrible rainstorm which flooded the basement again and nearly paralyzed the furnace. Neighbor to the rescue. Sally had lived in Fayson Lakes for twenty years and knew everyone so she located some sort of professional to "fix" the basement. Everything in my life now needed fixing. My growing depression made any new crisis look like a calamity. Getting up, fixing bottles, fixing breakfast, making lunches, feeding babies in tandem, fixing breakfast for Cliff, making beds, doing laundry, finally getting a shower myself, scheduling a trip for groceries when Cliff was home and awake. A colicky baby, a sleep deprived husband, a bewildered toddler, a nine-year-old and an eight-year-old with school crises and a mom who had become a shell, numb with pain.

FIFTEEN

Crashing

Black was becoming my companion; first a shade of gray, darker than silver but with a glimmer of light penetrating my morning routine, that time when I told myself it really wasn't so bad. Someday Scott would sleep through the night, someday we would live like a regular family, someday both babies would be able to sit up, someday I would be a teacher again. In this pep talk I told myself Cliff was really trying to help. We were both caught. That's when the strands of light in the silver shone through. As the sun dipped from a horizon I couldn't see, my shade of gray became charcoal suggesting my life resembled ink blots that were merging into one very dark puddle.

Prior to Christmas, Cliff suggested he take Tami and Ray to the Macy's Thanksgiving Day parade. They would ride the bus into the city, get off at the Port Authority and make their way uptown to the parade site. This would be their first trip into the city, a highlight of the holiday season for them. I was right; they came home exhausted but brimming with excitement. Their faces were aglow. I hadn't seen this kind of excitement since our trip to Disneyland years earlier. It had been a magical day for them. I looked at Cliff and smiled. I was happy he had taken this time for his children.

Christmas isn't Christmas without a tree, and we needed to select it as a family. Saturday morning after pancakes seemed just right. I bundled Scott into his snowsuit and filled the diaper bag with his necessities. Tami got Billy ready, talking to him about this adventure, his first real

Christmas. She had already talked to him about Santa Claus and read to him his Golden books about Christmas. I always knew when she was with him by the way he giggled. She was the most important person in his life.

All aboard and off to the tree lot where we oohed and aahed over the many possibilities. It wasn't the tree that was memorable; it was the time together.

"What about this one?"

"No, it's too short. We want a tall, fat one," Ray reminded us.

At last Tami and Ray declared the winner, the one most perfect for our 1969 Christmas. It would have to go on top of the car; inside wasn't a possibility. Fortunately, Cliff was prepared with rope. And I was prepared for hot chocolate at the stand.

Santa came right on schedule. I fixed a turkey dinner and Cliff didn't have to go in to work until his midnight shift. It wasn't so bad; we could do it. I could do it even if I had to pretend things were always like this. I could make this family function like a real one even if I would mostly have to orchestrate it alone.

Early January, mid January, late January. An endless month. How can thirty-one days feel so much longer than twenty-eight or even thirty? Darkness was now my companion. Before the month ended, Cliff came home to announce that he had put in for a four to midnight shift on a desk handling truck hijacking. That would mean a second promotion in just a few months. He was being recognized in this office as he had in Jacksonville. For Billy, Scott and me this shift would be better than the night shift as Cliff would be home during the day until 2:00 when he would leave for the bus. For Tami and Ray, it meant they would only see him on the weekend unless, of course, he was called out. For me, it meant long evenings as I often watched for his car lights to turn in the driveway sometime after 2:00 a.m.

The worry factor was still present. Even though Cliff was supervising a desk, he often participated in arrests and raids. In New York this was serious business; working with the NYPD was often dangerous. Just a short time ago an undercover FBI agent had been "outed." In the past I hadn't worried about other agencies Cliff was working with. Now my worry meter was escalated.

Snow fell, and out came the sleds and ice skates. This was a new season for Tami and Ray, and the possibilities weren't lost on them. They now had developed neighborhood friends who introduced them to the magic of winter.

Weekends we all needed Cliff. Repairs had piled up, the car needed servicing, and we all needed attention.

"Hey, it's Saturday. Let me sleep a few hours, and then we can do something," Cliff said. "I'm going to see if Tami and Ray want to go ice skating. If you could take Scott to the store with you, I think I can manage Billy at the lake." He smiled at me.

I didn't smile back.

"No, that won't work. You aren't going to take a fifteen-month-old to the lake. I'm not even crazy about Tami and Ray skating on that ice."

"You don't want them to do anything."

"You're right. I want them to do everything, all the things that are safe." He walked past me into the living room.

That's what we were doing now: passing. Passing carefully.

Timing is what it's about sometimes.

The babies were napping, Tami and Ray weren't yet home from school. Cliff might be rousing from his daytime sleep. I eased our bedroom door open to see his eyes half open. I walked over to my side of the bed. We didn't share this bed much anymore. I slept fitfully with nighttime feedings while he worked mids, and he slept while I managed the family's days. I curled up beside my husband with my head on his chest. He felt warm and strong. I wanted to lean on him and know I was supported and protected. He held me tighter. I was saddened that this was the most intimacy we'd had since Scott was born. I lay there quietly, pretending all was well with us.

"This crazy schedule of mine isn't so great, is it?" he asked.

"No. I miss you. How long will this last?" I wasn't sure I wanted to know.

"Probably six months at least. All the shifts are extremely busy, and that I like. Plus, not only do I have a desk to supervise, but I also get to go on the raids."

"I'd rather not know about that part of it. In fact, I'd like to take a leave from being your assistant here at home." I was under water without worrying about whom he was chasing next, and whether the officer next to him was on his side.

"What do you mean? I can't control who calls here."

"Maybe tell them to call you at the office. Look, I'm not doing so great, and for a while I'd like to pretend you're not an FBI agent."

"That's pretty unrealistic. What do you want me to do?"

"Don't tell me your stories about your raids, near misses, arrests and how you and yours are getting a handle on organized crime. I know more about these mafia families than I do my neighbors. Let's see, there are the Bonannos, the Gambinos and the Genoveses, right?"

"Well, who am I supposed to talk to, to share with? I thought we were a team."

"Maybe we were, but one member of this team is injured, on the DL or whatever you call it. Cliff, listen to me. I need help. I'm a single mom here with four kids. I'm isolated, and I nightly imagine the worst, that knock on my red door late at night telling me you're dead."

"At least I have good insurance." This was his standard reply always accompanied by a smirk, which I had ceased to find humorous.

"I don't want insurance. I want a partner, a spouse, a husband. And I, too, need someone to talk to, someone who listens." I rolled over to the sounds of nursery noises. Tami and Ray would be home soon, and I would listen to their school tales.

When Cliff left, I pretended to be sleepy. I washed my face, brushed my teeth and turned back the bed. When the car backed out of the driveway, I walked to the kitchen to fix a bottle for Scott and a glass of wine for me.

How does a relationship get to this point? I asked myself this question nearly every night as I sat and waited for him to pull in the driveway at some obscene hour. I told myself things were going to be okay someday. We had just hit a rough spot or two, or twenty. Maybe if we had time together. As if in answer to this possibility, Cliff came home with an idea.

"Honey, I know this has been a tough stretch so I was thinking maybe we could get away for a weekend, celebrate my desk promotion?" He winked at me suggestively. "I talked to my mom, and she said she'd come out and babysit for us. What do you think?" He was all smiles as he took off his coat and placed his gun and credentials on the bureau. "Where would you like to go?" He said all this positively as if I would jump at the chance. I had no energy to jump at anything.

"I don't know. I'm thinking about your mother. This is a lot for her to take on. Let me think about it."

"Mom isn't working so she said she's free anytime. Maybe in a couple of weeks? And how about the Poconos?" He handed me brochures he'd picked up from the travel agent.

"Fine." And so it was.

"Honey, I told the office 'no calls' this weekend so this is our time to ourselves. It's good to get away, isn't it?" He reached over for my hand, a gesture I had always loved.

I didn't respond. It seemed to me an odd statement. He was always away.

"You're quiet. We have two whole days at this nice, quiet place. Is there anything special you'd like to do?"

"Nothing. That's what I'd most like to do. Breakfast when I wake up, maybe a walk in the snow and dinner at this lodge. Truthfully, I'm too tired for anything else." At the moment I'd even lost interest in conversation.

Looking back, I have no recall where Cliff and I went, what we did, or what we shared on our weekend retreat. I just remember getting into the car, driving off and getting back in the car for a return trip home. It was as if the grayness of my life were spreading into all I experienced. Goldie fared, but not well. Tami, laughingly, told me, "Grandma put Scott in the closet. He cried like he always does, and he was keeping Billy awake so she put him in his carriage and wheeled it out into the foyer." I nodded. However Goldie had solved the problem was fine with me. Goldie returned home, and Cliff was back on schedule as were Tami and Ray. Billy, Scott and I had no schedule. Nothing in my life ran on time. The unexpected was becoming the norm.

Almost.

One morning I heard Cliff on the bedroom phone with his mother, again thanking her for coming out to babysit. I heard him say, "Yeah, that's probably a good idea. Okay, I'll pick him up."

"Who are you picking up?" I thought it might be his younger brother.

"That was my mom. She loved being here with the kids. When she got home she had an idea which I think is a good one." His ideas scared me.

"Oh no, I don't think I need one of those. Great ideas rank right up there with 'opportunities.' I've seen both, and rarely have they been impressive." I turned from capping the last baby bottle to see what his expression was telling me. "You may as well tell me, but if it's anything else on my plate, the answer is 'no.'" He followed me into the kitchen, talking rather quickly as if to mitigate what he was about to tell me. If he talked fast, maybe I wouldn't have so many questions.

"Well, you know how my mother is about dogs?"

"Yeah, she has about a half dozen of them."

"Well, she's just rescued a really nice dog, a red Vizsla, about four years old. She wants to find him a nice home and thinks this is exactly what our family needs. He would be great for the kids and would be a good watchdog for you. I know it's lonely here at night." He was smiling, actually smiling. My mouth had fallen open at this absurd suggestion.

"NO. NO. NO. The last thing in the world I need is a dog. I'm already drowning. What could she be thinking? She was here; she knows what chaos we're living in…."

"Let me finish. This Vizsla is a hunting dog; he's four years old, housebroken with all his shots. He doesn't shed so we don't have the allergy problem. The kids would love to have a dog; actually, they could take care of him."

"You haven't said anything to them yet, have you?" I looked at him with an unbelieving stare and a continuing shake of my head. "Cliff, no. No dog."

"But I told my mom we'd try it. If it doesn't work, we can send him back." I recognized his pleading look; it translated, "If you don't give in, everyone will hate you."

"You already made this decision before you even talked to me? That's what I love about this partnership; there's only one decision-making partner, and it isn't me. Call her back and tell her not to send this dog." I turned my back and walked away. He followed me.

"Please, just try it. She's already bought his ticket. I'll pick him up in Newark. I promise if it doesn't work, he'll go back to Toledo."

Baron, the large, energetic, red Vizsla, bounded in the door to meet his new family. Tami and Ray decided he needed a walk, but with one dramatic lunge he broke free with Cliff and the kids chasing after. I closed the door hoping in his escape he would find another more suitable family.

Baron loved to run so that's what I let him do. In the mornings after I saw the kids off to school, I fed Baron, then walked him to the front door. I patted his head and opened the door for him. He and I had an understanding about freedom. We both needed it. Only one of us could run at this moment; I conceded he could run for both of us. "Go get 'em, Baron, go find whatever it is you're after." I watched as he bolted from my side through the open door, across the path and driveway toward somewhere. What was calling him? An earlier home where he was free? A home whose master was engaged with him? I watched him race down Standish Lane toward the East Lake and out of sight. Sometime in the early evening he would return snowy or muddy to reunite with Tami and Ray. They would take him, along with his muddy paws and other debris, to their upstairs quarters for the night. He knew where he lived and didn't appear to want to leave just yet. Maybe he was weighing his options as I was weighing mine.

"So, Baron, what do we do now? I don't dislike you, but your presence here reminds me of yet another failure. I look in your eyes when you come home at night, and I see distance, distance from us coupled with yearning for a place perhaps you haven't identified. I know that space, Baron, and I won't contribute to your confinement here."

And Cliff? How would he react?

"Okay, we tried it. It hasn't worked. I'm the dog's caretaker, just as I knew I would be, and I don't even like him. I don't want Baron or any dog. Call your mother; he's going home."

"I just hate to call my mom and tell her we failed," he said.

"I didn't fail. I never wanted this dog in the first place. And he doesn't want to be here. My decision is final. Call her and send him back."

Cliff called his mother who tried desperately to convince him to reconsider. I prevailed. Baron was on his way back to Toledo. I patted his head as he left.

February crept in with whiter snow, the sun peeked through the clouds a little more often, and spring was within shouting distance. But the black hole of depression beckoned from the wings of those endless winter evenings as I sat before a blazing fire, staring into its flames divining answers that didn't come.

Memorable experiences are often those that aren't significant in and of themselves. It's the timing of when they occur. It's one more sadness in a string.

I had waited until after the new year for Scott's well-baby check up. That way I wouldn't have to worry about getting home in time for Tami and Ray's return from school. On the designated day we all piled into the car, Ray in front and Tami in back with Billy and Scott. The check up went well except for the trauma of shots for both boys.

Returning from the doctor's office, we pulled into the driveway. No more check ups for another month. I parked in front of the garage door, activated the opener so we could walk through the back door of the garage into the gravel play area and on into the house. Just as the five of us approached the open door, I saw Billy trip in front of me, just out of arm's reach, on the threshold and sprawl face first into the gravel, his screams threatening to alarm the street. "Ray, here, take Scott." I handed my screaming baby to a less than eager older brother. "Tami, run, get some ice." I ran to Billy to see blood pouring from his chin. I grabbed a diaper from the bag to apply pressure to the gaping slit. Carefully, I lifted the diaper to determine the damage. His little chin looked like someone had attempted to slice it in pieces like an apple. I picked him up and placed the ice on the slice. He wasn't going to calm down until the ice numbed the ugly cut. Only one action to take: drive back to the pediatrician, hoping he would stitch the gaping gash and not send us to the hospital emergency room.

Inside the car once more, this time with two upset kids and two screaming babies, I shakily retraced my route. Looking like lost refugees, we walked back into the doctor's office to the amazement of the staff who took one look and said, "Come on back. Let's fix you up."

Trying to lend sanity to the situation, the nurse said, "Gee, you were just in here. You didn't get very far, did you?" She was trying; she was going to get this little family fixed up. Tami sat in the chair and gave Scott his bottle to finish, which was a start. I held Billy in my lap while the doctor numbed the chin and sewed my beautiful child back together. Billy was crying, I was crying, and I suspect the doctor wanted to cry.

I should have held Billy's hand. I should have been watching more carefully. I'd been through stitching up children before; why was this experience different? I knew why; the train I was on with Cliff had derailed. He had the Bureau, and I had the kids.

We filed from the office like the wayward family we were, dirty, bloody, tear stained, lost. The car was quieter going home. Scott was finally asleep, Billy's pain was gone, and Tami was holding him. Ray sat in front with me. I looked at him and thought, "My oldest son will never have children."

We were home; dinner was grilled cheese sandwiches and tomato soup, my old stand-by in time of crisis. A nice warm bath would help. Everyone was finally in bed, exhausted from the ordeal of the day. I hadn't even asked Tami and Ray how their day at school was. Silence filled the house as I filled my wine glass and sat before the fire Ray had built for me. I sat and listened to the silence.

Cliff called about midnight as he was leaving the office, his policy of checking in. "Gosh, this day has been chaos. This new desk I have is hectic. It seems any truck on the road is a target for truck-jacking. I hope the Port Authority isn't too bad. Catching the bus at this hour is no picnic."

"Be careful. See you tomorrow. I don't think I'll wait up for you tonight."

"Yup. Oh, how was your day?"

"Fine." He might notice Billy's bandage in the morning.

A cozy fire, a glass of wine, three children asleep, one baby waiting for his last bottle. All suggesting warmth; yet, coming from within my heart's deepest, darkest recesses, existed a black hole that with the passing days beckoned me closer. Each of my thoughts this night was a distorted photograph. Now the wine was warmer, along with my body's extremities; however, a disturbing chill lingered. One more day, could I get through one more day? And after that?

Mom? Call me. I need to tell you everything that's going on, to tell you I need you, to ask you how you made it through rough years. Can you come closer where you can really hear me but no one else can hear us? I'm crumbling under the pressure to be the perfect mom and wife. I'd even settle for being an average one. It's all too much. I'm locked in this house with my two babies in the darkness of winter days and nights. The trees that spread their huge be-leaved branches in summer to shield me from the sun are now skeletons reminding me of the barrenness of my life. I talk to my house, and she stands firmly beside me reminding me of the strength in her solid walls. But she isn't you. I need you, Mom.

What do I do? You've told me not to pile so much on my plate. Okay, what do I take off: the kids, the house, the car, my bridge group, my only outlet? I can't leave this mess. I could never come back to you and Dad saying I failed. But I am failing.

What can you tell me? Tell me something. Tell me you love me in spite of. Tell me it will turn out. Talk to me.

Many times I had picked up the phone, put it to my ear and started to dial, then hung up because I knew I would cry. The call I wanted to make I couldn't. So I continued to stuff it all down just below my heart where I urged it to stay until….

I folded my arms around my head, closing out all sound but that of the fire and willing my mother to hear what I was afraid to speak to her or anyone. If I said I was a failure, I would be. If I said I couldn't go on, I wouldn't be able to. I told myself I should be able to do better; I certainly had practice. Multiple moves, practice making difficult decisions and an absentee husband had provided me with skills for a role I never wanted. I had opted for a partnership; I got a solo act.

There wasn't a way out, was there? I couldn't quit, and I couldn't let anyone know how I was really feeling, not even my closest neighbor friends in my bridge group. We often played at my house so I wouldn't have to get a sitter. These three women had never known an FBI family and were curious.

One Wednesday evening we sat before my fireplace, fire glowing, candy and nuts on the table and cards dealt for the first round. Tami and Ray were upstairs, and I had put the two babies to bed. In the midst of play, Scott began to cry. I nodded at my friends to indicate I heard him. "He'll go back to sleep if I leave him alone," I said. Not to be. His cries escalated while I sat motionless, unable to play my cards or move from my chair. Something like a spreading darkness had overtaken me. I sat immobilized. Billy would soon be awake, yet frozen I looked at the hand I'd been dealt. I laid my cards face down and grasped my head with both hands as if to squeeze all the sorrow and helplessness onto the table. Tears rained on my folded cards while around me my friends were scurrying. I looked up; Donna had Scott, Susan held Billy and Mary was fixing bottles. I placed my vacant hands on the seat of my folding chair to push my quivering body upward to care for my boys.

"No, Sandy," said Donna. "Let us do this. We haven't had babies for a while." She placed her vacant hand on my shoulder. "Go in the family room and lie down. We want to do this for you."

Curled up on my side, I allowed my weary body to release its stash of tears onto an available receiving blanket. The room grew quiet, and I felt my friends' presence. I sat up, extending my hands in gratitude. Tomorrow I would feel guilt over this lapse. Is that what they call it when a person has shoved so much stuff down into that space where no one can see it and you vow not to feel it?

Donna stayed with me for several hours that night without asking or even encouraging me to talk about all the feelings lurking in that dark space. I loved her for these moments. She left me in the quiet of my space where I stayed until the phone rang.

"Hi, honey. Look, I'm not going to be able to come home tonight. We just had a big truck hijacking case break so I'll work until we get some resolution and then crash here. I'll be home sometime tomorrow."

"Okay." It didn't matter that he wouldn't be home. Nothing mattered.

This insidious mold called the Bureau had crept into every aspect of my life. It had usurped the person I used to be. After hanging up the phone, I shuffled into the bathroom before bed. Glancing into the mirror, I didn't expect to see a young exuberant woman staring back at me, but I didn't expect to see a lifeless ghost either, one whose countenance revealed defeat. "Who are you? I don't know you. I once knew you, didn't I?" No smile of recognition from the image. Her colorless eyes looked like a cataract film had overtaken them. An ashen complexion that makeup couldn't fix: a waxen image. Something had crawled inside to kill her.

Instead of going to bed, I walked, shoulders slumped, back to the living room for another glass of wine beside the fire's final embers. Seated, I stoked orange glimmering coals to encourage yet more heat for a winter's chill that wouldn't leave me. Sitting cross-legged close to the fire, begging it to fill me with its warmth, I reflected in the quiet of the late hour. I was getting dangerously close to the edge. I just had to take one step. The alluring swirl of blackness enticed me. It would be easy. I had plenty of pills in my medicine stash. I had my .38 Snubby I'd never fired. Tami and Ray would be fine; the babies wouldn't.

I curled up on the floor closest to the dying fire and cried.

SIXTEEN

Reaching down, reaching in

Morning comes late in the winter months. Windows yawn to reach for light. From my curled bedtime position in front of the now expired fire, I could hear sounds of movement upstairs and Scott in the nursery, not yet crying. I hastily dressed in yesterday's sweats and began the morning routine of breakfast, bottles, and lunches for Tami and Ray. I moved from the dishwasher to the cupboard to the refrigerator as an automaton. My body followed what it was receiving from my brain. Fortunately, I could follow this routine in my sleep.

"Hi everybody. Tami, you look pretty this morning. Ray, be sure to wear your boots. Have a great day at school. Billy, are you hungry? Let's get you in your highchair. Scott, how about taking your bottle in your baby seat?" I rattled on in a way that seemed familiar to me; at least someone's voice was echoing in my ear. I was still alive.

Tami and Ray grabbed their coats, backpacks and lunches and gave me a kiss as they walked out the door. I returned to the kitchen for my first cup of coffee and noticing I had used the last bottle of formula, I began to pull the components from the cupboard, cascading the powder over the counter, its flakes floating into my coffee cup.

I looked at the mess, grown from a spill to a massive mountain. Robotically, I reached for a sponge to clean up the now sticky glue, which resisted my attempts first to brush it into the waste can and then to rub it into firm globs with my sponge which only served to expand the scope of the clean up. Now my spill had become one more morning challenge whose pasty face looked up at me from my countertop. I could feel that seductive black hole growing closer. It beckoned me to take one more step. I placed my face in my arms on the red laminated breakfast bar and sobbed. "I can't."

My yellow wall phone stared at me. I stared back asking for help. Not my family, not neighbors, not anyone who knew me. Maybe a medical person. But my only doctor was my obstetrician, an odd choice but the first number at hand. Cautiously, I dialed. I recognized the receptionist's voice from my visits to the office. She would help me; I could hear it in her voice.

"I can't do this. Please help me. I have two babies, an eight-year-old, a nine-year-old and a husband who's never home. I can't do this any more." I was rambling to a person I didn't know. "Please help me." Sandy Browning, this independent young woman from the Midwest who thought she could make anything work now knew she couldn't. Her world was no longer grey; it was black. A curtain had descended on what felt like the final act.

"Don't hang up, Sandy. You just had a baby with us a short time ago. Let me pull your file and get some information. Stay on the line. Promise me you won't hang up." Her voice was now stronger, firmer, in control.

Stay on the line? I was on the line, the end of the line, the one leading to despair. I needed a way out. Pills, razor blade, gun, gas. All the options resurfaced as I waited for help. I was a failure. I couldn't handle my own life. God, these poor kids. Dad working all the time. Mom barely functional. I couldn't do this to them.

"Okay, here's what I need you to do. Call your husband or a sitter for the babies. I've spoken to Dr. Arthur's office, and he will see you when you arrive. He's a very fine therapist; he can help you. Can you do that? Our other resource is to call the ambulance. Are you able to drive?"

"Maybe. Yes, I think so. I've never done this, seeing a therapist. Will he think I'm crazy? Will he tell me to get hold of myself? I don't think I can find myself let alone help myself."

"No, honey, healthy people see therapists every day to help them with problems. He sees lots of people like you. You need a professional you can talk to in a place that's safe. Promise me you'll do this."

"Promise. Just tell me I'll get better."

"Yes, honey, you will. I'm going to call and check on you shortly to make sure you've gotten a sitter."

I thought about the sitter situation. Maybe Cliff could get home to watch the kids. I'd wait until I talked to him.

I reluctantly hung up my lifeline and looked around at breakfast mayhem in the kitchen, laundry to be folded and babies who needed to be tended. At the moment they were contented in their surroundings. I poured myself another cup of coffee and shakily grasped the phone. The sitter could wait; Cliff could wait; I needed to talk to the strongest person in my life. I had never before called my dad at his office. He was in, and his secretary put me through.

"Dad, it's me. I'm so sorry to bother you." As soon as these words left my lips, my voice began to quaver and words stammered from my throat. "You've always told me I was so strong that I could handle anything. You were wrong, Dad. I can't handle anything." God, I sounded like a slobbering baby.

"Wait, honey, slow down. I'm not going anywhere. Tell me what's happening?"

"I'm sick, Dad. I cry all the time and can't handle anything. My world is like a black hole. I called my doctor this morning, and he's referring me to a psychologist. You always told me that the only people who used these quacks were those who were so weak they couldn't stand on their own two feet. I'm calling to tell you I'm one of those people. One of those weak people, Dad. That's who I am." My words rambled as if I had a time limit to get all this out. My dad had no tolerance for weakness. Better now he know who his daughter really was.

It was a few seconds before he spoke. "Honey, you're my strong, beautiful daughter. I admire you so much. You're a wonderful mother and wife. It sounds like right now you just have too much to handle. I think seeing a counselor is exactly the right thing to do. Probably more people should do what you're doing."

"Dad, I know what you've always said about these people. But I'm drowning, and this was the hardest call I've ever had to make. You're the most important person in my life, and I've failed you."

"No, you haven't failed me; you never could. I wish I could be there with you."

"I miss you, Dad."

"Mom and I will be out soon. A few weeks ago I told Cliff I'd come out and help him with some repairs." A visit now would not be right for either of us.

"I do want to do a couple of things though," he said in his executive voice. "I'm going to send you a check for your counseling sessions, and I want you go as often as this person thinks he needs to see you. The other thing is, I want Cliff to look for someone to help you at home with the cleaning, laundry and babysitting so you can get out once in a while. Promise me you'll do this. I'm going to check next week to see that you have people on board for help." Dad's voice was one of authority.

"Okay, Dad. I'll get someone."

"Honey, I want Cliff to do this. I love you, honey, and you know I'll always be here for you. Right now you need to call Cliff. You may be surprised at how he responds."

"Dad, please don't tell Mom. I'll call her after I see the therapist. I know she'll worry." And well she should.

Scott had thankfully fallen asleep in his baby seat, and Billy was tired of his chair so I released him to his stack of toys. Control. As long as I had things under control, everyone was at least safe. I dumped my lukewarm coffee into the drain, loaded the dishwasher with breakfast residue and thought about my conversation with Dad.

My next call was equally painful. At least Cliff was now in the office on a desk so I could reach him.

"Sorry to bother you. I guess you must have had a busy night. Are you coming home soon?" My voice sounded shaky, uncertain, as if I didn't want to say any more.

"I'd like to get home for a nap before my shift at 4:00."

"I need you home. I can't go on like this. If you need to take vacation time, so be it, but I need to meet with a therapist today, the sooner the better. He's expecting me." My sentences were all jumbled in no logical sequence.

"What happened? You were fine last night when I called from the office."

"No, I wasn't fine, and I'm not fine now. How would you know anyway? I need you, Cliff, for lots of things, but right now I need you to be a father and come home and watch the babies so I can see someone who can help. If that's not possible, tell me, and I'll find a sitter."

"Honey, everyone has bad days. It will take me a while to get home so make your appointment as late as possible. You might call a sitter as a backup."

"A bad day? Where have you been for the past few years? Have I done such a good job of keeping it all together that it seemed I was okay?" Or didn't he want to see it? I was screaming for help, admitting I was over the edge. I needed a safety net. I knew my problems were an inconvenience. Cliff was a busy man, and he had a long commute home. I was even feeling maybe I shouldn't have called him. I was a problem he didn't need. I had a problem I didn't need either. My inner voice told me I was on my own and I'd better figure it out.

"Okay, I should have known my problems would need to fit into your schedule. You couldn't just drop things for my emergency. You see, this isn't a bad day or a bad week or even a bad year. My world is shattered." Even as I spoke I could feel my body's walls splintering from the inside out threatening to burst into thousands of toothpick sized pieces.

"I can't believe this call. Things are hard for me, too. I'm just trying to do the best I can to support this family. I can't be here and there both."

"You helped create this mess, and you share in the responsibility. It isn't all about money and your job, you know. Building a family is hard work and takes two people."

"Right now I can't be home. I'll leave as soon as I can, but I know I can't be there before 6:00."

"I'll see if I can find a sitter; if not, I'll make my counseling appointment for 6:30 or 7:00. The doctor's office said he works evenings. Cliff, I'm sorry to make it difficult for you, but I need help."

"I'll be there by 6:00."

Cliff pulled into the driveway around 5:00 as I was feeding the children. It was a pretty gloomy house: Tami and Ray, who seemed to be arguing about everything, two hungry, crying babies and one barely functional wife. Cliff quickly changed clothes and dug in to help. I turned the family over to him, showered and left for my appointment. Driving, I began to feel maybe I wasn't as sick as I felt, maybe I was exaggerating things, maybe a session or two to talk to someone and I would be better.

I found myself hesitating, driving slower until I pulled into the driveway of the counselor's home, feeling uncomfortable and ashamed but not enough to cancel the appointment. The small porch entry at one end of his home was inviting with planters, which soon would be overflowing with color and a dark plum colored door with a small hand-lettered sign welcoming me to come in without knocking. So I took my first step to gain control over the direction of my life. I opened the door and stepped over the threshold feeling I was leaving something behind. It felt right to be here. The small attractively furnished waiting room pulled me in with its soft lavender walls, classical music, candles and upholstered barrel style chairs inviting me to relieve myself of whatever my burdens were.

Any trepidation I had entertained on the drive faded when Dr. Arthur introduced himself and invited me into his office where he gestured to me to have a seat on the couch. I felt reassured knowing other people like me had sat here looking for help. I looked up as he walked to a chair across from me, not so close as to be imposing but close enough to be reassuring.

"Sandy, I got a call this morning from your doctor. I'm really pleased you're here. You have to understand that whatever we talk about in this room stays here. This is your space. You're safe here." He looked directly at me assuring me he spoke the truth.

I nodded. " I'm not sure I know where to start. How do I do this?" I could feel the emotion swelling. Words were going to be hard to form with the lump forming in my throat and the tears already falling.

"Let's start with a little information about you. Who is Sandy Browning? What has she been doing for the last ten years or so? Where did she grow up? Start wherever it's easiest."

So I did. I opened my mouth to form words; what came out sounded like disorganized gibberish, but it seemed to be gibberish he understood. He nodded that he was hearing me, and then I talked and talked some more. Words and thoughts ran together. He listened. At the next pause he said, "How about we recap some of these thoughts; you let me know if I'm understanding the sources of this terrible place you're in." This time he talked, and I nodded as he put into order my muddled thoughts. He had heard me. He suggested we meet twice a week until I was feeling better. I'm not sure what I told this man, but I knew I was breaking the ice with myself.

I pulled up to my red door feeling like I could make it another day.

Cliff was sitting on the couch feeding Scott when I walked in. I hung my coat in the closet and ambled into the kitchen for a Coke.

"Would you like a drink?" I asked.

"No, I had a snack while you were gone. How was your session?" For the first time in a while, I thought I could see concern.

"It was good. Dr. Arthur's a very nice man. He doesn't say much; he mostly listens. For a while I'm scheduling time with him twice a week."

"Wow, that's quite a schedule. That's going to be pretty expensive. I'm not sure how much the insurance will pay. And I'm not sure I can always be here for your appointment times."

"I know all that. Don't worry about the cost. Dad is sending me a check for the sessions, and I'm going to line up a sitter for at least the next month." I nodded as I confirmed I had this small part of my life in hand.

"Oh, I didn't know you'd talked to your dad."

I could tell he was asking for more information, but my response was a simple, "Yes I've talked to him."

One particular therapy session found me beginning to validate myself to myself. This came after a series of meetings where I talked and Dr. Arthur listened, sometimes offering comment but mostly asking questions for clarification. After several weeks we began to discuss tactics such as boundary setting that I could use to handle everyday stresses. What could I give up to gain control over more important aspects of my life? Could I lower my expectations for Cliff's involvement in the family so when I accepted social invitations, I accepted only for myself? Could I discipline myself to not answer phone calls late at night, which most often were from informants?

I learned it was okay to concede that I needed help. I hired a cleaning person and a babysitter to come in once a week, which would free me to get out if only to shop for groceries. I had to convince myself that this wasn't an admission of incompetence on my part. It helped. So Dr. Arthur and I continued, working slowly to rebuild my confidence. At this point it wasn't about my marriage, it was about me rebuilding my strength.

It was time for a talk with Cliff. I poured a Coke for him and a glass of wine for me and sat down next to him on the same brown couch where we had once held our family planning meetings.

"I've been in counseling a while now and feel like I'm ready for a talk about us and our future."

"That's probably a good idea. We really haven't talked much since being assigned here. This office has been crazier than the previous ones, I know. And then I have this god-awful commute. So what's up?" He smiled as he looked at me. I got up to turn the TV off; I certainly couldn't compete with that.

"You're right, it is a bit about this office. You say I don't understand your job here in New York. But, that's not a big change, is it? These assignments have all been difficult. It would probably be best if FBI agents were single. But, that being said, I'd like to talk about what we can do to get out of here."

"We've talked about this before," he said. "I know you feel trapped here, but the only possibility I see is to be selected for the Administrative Track which would probably mean a year or two here as a supervisor coupled with a recommendation for a supervisory position in Washington, D.C." This sounded like something out of the Bureau Handbook: carefully chosen words.

"I'll take it. Make this happen. You're already a supervisor, so that should count for something. I won't stay here. You can find a way to get us out, or I'll eventually find a way to leave on my own." I half believed what I was saying. No, it was more than half.

"I thought things were better since you started the counseling." He wrinkled his brow in confusion.

"They are." How did I make him understand it was the lifestyle; it was the loneliness; it was being in a marriage without a partner.

"I am getting better. I now have someone to talk to, but listen to me. I have no husband. Do you hear me? I have no husband! Have you heard this before? I think so. If I'm going to live by myself, it will be somewhere other than two hours from New York. Winter is as dark as my spirit. I wait longer each day for the sun to shine through my windows. The cheeriest part of this whole community is my red front door."

"What do you want?"

I paused. How many times had I asked myself this question? I wanted change, an out. I'd even settle for another move.

"Out. I want you to figure a way to get us transferred from here. You mentioned the Administrative Track. Do that."

"I hear you, but this is my career."

"Then get a new career. Start looking for jobs in California or somewhere. I won't live here the rest of my life." I wouldn't cry either, not this time.

It was counseling night again. I fed the children, put on my coat and left. I started my car, my lifeline to the outside world and a connection with someone who was helping me. Driving home, my little house looked so welcoming from the road. She had become my ally and my refuge.

Removing my coat, I settled down on the trusty brown sofa, a repository for tears, a few serious discussions and even spilled baby formula. My depression hadn't loosened its grip; but in the safety of my warmly lit room, I began to feel a glimmer of light piercing the blackness that had surrounded me.

As the weeks progressed, my daily load began to feel a bit lighter as I tended to my growing family. Cliff helped with the house, which was a first, and devoted more time to Tami and Ray. I continued to voice my frustrations, and Dr. Arthur agreed that while I probably wouldn't have chosen an FBI lifestyle, I needed to figure out how I could stay sane and stable within the Bureau bureaucracy. Some of his suggestions worked, and some didn't. In the late evenings while Cliff worked, I still sat by the fire, staring into the embers for answers. I still talked to my house asking her what other women in my position had done. I tried to settle for what I had around me and feel contented. It didn't always work, but over time I was feeling stronger.

In the meantime summer arrived and with it a breakthrough of light into my life. Both babies were now sitting up which meant I could put them in the double stroller and go for a walk around the neighborhood, down to the lake where I could watch Ray and Tami paddle our rowboat. We all went to the pool where Tami and Ray took swim lessons and swam for the team. I watched from the baby pool. Finally, summer was here, and I was outside where it was green and filled with flowers. The hardwoods bent and swayed in the breeze, offering us blessed shade on those sultry days. I moved all the important family events like meals, reading and playing games onto the screened back porch. My face became tanned, and I felt warm. Inch by inch, my beautiful landscape encouraged me forward.

Cliff's time with us was still limited as he working on the illusive supervisory appointment to a desk in Washington D.C. Finally acquiring the minimum experience, he applied for a position in Washington. It was a long shot.

In the fall of 1970, as I was clearing our breakfast dishes, Cliff called. "I have great news. The leadership here has recommended me for a supervisory position at the Seat of Government in Washington." I could hear his excitement. Maybe he could salvage his marriage with this next assignment.

"Does this mean we're out of here?" I held my breath for his answer.

"Not quite. I still have to go to D.C. to interview with Mr. Hoover. He approves or rejects all applicants for administrative positions." This would be his second interview with the Director.

"Oh no, this could be a huge obstacle." Everyone was terrified of Hoover who was in charge of everything. Cliff's future with the Bureau and my sanity hung on this interview. Cliff had spoken with other agents who had gone through this process and prepared himself the best way possible. Finally, ready, he took the train to Washington.

I waited.

Normally, these interviews with the Director lasted no more than fifteen minutes; Cliff's interview lasted forty-five minutes. He called me following the meeting and when asked how it went, because our whole future rested on this interview, he said, "I think it went fine. Mr. Hoover asked me what I was looking forward to in my Bureau career, and I said 'I want to come to D.C. and work for you.'" Now, possibly, Mr. Hoover would grant Cliff his request.

And that was true. He did want to go to D.C. and so did I. I was putting all my chips on the come line. Washington D.C. had to be better. It would be better: a new house, a new desk job with regular hours, a real support neighborhood for me. It had to work.

Upon Cliff's return to the New York office, the Assistant Special Agent in Charge called him into his office saying, "We have a dilemma; we received a memo from the Director which says, 'Transfer this agent to SOG as soon as possible.' We're not sure what that means—days, weeks or months, and since no one wants to ask the Director to define 'ASAP,' we're cutting your transfer orders to Washington immediately. Plan on reporting to your new assignment in D.C. in thirty days."

Cliff's first words to me were: "How soon can you have the house sold and be packed to move?"

"I don't know about the house sale, but I can have everything else ready in a week. Bring home the new moving requirements, and I'm ready." I had moved so many times, I could organize our transit in my sleep. We had remodeled our 1920s house with the white picket fence and heavily wooded lot to present herself well to prospective buyers. I knew she would sell quickly. She was quirky yet proud. In our eighteen-month residency we had redone the kitchen, fixed the screened porch, painted the interior and exterior and more importantly, I knew she would welcome the next family with her charm. Like every other house, we had created a welcoming home in a very short time.

"Are you serious? You don't think I'll have to go on ahead like we have in the past? We have a lot to do—sell the house, pack and on and on."

"No, we're going to make this move together. I'll start the list, and we'll divide up the tasks. If this is the way it usually goes, you won't have much of a work load here in the next thirty days so you should be able to dedicate yourself to this move."

"Okay, I get the picture."

Hopefully he did. I was running this show. "I'm one very experienced and motivated lady. I want out of here. I never see you; I don't know you. I'm living with a stranger who shows up now and then. You were sent up here to work the mob, which was troublesome enough. I'm fearful every time you go out on a raid. You know that thing I have about being a young widow. I'm ready—let's go."

We had new moving regulations this time. Mr. Hoover was entering the modern age. This time all travel and moving expenses were covered, even for family members. In addition, the Bureau covered the cost of a house-hunting trip to the new location. So we packed up and drove to D.C. to find our new house. Cliff had been talking to a realtor about our requirements, so the agent knew what we needed and had properties lined up before we got there. One of our possibilities was a new-build in the King's Park West subdivision in Fairfax, VA. We liked the house plans and the location. Fairfax County schools were rated the best in the nation at that time. We selected the plan, the lot and picked out all the special things that would make this a lovely home for us. It wouldn't be ready for six months so we solved the problem by renting a furnished townhouse in Alexandria. I would drive the kids back and forth to school, but even that was fine because I got to watch my new house being constructed.

In thirty days we left. The first people to look at 8 Standish Lane made us an offer, and we were set to go. As Cliff backed our blue station wagon out of our driveway, I looked with fondness at my old friend with her red door and knew she was wishing me well and would welcome her new residents just as she had me.

Part Five

Do you ever feel as if it's the first day of the rest of your life?

Washington D.C.
1971-73

SEVENTEEN

If it looks like the perfect place, it might be

Running isn't always a bad option. Cliff called our move to D.C. a transfer, a promotion like other transfers. Only, for me, it wasn't like the others. I was running, setting world records in my need to distance myself from my recent depressive crisis. New Jersey was a past I didn't want to be reminded of, and it took years to acknowledge to myself the shame of my suicidal crisis. It was shame for something that shouldn't have happened to me but did, a shame of failure hanging over me like that seductive black cloud beckoning me to slip over the edge to the end. In future years I would feel shivers down my arms and a rush to change the subject any time a discussion turned to Cliff's exciting New York mob encounters or when people innocently asked me about my experiences in New Jersey. I would only answer something inane like, "It was okay." Then I would change the subject and walk away. The scars from that period of my life ran deep, too deep to ever share with anyone.

So while I rejoiced in our new assignment, that little voice cautioned me: be happy, act happy, but be cautious.

Leaving 8 Standish Lane, I took one last look at my friend, my Cape Cod sanctuary. I had cried for joy at the news of our transfer; I had cried because it is what I always did when faced with change.

Two in the far back, two in the back seat and two in front; six of us piled into our dark blue Mercury station wagon, a gift from my parents.

They couldn't always be close physically, but they often helped me in surprising ways. My dad's answer to problems was to throw resources at it like the gift of this station wagon.

It was warm for early December as we rolled into the nation's capital and I recalled my first visit here. I was in high school, and Dad was in the process of building a new manufacturing plant in Delaware when he asked my mother, sister and me to accompany him for a mini-vacation to the nation's capitol. I remember my anticipation as we drove east and my awe as we made our entrance into the city in the late evening and how the monuments' illumination brought forth chills of something I later identified as patriotism. Dad pulled into the area of the Lincoln monument where we walked respectfully up the steps to Lincoln himself. I stood there a long time reading his quotes engraved on the walls and marveled at my good fortune in having parents who afforded me these experiences.

Now as we drove past the monuments and the White House, I listened to the kids' ooh's and aah's. What a great place this was going to be for them. It would be history live. And since we could be here as long as five years, we wouldn't have to rush through our education. Every week we could explore a new piece of national heritage. And besides the city itself, there was Mt. Vernon, Monticello, Manassas, Gettysburg and more just a few miles away. I smiled to myself as these thoughts traversed my mind. This was going to be a wonderful adventure.

"Cliff, I can't believe we're here. I'm so happy I could cry." I reached for his hand.

"Don't cry. Just be happy," he said, squeezing my hand.

A new place. A new start for a tired marriage. A new attitude and image. A healthier me. That was my wish list for this relocation. Cliff's job would be different. He would be assigned to a desk supervising cases as opposed to actually working the cases on the street meaning he would be safe from eight to five. He would be home for dinner and no undercover or night raids. On the weekends he wouldn't have to call in every two hours. And they were paying him more money. The sacrifices we had made had paid off.

Over the years my personal observation has taught me that when people move to a new location, they believe they are starting over. They aren't. They're just extending what has gone on before only this time it's a new physical location populated by a different cast of characters. All the past baggage moves with them. I didn't know that yet in 1971.

When packing up my boxes for the move, I had cautioned myself to proceed slowly in my enthusiasm for this latest transfer because I so desperately needed it to be the answer for our relationship and my personal health. I had now been off the steroids long enough for the side effects to have lessened. Swollen face, sore joints and drastic mood swings were disappearing. Although a few emotional scars remained, with professional help I had learned I was stronger than I thought I could be; in time of trial I really could pull through. These painfully acquired skills certainly should be good for something.

Moving into a new city had once again inspired me to empty the debris from the stored memories and refill them with new dreams. The dream part was easy. Leaving behind old issues and baggage from previous moves was more difficult.

As the new year rolled in I felt like I was on a vacation. Being in a furnished townhouse in the heart of Alexandria within walking distance to shops wasn't so bad. Cliff was settled onto a criminal desk at headquarters and appeared to be adjusting to the numerous protocols and policies that accompany any bureaucracy. He rode the bus to and from his office, and I drove Tami and Ray to and from school each day as we watched our home being built in a bucolic blend of residential and rural with woods just right for playful imagining and the cows meandering in the neighboring field.

Building our new house seemed symbolic of this new start. We hadn't built one since our first house in Delaware. When it came to the color for the front door, the builder's representative told me a standard color came with the house. I asked if that had to be the case, that it was important for me to choose that color for my new house. She left the room to consult someone and returned with a small palette of colors. I smiled as she handed them to me. I knew instantly it had to be a strong color, a beautiful teal green. It was settled.

It was finished; our house was ready for us. It had been nearly six months since we had watched the movers take away our treasures from 8 Standish Lane. Excitement was our companion as the movers carried our treasures from the Allied van into our brand new, four bedroom, three-story home with no history of abuse, neglect or conflict. No knots to cover with paint, no leaky basement. Clean and pristine, built just for us.

May 8, was the day, just a week after the Mayday demonstration against the Vietnam War. Half a million people demonstrated, marched and conducted sit-ins. The group's aim was to shut down the government by making it impossible to get into or out of the city. The effect was especially disturbing to workers like Cliff who endured throngs of hippies spitting on cars and throwing obscene signs.

"I'm glad you made it to work and back. I've been watching the TV reels, and it looks like it was messy." I had noticed an expression of exasperation as he walked in the door. This wasn't his first experience with demonstrations.

"I wanted to run over those filthy, long-haired bastards. Wearing and burning the American flag and spitting on the very people who are trying to protect this country." He threw his coat across the arm of the sofa with a flourish.

"I could tell it was difficult," I said. "Would you like a beer or something?"

"No, thanks. I just don't think you know how hard this is to take sometimes."

"Maybe not, but I do know hard. I've had plenty of experience in that department: moving is hard, raising children is hard, keeping a marriage together is hard." Dodging demonstrators was a mere inconvenience.

Opening the enticing boxes coming out of storage wasn't hard. It was like a second Christmas, an adventure. Box openings were part of our FBI history, but this experience was different. Finally, after thirteen years, I was able to unpack the wedding china, silver and crystal and place them in the new dining room cabinet I'd found in the classifieds. I unwrapped each tissue wrapped piece, placed it in the warm sudsy water, dried it carefully and arranged it in its place of honor. These treasured pieces had made it home at last. No more boxes for them. They and I were ready for some celebration. What better person than my mother to join me. Mom's arrival was timely in that not all the boxes had been emptied, and I still needed to find or make curtains and drapes for the windows.

"What do you think about this bay window?" she asked. Before I could reply with ideas she said, "Why don't we go shopping on Saturday when Cliff will be home. I think we can find something beautiful." She was smiling, almost giggling.

"Sure. I have a little money budgeted but probably not enough to get everything. My first priority is to find something nice for the living and dining rooms. Also, I haven't decided what to do with the kitchen bay window. Maybe blinds? It's up high so people really can't see in." We walked from room to room measuring and discussing possibilities. When Saturday came, we were ready.

"It's so good to see you smiling again. You love it here, don't you? And your new house is so beautiful." She reached across the seat of our brand new blue LTD station wagon and patted my knee.

"Yup, it's good, Mom. I feel like I've come home." I knew Mom was heading to a discussion of my marriage, an uncomfortable place for me.

"I'm happy for you, honey. I think of you every day and pray things are better." Her downcast eyes told me she wanted me to share more with her. As I focused on the drive home, I thought of the make-believe letter I'd written her in New Jersey. Dad would have told her of my debilitating depression, that terrible space I'd been in.

Sometimes it's what's not said between mother and daughter that is the most poignant. Although I protested, Mom insisted she had planned all along to decorate my windows for me. They turned out as beautiful as she promised. Her visit wasn't about windows.

Before she left I suggested we celebrate our decorating with a nice candlelit dinner in the dining room featuring my wedding china and silver, knowing my husband would be present.

"Hi everybody. Hey, what's the occasion? I smell candles, and look at the table. Who's coming?"

"You are. I'm celebrating two events: your new job that allows us to do things like this and Mom's visit. Pretty nice, huh?"

The kids had never seen me decorate a table this way and reacted accordingly. Scott and Billy loved the candles; Ray asked if he had to change his clothes, and Tami said, "It looks beautiful, Mom." I looked around at my remarkable family and promised them and myself we would have many more such celebrations.

And one of those would be the day we finished our walk-out lower level, our first really major project together. With Cliff's new schedule and his promotion to a GS 14, we finally had a little more room in our budget and time in the evenings to make this project possible.

"Okay, your mom had some good ideas," Cliff said. "I think we'd better get this project rolling before the Bureau decides to send me somewhere else. The first thing we'd better do is lay out the space with measurements." He grabbed some sheets of graph paper and a pencil, ready to go. He grabbed my hand as we headed for the stairs.

"I'm thinking a large family room where the sliding glass doors are and a medium sized laundry/storage room. I don't think we can afford to put another bath in, do you?" I asked.

"Probably not, but the plumbing is already in the laundry room so the cost might not be too great. We can price it out."

We carefully measured the space, drew multiple plans, shopped for materials and figured costs. He favored one look for the paneling; I favored another. I wanted cedar shingles; he wasn't so sure, nor were the sales people who advised me shingles were for outside. I told them I was putting them inside. So we compromised; he chose the paneling, and I chose the shingles. I loved those long evenings and weekends we worked together to create our new living space, side by side trudging downstairs for two or three hours of physical labor. I wasn't very good at the heavy stuff, but I could staple the wood shingles to the north wall.

"You know what? It's coming along. Look at my wall. The shakes are even somewhat level. I don't think they have to be perfect, do you? I kind of like the ragged, uneven look, and the cedar makes the room smell so good." I moved back a few feet to gauge its effect from a distance.

"Your wall is looking pretty good, better than my paneling project." Cliff pointed to what would soon be a paneled wall. "Maybe with some pictures hanging it will look better, and no one will notice the mistakes."

Our completed laundry, playroom, and TV room called for a celebration, just a few neighbors who were also in the throes of finishing basements. Our immediate neighbors worked for the federal government: Army on one side, Navy on the other side, Air Force across the street and more FBI families on adjoining streets, giving me a support group not unlike the one I had in Houston. My two best friends, Fran and Doris, were military wives who understood isolation and loneliness. Over afternoon iced tea we would share experiences and nod in understanding.

I loved the feeling of walking the neighborhood, waving at those outside and knowing they were like me. I didn't have to pretend I wasn't FBI.

This wasn't all we had celebrated together. Landscaping had turned into a neighborhood activity with everyone helping everyone else with fences, shrubs, trees, flowers and, oh yes, poison ivy which covered Billy's arms and legs with itchy, red splotches. We were drawing boundaries with our fences and planting brightly colored flowers, shrubs and gardens to enhance the beauty of our comfortable homes.

As Cliff and I cleaned up after the party, gathering paper plates and glasses, I saw an opportunity.

"Nice party, huh? It looked like everybody had fun. The Drapers really liked our new family room. In fact, they may try wood shingles on one of their walls." I pointed with pride at my cedar wall.

"Yeah, it was nice. I'm glad we did it. Maybe celebrating these basement finishes will become a tradition. I see the beer's all gone; that's usually a good sign." He smiled in my direction leaving me an opening.

"Cliff, let's stay here forever." I tilted my head in affirmation.

"Forever? That's a long time." He paused in his picking up.

"I feel like we belong here. Tami and Ray love school; Billy and Scott are in a preschool program, I'm helping out at their school, and for the first time ever, I feel like I have a husband and a life." I asked my voice to convey a positive tone.

"You're serious? You're actually suggesting we stay here?" His expression told me he had never considered such a direction. After all, we'd been moving our whole married life, and he was aiming for a higher position in the Bureau, which would mean more moves.

"I love it, it's beautiful, and there's so much for us here. I feel like I'm in the center of everything important that's happening in the world."

"Well, we're in the center all right including these damn demonstrations. There's one problem though. A permanent assignment isn't likely as long as I'm on this Administrative Track. We might be here four or five years though." He was speaking more slowly as if he were actually considering what I was saying.

"Well, that's something." Four was close to five even though I knew with the FBI he couldn't predict the length of our stay. "What if you got off this track? The Bureau has thousands of people here. Maybe, there's another position you'd like. A permanent one. Maybe a field position at

WFO (Washington Field Office) or a different kind of job but one still interesting." I had to hurry while he was still listening.

"Not likely, even if I did want a different job, which I don't. Look, honey, we knew when we came here that I was on track to move back to the field as an Assistant Special Agent in Charge." He was nodding that surely I remembered.

I nodded in return. I did remember what this assignment was about. "I was just thinking how great it would be if Tami and Ray could finish high school here or at the most have one more move. That would get Billy and Scott half way through elementary school." I looked for a non-verbal response. His scowl told me he didn't want to have this conversation.

"So far, they've adjusted just fine," he said. "Right now we aren't moving anywhere."

"I'm just saying that I would like it to stay like that. I like having you home."

Ignoring my last statement he announced, "Look, this desk job may look like the ideal for you, but it isn't all that perfect. At first, I felt genuinely lucky to have been tapped for a desk here at headquarters, a fast track to advancement, but after almost a year I see it differently. It's extremely competitive, and there's an air of secrecy about the whole place. I've been warned about people I shouldn't speak with and never to discuss cases in the halls or elevator or even with my office mate. It's not like being in a field office where everyone works together. From where you sit in this nice house with plenty of friends, it probably looks ideal, but..." He paused to see if I were listening. I was.

"No job is ever perfect, is it? Finding that balance that's right for a family is difficult. At least we're talking. I was talking to Nancy this week, and she said they're talking about requesting a transfer from the lab here back to Utah. They're Mormons, and they miss family."

"Yeah, Dave's mentioned it in the carpool. He likes the work, but Nancy isn't very happy."

I looked over at him and smiled. He had one last point to make. "I'm the one who has to do this job, and I'd like you to believe I'm making the best decisions possible for my career and our family." His point was made. He reloaded the last garbage bag for the trash and turned toward the stairs.

I looked at this handsome man with so many wonderful qualities and wondered why he couldn't hear me. Did he love me?

EIGHTEEN

Dissent

It was one of those early summer evenings when everything feels just right. I had made my famous potato salad, and the grill was ready for the hamburgers. It wasn't boiling hot yet; even the infamous D.C. humidity was a tolerable level. A perfect setting for an outside picnic on our brand new redwood table.

"Well, what's new with everybody," Cliff asked. "Anybody do anything fun today?" It had been a busy day for everyone. Ray had gone to the park with Brad; Tami, Billy, Scott and I had gone to the library. This was going to be a fun summer here in our new neighborhood. I already had the kids lined up for camps, which seemed important since we didn't have any kind of family vacation planned for this summer. Our vacation funds had been diverted to our basement finish and landscaping.

"And how was your day, I asked."

Cliff turned his attention to me and shook his head. "With these darn anti-war demonstrations going on, getting into and out of the city is a nightmare."

"I've seen the latest news clips on TV. A lot of people feel strongly about this war and think we should be out of it." I counted myself among them but rarely played that hand, one that would not be regarded well in this household although I felt strongly that Tami and Ray should see and hear both sides of the argument.

"Afraid so. What people don't realize is this bunch of rich, filthy, braless hippies are actually part of a larger conspiracy to overthrow our government."

"Do we actually know that? I know Hoover hates the communists and thinks they're behind most, if not all, of these groups."

"No, you really don't know anything, and neither do the American people. The identities of these groups are classified. Even I'm not privy to all of it." He looked at me as if to say this should end the discussion.

"But maybe we need to know. If we did know what this was all about, maybe we'd know which side to support. Should only a few people know what's going on?"

"American foreign policy and decisions about war should be left in the hands of those who know best."

"And who would those be? Generals and politicians who profit from the war itself?"

"You're sounding like a radical. You shouldn't spout off about things you don't know anything about." He turned toward the hamburgers and the kids clamoring to be fed. This had turned into one of our family discussions, the kind I had initiated during these mealtime conversations with Tami and Ray in Jacksonville. Once the picnic was on the table, our conversation expanded to include the kids. The rules were the same: everyone was allowed a voice, and no questions were off limits. I looked around the table at the curious eyes now considering their dad's position on the anti-war protests.

"They probably could look nicer, but they do have a right to speak freely and to dissent," I said. "That's what this country is built on."

"What's dissent?" Ray asked. When he spoke up, Billy sat up taller to hear how this was going to play out.

"We talked about it in school," Tami said. "It's when you disagree with someone about something, something really important, and you speak out about it."

"That's right, and we have to protect our right to disagree when we believe our government is wrong." I looked at Cliff and tried to gauge how strongly he was going to react. That he and I disagreed was no secret.

"I can't share much, but the FBI has information on these protestors that it hasn't shared. Kids, the communists may be behind this whole movement." That had been Hoover's explanation for the civil rights movement also.

"On that note," I said. "Shall we go to the park or the pool?"

As I gathered the plates and bowls onto the tray, Cliff grabbed my arm, but he wasn't smiling. "I don't like it that you're always disagreeing with me."

"Let's talk later," I said.

For the sake of the kids, we dropped our discussion, got our suits and towels and headed for the pool. Mostly tired and clean from our playtime, we headed home for snacks, stories and sleep.

It was our time so we, too, settled in with some ice cream. The house was quiet, inviting some introspection and conversation. I had wanted to ask Cliff about an incident involving the FBI last spring.

"Isn't this nice? I love having you home even if we don't agree on everything or sometimes anything." I snuggled up closer to him on the now almost ragged brown couch, which had been relegated to our new downstairs family room. God help us, it probably wouldn't make another move.

"I like being home. The pool was nice, wasn't it?"

"Can I ask you something unrelated?"

"Sure, shoot."

"Do you want to continue our discussion about Vietnam that we started at dinner?" I turned to face this man who shared my house but certainly not my views on so many issues. Sometimes when I looked at him I saw a man so different from the one I married. Is this the way he saw me?

"I don't know that there's much to discuss," Cliff said. "I work for the government, and I can't condone this kind of action for any reason." By action did he mean the protesters or my views?

"Yes, but you did condone it in Selma. You'd call me so upset every night about the situation there. Don't these people have the same right to rise up against what they think is wrong?"

"These are communists; they want to overthrow this government."

"No," I said. "They want the war to end. I want the war to end. Our soldiers who are dying over there want the war to end."

"Another thing. I don't know that it's healthy for the kids to be hearing this kind of discussion from their parents."

"Why? Because we disagree? They need to know there are many sides to an issue. You and I can be an example for them to see how two people can disagree but still love each other."

"Okay, I see your point. Not sure I agree, though."

"I do have another issue I'd like your take on." I made eye contact to see if he were receptive. He shrugged.

"This break-in at the Media, Pennsylvania resident FBI office. It's certainly gotten a lot of news coverage lately. How could this happen with an FBI office? Some files were stolen or something."

"Yup, the burglars did steal some files relating to current investigations. There's a lot of scuttlebutt at headquarters, and we've been told to talk to no one, not even our families."

"Am I family, or do I qualify as an insider?" I smiled as I said it. Sometimes I didn't know which I was. "According to the news, some Citizen's Commission to Investigate the FBI has taken responsibility for the burglary. Apparently, someone leaked the contents of these files to the media, which included investigations into a senator's daughter. Is this correct, or has the media fabricated this whole thing?"

"You seem to have been paying a lot of attention to this media attempt to embarrass the Bureau."

At that moment I remembered Cliff's early caution to me: whatever you do, don't embarrass the Bureau. Well, someone had. Someone inside.

"My real questions are these: was this an agent or an informant who leaked the content of these files, and why is the Bureau investigating the activities of private citizens?" I had been conflicted about this whole informant picture from the get go. To me, this leak came from inside.

"The Bureau is trying to keep Americans safe through all this social turmoil, and that means investigating groups or individuals that may be subversive. If we don't know what's going on, we can't predict their behavior like planting bombs and killing law enforcement." Cliff spoke as if giving a press conference.

"When does that impinge on a person's right to privacy especially if he doesn't know he's being investigated."

"Sometimes safety overrides."

"But it shouldn't, should it? To think the Bureau might be tracking me if I were on the membership list of one of these 'subversive' groups is creepy. That can't be right."

"That's why I told you in Jacksonville you could not get involved with any civil rights group. You have to know by now that as an FBI family we have to live differently."

"But I can talk to and take messages from your informants, and I don't know if they're working for you, themselves or the FBI. It's an uncomfortable position."

"It probably all seems contradictory, but I work for the Bureau, and I'm dedicated to follow its line. And because you and the kids are attached to me, well, you know..."

To follow the Bureau line. Maybe compromise my values? Then what becomes of me?

NINETEEN

Changes

Change was afoot.

I could tell by the expression on his face: that winning smile that said, "I know a secret."

"Okay, something's going on. I can see it." I smiled, thinking it must be related to his current desk assignment.

"Well, I got big news today. I'm being assigned to the Inspection Squad, the next step up the administrative ladder, which means I'll be part of a team going around the country inspecting offices. I'll be out with the team for three weeks of the month and then back home for the fourth week." His expression was contemplative as if he, himself, were thinking of what this would mean.

"Gosh, it's a lot quicker than you'd thought, isn't it? Didn't you tell me it would be two to three years before you were called up?" I actually smiled with pride at his selection.

"I know. It's sooner than planned, but that's great. It'll sure be a different experience from what I've had on the desk or in the field. I remember being in Jacksonville when the team came in. It was challenging."

"You'll be better than they were."

"I knew it was coming, and I'll be glad to get it behind me." He spoke hesitantly as if with reservation.

"You should get to see some interesting places, and you like to travel. I don't know about the work itself…. Probably a good assignment to get out of the way."

"That's probably it. No one in these offices likes to see the Inspection Team come, and they love to see the inspectors go. Kind of like an IG inspection in the army. Not a popularity contest, that's for sure." His voice was softer than usual as if he were studying the ramifications of this new role. I wasn't too worried about this stint; we had weathered more trying times.

While a supervisor on the airplane hi-jacking squad, his greatest challenge had been the D B. Cooper case. Why is it Thanksgiving brings forth so many kooks? This whole incident had started Wednesday evening at the Portland airport. A man calling himself Dan Cooper purchased a one-way ticket to Seattle, seated himself in the rear and told the stewardess he had a bomb. He handed her a note saying, "You are being hijacked." He demanded $200,000 in cash, four parachutes and a fuel truck in Seattle.

Cliff was contacted immediately as this was his desk; it was his investigation to coordinate. It was a tense time and the first real test of his ability to manage a high profile investigation from Washington. D. B. Cooper supposedly parachuted from the rear of the plane, but no trace has ever been found. While this was exciting for Cliff, he obviously missed being on the ground for the investigation and the action in the field. For me, having him safely behind a desk was much preferable to having him involved in a shoot out on some tarmac.

For the children and me, this inspection assignment meant Dad would be away again; he wouldn't be coaching Ray's little league team as he had a few months previous, nor would he be with us on those Sunday excursions to the museums and monuments. But, this assignment would also end.

My practice in being alone in other assignments and handling the household stood me in good stead for this new one. I felt comfortable here and confident that nothing could significantly shake me. I was feeling better than I had in a very long time.

The inspection assignments came and went throughout the summer. We celebrated those weeks Cliff was with us. But there is always someone or something to shake us from our comfort zone. So it was on that quiet Sunday evening in our safe and secure neighborhood as the sun slithered across the horizon into nothingness, that I settled into my softly tufted chair with one of my many books in progress.

The children slept upstairs after hectic hours of pretending what might be in a make believe world where all is possible. I dreamed along with them, remembering those days of my own imaginative childhood when limitations didn't apply. I must have nodded off, a dream from which I was awakened around 11:00 p.m. In this state between waking and sleeping, I reached for the ringing phone. *Must be Cliff, except it's a bit late for his call…*

"Hello."

Silence

One more "Hello" thinking Cliff had a bad connection from his hotel. Then a male voice, muffled at first, then louder.

"Sandy, I'd like to come over."

"Who is this?" I asked pleasantly, still thinking I may know this person. Maybe my neighbor Gary. On the other hand, maybe I didn't know him, and my heart began racing. No stranger to obscene and threatening calls associated with Cliff's work, my mind flashed backward and forward making craziness of this situation. An informant gone beserk? A prank caller? Someone disgruntled with the FBI? Somebody stalking me?

"You know who this is."

No, I didn't know this person. Of this I was now sure. In my memory I could find no match for this raspy voice. But he knew me; he had called me by name. Was he really calling me, or did it have something to do with Cliff?

I slammed the receiver, made sure all the draperies were closed, rechecked the door locks and raced upstairs to be sure all was well with the children. Sound, peaceful sleep. Since the caller didn't phone back immediately, I felt somewhat relieved that this was a crank call or at least one not intended for me. But he had called me by name, not that there weren't other Sandys.

Feeling more relaxed and now comfortably settled in for a night's sleep myself, the ringing of the blue Princess phone on my night table sounded like an invasion of artillery. I let it ring hoping its deranged voice would cease. It didn't. This time I picked it up without saying "hello."

After what seemed an interminable time, my hands shaking on the receiver, the voice said, "Sandy, why did you hang up? I want to come over."

Again, I slammed the receiver. My wakefulness heightened my senses. I imagined noises two stories down and questioned whether I had locked everything. I smelled smoke, saw shadows, heard voices until my raw nerves demanded I get up and start my day, five hours earlier than normal. Should I have called the police? No, these were only crank calls; the cops wouldn't do anything. My husband was an FBI agent; he was the one to take care of this.

I was able to catch him at his latest inspection site. "Cliff, it may be nothing, but last night I got threatening calls from some guy who says he's going to break into the house. I think he might be serious. I haven't yet called the police because I figured they couldn't do anything except maybe suggest a trap on the phone line. I know you're stuck in the field. I just need to know how to handle this. I haven't said anything to the kids."

"Listen, honey, it's probably just a crank. Go over and talk to Gary about the situation. He's home and can actually see our backyard from his deck. I feel pretty sure this is some nutcase or a person looking for someone else."

"But he used my name. What about some of these wacky individuals you work with?" After nearly ten years in the Bureau, there was quite a list of these "questionables." My caller seemed certain he had the right person.

The next day followed uneventfully except for that knot in my stomach that had plagued me on previous occasions when I felt I was being targeted for my close proximity to the FBI. No calls during the day. Maybe last night was a fluke. Or maybe my caller was working. Maybe he had the wrong number, and maybe he was really calling a person named Sandy, a different Sandy. Maybe tonight would be peaceful.

Around 12:30 a.m. when I was reasonably satisfied that we were safe and I was sufficiently tired to fall asleep, I went upstairs after turning on the outside lights and double checking the locks. I didn't turn on the bedroom lights, just in case he really was serious about a visit and was loitering outside with binoculars or something weird. Hall light on, babies sleeping soundly in their room at the top of the stairs, Tami and Ray asleep in their rooms; all was secure. If he broke in, I would be able to see and hear him on the stairs and hallway. Perhaps a watchdog was a good idea after all.

I climbed into bed, this time with my loaded ".38 snubbie" under my pillow – just in case. I despised guns, but life in the FBI had brought its challenges, and I now stored this lethal "friend" in my nightstand drawer still not convinced I would ever be able to fire it. Lulling myself into thinking I had made something out of nothing, I slipped into light slumber.

Brrring…Brrring…Brrring…Brrring

From a troubled sleep, I vowed I wouldn't answer. As if on command, the ringing stopped. Then started again. Then stopped. Then started again. Knowing I could not endure this all night and afraid to unplug the phone, I cautiously lifted the receiver to my ear.

"Answer when I call. I'm coming over. I was at your house last night, but all the doors were locked. I'm coming over again. Don't lock me out." Click.

Trembling and tearful, I called Gary, my trusted neighbor, whom I had briefed on the situation. He said he would go onto his back porch under cover of darkness where he would watch for any movement in my backyard.

This time the seriousness of the threat forced me to call the police. Maybe, if this person were nearby, police presence would scare him off. In my terrified state I grabbed my gun and went halfway down the stairs with the revolver pointed so if he were in the house already and tried to come up to the bedroom level, I could shoot him as he approached. Tears streaming down my face onto my neck, I sat and waited, shaking with fear. Could I shoot someone? I had always said, "no." But now my response might be "yes."

Wait – what was that noise? Did it come from the basement, our walkout level? Did I see a light? I prayed the basement lock was strong enough to keep him on the other side. Backyard trees formed eerie shadows swaying like elongated monsters beckoning to me, luring me into their clutches. Does fear smell like a mixture of sweat and tears, or is it more like rotten flesh? What color is fear? That color wasn't in my pallet. And death? Is it always black? Jumbled thoughts raced through my mind perhaps in an attempt to keep me in the present. My children's lives could depend upon my ability to remain in control.

Sitting on the upstairs steps, praying for safety, the minutes crept at a dreamlike pace. Was this really happening to me? Had the other incident in Jacksonville also been a dream, or was it a practice run? What about the incident when I was thirteen and alone with my sister on our farm. Our parents had gone to a community meeting down the road. As I was sitting in the living room doing homework, I heard a knock at the kitchen door. I got up and walked to the door and saw a young man in a white sailor hat; he looked just like my uncle until he turned around. Just in time, before I opened the door, I saw it was a stranger. He motioned for me to let him in. I backed into the living room hoping he would leave. Instead, he followed me, peering at me through the curtainless living room windows. Dad hadn't yet installed window coverings to block out such intruders. I moved into my parents' room to the phone. When I picked up the receiver, there was no dial tone; the line had been cut. I crawled under the bed where I could hear him rummaging outside. Terrorized, I prayed for my parents' return. After what seemed like an eternity I heard the door open and prayed it wasn't the intruder. I screamed and cried when I realized my parents were home. My dad went to the neighbor's and called the sheriff. It seems we had a would-be intruder with some mental issues who frequently tormented the farm families.

I carried the remnants of this experience with me to my persistent caller.

When the bright lights of the police car scanned my house and the officers knocked on the door, I answered it, weapon and all.

"Ma'am, put the weapon down slowly on the floor. Is it loaded?"

I shook my head and knelt to the floor, placing the Snubby on the entrance rug.

The officer leaned to pick it up, keeping it pointed toward the floor.

"When we leave, I want you to put this gun back where you keep it. It's very dangerous for you to be walking around with it," he said.

"It's also dangerous not to have a gun when this creep breaks in. My husband is a special agent with the FBI, and you know the terrible people this profession attracts." I looked at him until he nodded.

"Have you talked to your husband about this?"

"Last night but not tonight. He's out of town."

"Do you have any idea who this might be? Anybody suspicious?"

"Scummy people come by the truckload with this job, so it could be anybody." Tearfully, I told him what had been transpiring with the phone calls. He suggested I arrange for a trace on the line

"Listen, we drove around the neighborhood but didn't see anyone suspicious. If this continues tonight, call us again. We'll sort of hang around your neighborhood."

It was time for Cliff 's personal investigation. He now had a case involving his own family.

The next morning arrived all too soon. Five of us were seated at the breakfast table when Ray asked, "Mom, what was in the dryer last night?"

"Nothing, why?"

"I heard something going 'clunk, clunk' like sneakers when they go round and round in the dryer."

"No, you must have been dreaming."

Tami accused him of always hearing things and suggested he had probably dreamed up the whole "sneaker in the dryer" thing.

Ray and Tami ran out the door to catch the bus for school. Billy and Scott were secured in their high chairs finishing breakfast so I started down the basement stairs with the laundry. Four or five steps down, I felt a breeze. My heart froze. I stepped down a few more treads where I could see the family room draperies billowing inward. A previously locked sliding glass door was now open. He'd come in, hadn't he? Should I continue downstairs or run back up into the kitchen? Shaking, I decided to continue down the steps, my legs now shaking in tune with my shoulders. Going toward the laundry room with its two large windows over the appliances, I again felt the chill of cold air from the open window. In a flash the situation became clear. My caller had entered the house via the laundry room window. Ray, whose bedroom was directly above, had heard the mini-blinds rattle as our intruder entered. When he couldn't get access to the second floor through the bolted basement door, he had exited via the sliding glass door. More terrified than ever, I placed my hands over my face screaming silently into my trembling fingers. Not sure if the person were still hiding downstairs, I shakily closed the basement windows and sliding door, crept up the stairs to the kitchen, locked the basement door, poured another cup of coffee, and sat down with Billy and Scott.

Black coffee wouldn't be a solution, but it might keep the eyelids open in order to deal with any new developments.

Before I called Cliff, I phoned Gary, but he had already gone to the office. His wife said she would contact him and have him call me.

Trying to maintain some sense of calm, I called Cliff, who was still in Colorado.

"Cliff, he was here. He came into the house through the laundry window and out the sliding door. He left them both open. I'm terrified. This isn't a prank caller; he's serious. I guess I can call someone to put different locks on the basement windows." I was speaking to myself as much as to him.

"Look, enough is enough. I'm catching a flight home. Don't tell anyone I'm coming just in case it's someone we know or who lives close by. I'll order the trap for the line. We want the caller to call again when I'm home, but we don't want him to know I'm there."

"Okay, but I'm going to call the lock people. Call me with your flight info. and I'll pick you up."

My day was busy, but my nerves were on edge. I had asked Gary to come over to check on the basement to be sure no one was hiding down there. All appeared to be in order so we re-secured all windows and doors to thwart another entry. Dreading the darkening hours, I stayed up later than usual, curled up on the living room sofa with my book in hand and my .38 at my side. Unable to keep my eyes open any longer, I trudged upstairs to another restless night. Almost in sync with my retiring, the phone rang.

"I came to see you last night. Why did you have the basement door locked? I told you I wanted to come over. I'll be back, and I'll get in, so don't make it hard for me and don't hang up when I call. If you do, I'll just call again and again and again."

"Who are you? How do you even know me?" I screamed into the phone before I hung up. Crying hysterically, I called Gary who came over to await the next call. But I knew it wouldn't come. Gary spent that night on his screened back porch so he could watch my house. And my caller could watch Gary.

I decided not to call the police again. The last time they acted like I was a hysterical wife, which I was. Gary was aware of the problems, and Cliff would be home the next evening. I could make it one more night without sleep knowing my husband would be home, hopefully before the next call or break-in.

Once home from the airport, Cliff ordered a trap on the line, hoping for another call. There was one call, not long enough to trace. And then the calls ended. Almost simultaneous to the ending of the calls, one of our neighbors, without explanation, sold his house and moved on. Was he the intruder? Or was it a disillusioned informant or someone Cliff had arrested and was now free? It had to be someone who knew when Cliff was out of town and when I was home alone. This frightening incident caused me to examine how well one person really knows anyone in her life.

My space, my home, had been violated, making it easy to lose trust. When this nightmare was over, I remained haunted by the image of a young woman who looked like me sitting on the stairs close by the front door with her revolver loaded and pointed. Could I have really shot the intruder? I believe in that moment I could have.

TWENTY

What? Where? NO!

Fall began its tease with morning temperatures just a little cooler promising my favorite season would soon shower me with color.

I had adopted a new fashion look, I'd bought my first new car, and I could feel my confidence burgeoning. I was happy in my community, and I loved the energy of D.C. Cliff would soon finish his tour on the inspection squad and would return to his desk job with regular hours. Winter would come, and we would take up the skiing we had started last season. My world was brighter than it had been in years. Homeostasis, however, doesn't last.

On his final inspection assignment, Cliff called from Durango, Colorado, his rapid speech a sure sign of his enthusiasm. "Hey, you should see this place. Durango's a beautiful small mountain town that looks like a postcard. You'd love it. I didn't know the Bureau had offices in places like this. I wish you were here."

"You've fallen in love with lots of places you've inspected this year. Maybe we could plan a Colorado vacation. That could be fun."

"Yeah, we could even come out here to ski. Gosh, it'd be so great to live in a place like this." His voice sounded like a commercial for the town. "Lots of Indian reservation cases though. They tell me that's pretty frustrating work." Was this an "on the other hand" statement?

"I've never been to Durango, but I was in Colorado once as a child, when we took a family vacation west. When are you coming home?" I was ready for this inspection phase to be over. We missed him.

"I'll be here for a couple more days. Then it's back to Denver, which isn't too bad either. So probably another four or five days. By the way, I just found out from the SAC in Denver that he's opening a new resident agency in Glenwood Springs, not too far from Aspen."

"You keep calling and talking about these fabulous places," I said. "What's this about?"

"I guess I get carried away, but I was thinking that this Glenwood Springs might be a great place to raise a family. You know, just settle in and forget this rat race."

"I like this rat race, and so do you. This is what we've planned and sacrificed for, and it'll all be worth it in the end. That's what you've always said."

"I know. This small town attraction is probably a fantasy. I'm a ways down the administrative road now and probably couldn't pull it off anyway."

"Good. Remember, you promised me five years here. A promise is a promise, right?"

"Yup. This would be a real long shot, anyway."

"Long shots make me nervous; getting into the Bureau was a long shot and getting promoted to D.C. was a long shot. I know firsthand about these 'impossibles.' Please, no more discussion. Let me stay where I am."

"I hear you, but since we're talking I can tell you I'm not excited about being back on a desk. You can't believe the bureaucracy, and now with Hoover gone, it's probably going to get worse."

"Maybe with Hoover gone, there will be some positive changes like the hat policy, having longer hair and sideburns, the ridiculous checking in every two hours and all the restrictions about the Bureau car. This agency could do with some changes."

"And some of them might not be so great. Already there's a jockeying for the Director's position among Hoover's subordinates like Mark Felt and John Mohr. All of that political maneuvering is going to filter through the ranks. It's going to be pretty messy at headquarters for a while."

In short time, President Nixon appointed L. Patrick Gray, an assistant attorney general as Acting Director of the FBI. A permanent appointment would come later. According to what I was reading and hearing from Cliff, Director Gray wasn't into any overnight changes.

Once back in Washington from the inspection tour and again assigned to a desk, Cliff ran into Mr. Gray on his lunch hour. Coincidentally, both men liked to use this time to run the Mall and the steps of the Washington Monument. Conversations ensued, and over a period of a few months they developed a relationship of sorts.

"Hey, I had a good talk with the Director today at lunch. I told him about my tour on the inspection squad and the opportunity coming up in Glenwood Springs and that I thought it would be a wonderful place to raise a family."

"It might be perfect for some family, not ours. What you should have said is that it might be perfect for you." I looked at him as he hung up his suit and shook his head.

"Why aren't you excited about this possibility? This would mean no more moves; the kids would be able to grow up in one place."

"And you would take a demotion, a pay cut and be back in the field chasing fugitives. Just the life I hate." I looked at him as he shook his head at me in disbelief.

I'd seen that tactic before. "Do you live in the same house with me? I love it here. We live in this lovely house in a great community, and we're finally making enough money to do extra things. Plus, you and I have more time together than we've ever had. That's the way I see our situation."

In the past he had been successful in wearing me down. This time I wouldn't give in. I had followed him like a subservient puppy dog because I didn't have a profession, because I was a mom with four young children and because I would be quitting on my marriage.

It wasn't to be the last of the discussion. A few weeks later Cliff came bounding in the door, his enthusiasm radiating from his expressive face. He had news.

"I spoke with Pat Gray today at lunch, and he said he'd checked on my request to go to Denver. From there we could be sent to Glenwood Springs. It's a slim possibility."

"Request? You made a request? We never talked about a request to go anywhere. You said someone was opening an office somewhere in Podunk Colorado, and I told you I wasn't going anyplace. Look at me. I live in this house; I'm your partner and wife. It's time you started treating me as such. You don't get to decide these things on your own, not anymore."

"I just threw it out there as a possibility."

"You threw what out there as a possibility? A transfer possibility to the new director? I suppose you've talked to the Denver SAC also. No discussion; you just plow forward greasing the skids to make something happen that I don't even want. Just like the letter you wrote to Hoover that got you in this organization. What's wrong with you? What's wrong with me?"

"I didn't mean it to come off like this. I guess I just got so excited. I thought maybe you'd had some time to reconsider. It doesn't look promising though." Was he referring to the move or to me?

"Good. I was hoping it would be no possibility."

"The best he thinks he can do is get me to one of two offices: Las Vegas or Denver."

"What!" I shrieked in a voice that frightened Scott and started his two-year-old tears flowing. "It's apparent you and Mr. Gray have been discussing this impossible dream transfer for a while. Have you told this new friend of yours your wife doesn't intend to move?" I picked up my crying child. I knew just how Scott felt. "Listen, I've followed you all over hell. If you put in paperwork to go back to the field and it turns out to be Las Vegas, this marriage just ended. I've followed you and this f-ing career all over the map, and I'm through." I marched with Scott from the kitchen into the living room. I didn't want to see or hear any more from this man.

He followed me. "Wait, I said it's a slim possibility. We aren't going anywhere. You'd love this town though. You can ski every day…"

I held up my hand, signaling him to stop. "I don't want to hear any more from you about this place, the one you've never even seen."

Still carrying Scott, I grabbed my purse and keys and turned toward the stairway and yelled to the kids, "Hey, everybody, I'm going to the library, wanna go?" We piled into my shiny white Pinto and left. I needed a place away from this man to forget this latest conversation. After the library, we stopped for ice cream. I could prolong an elevated discussion for only a limited time.

Good. No discussion tonight as Cliff was on the phone. Some Bureau business, I suppose or more Colorado finagling. I went to bed and pretended sleep. What to do now? Nothing and it would all blow over? Not likely.

So, I'd fight to stay; this much I owed to myself and my children. If only I had the financial means to be independent. I didn't, not yet.

Over coffee the next morning I decided to go on the offensive.

"Look, help me understand what's behind all this Colorado stuff. I've heard you complain about headquarters and all the bureaucracy here. So, is it that you want to be back in the field where you're gone all the time chasing fugitives, getting shot at, working to solve impossible cases and all that on-the-edge stuff? If that's it, why not go back to the field here? There has to be plenty of interesting casework right here, and we wouldn't have to move anywhere." At least this action would be a compromise.

"It's not just going back to the field although I love being in the middle of interesting cases. It's also about being in a nice place for you and the kids where I'd have more family time."

"A nice place? I love this place. I don't want to be anywhere else." I threw my arms over my head in resignation.

"I know you like it here, but think about it. In a nice small resident agency like Glenwood there would be no more commuting. I could come home for lunch. We could ski all winter and hike all summer. I would finally feel like I had a family."

"But what if this isn't the dream your family has? Cliff, I don't like the way this is going. I feel railroaded. This is all about you. What about the five of us who live with you? What about staying here and going back into the field? You didn't answer me."

"Listen, if I stay on this Administrative Track, we'll be transferred sometime, and taking a different job here is not what I want to do. I'm sick of dodging these raggedy-assed hippies on every street in Washington protesting everything that's great about this country."

"Oh, so it's not all about the job? By the way, in case you haven't noticed, we're in a very unpopular war and not everything is perfect here or anywhere. I suspect you'll find your hippies in Glenwood Springs."

For a couple of weeks a quiet truce reigned in our household. We avoided the transfer topic, and I was hoping the whole issue would go away while he was undoubtedly praying I would come around and embrace this latest "window of opportunity."

Then, on a Friday, a Black Friday, Cliff again broached the subject, this time with more urgency.

"Well, I saw Pat Gray today, and we're going to have to make a decision if we want to try for Denver."

I remained silent as I stirred the pasta sauce. I wasn't going to validate his statement with a response.

"Did you hear what I said?"

"No," I said. "That's my decision. If you're asking for my input, it's 'no.' It's all 'no.'"

He moved closer to me as I set the table. "Can't we talk about this one more time?"

"Look, I'm putting dinner on the table. I don't want another meal ruined over this topic. When we've finished eating, and the kids have gone to bed, I'll have a glass of wine and you can say what you need to say."

I walked to the stairway and called the kids to eat. He helped Scott and Billy into their chairs and seated himself. Dinner was quieter than usual as the kids picked up on the tension. Tami and Ray were more than ready to go upstairs to their rooms to read. Billy and Scott had baths and settled into bed with stories. I pulled my prettiest wine glass from the china cabinet and went downstairs.

"Can I start over?" Cliff asked. "I've never seen you like this. You've always been so supportive. The kids would love to go to Denver."

"Oh, sure, the kids. How do you know? When was the last time you actually sat down and asked their opinion on anything except as a way to put pressure on me? This time, Cliff, your tactics aren't going to work."

"Will you go?"

"I can't tell you right now. If I can figure out how to stay here with the kids and support myself, that will be my choice." I looked at him with sadness; another move, another set of challenges, always looking for something. For me these illusive searches had brought doubt and defensiveness. If the kids were just a couple years older; if I had a job; if I had just a bit more confidence.

"Look there's another issue here. You told me we were here for at least five years. We haven't even hit the two year mark. You lied to me."

"No, not true. I can't control how long I'm assigned to a place. They could transfer me tomorrow. I told you we could be here as long as five years."

"But they aren't transferring you tomorrow. There's something else," I said. "This whole family has sacrificed for your career, and now you're telling us it wasn't enough, that what you really want is to be a field agent, back where it's dangerously exciting. So you dismiss the sacrifices we made as if they were nothing since you've had this epiphany about your mission with the Bureau."

"Aren't you exaggerating? I've never misled you." His wrinkled forehead suggested he believed what he was saying.

"Oh no? What about the future the Administrative Track offers us: much higher pay, status in the community, a real Bureau family in a decent sized city? Now, you're telling me you really don't want that? Well, I do. I thought we were on the upward march to the top of this organization. What is this quitting stuff?" I slammed my glass against the table in disgust.

"It's not like that. I don't see it as a demotion."

"Well, it is. That's what they call it when you accept less pay and slide into a lesser position."

"I can't stay on this track and not move."

"You always bring up this moving stuff like it's something new. I know we'll eventually be moving from here, and that's okay with me as long as we're moving toward something. Cliff, what's this really about?"

"I'm not sure this is the right track for me." He lifted his arms as if he'd given up.

"Well, then get on another track. God knows there are plenty of career tracks here in D.C. Talk to Pat Gray about that possibility. He's connected. Another federal job would probably mean your pay would remain the same or higher. By the way, have you checked our finances to see if we can afford this great opportunity? We just now have reached the point where we're able to save a bit. Now a pay cut?"

My body felt disconnected from my jumbled head as I felt that black cloud of sadness approaching. How else could I say it to make him understand?

Despite my objections, Cliff had already talked to the kids. Living in the snow covered Rockies where skiing ruled was enough for Ray. Billy and Scott were too small to know a lifestyle other than moving. This would be Billy's third move in less than four years. It was different for Tami.

"Mom, we just moved here; I'm starting junior high in a brand new building, I have friends I really like here. I thought Dad said we'd be here maybe until I finished high school." Her voice tremored.

As the smart, cute new girl moving to a small town where everyone knew everyone else, she was sure to be a threat to some of the other girls. From my own experience of moving to a small town school as a 8th grader, I knew what my daughter would be up against. When I had earlier expressed my concerns to Cliff, he had pointed out that the other Glenwood Springs agent had a 7th grade daughter. They would have each other. Just like that, they would like each other. How did he know anything about girls or even his daughter, for that matter?

With each passing day, I dreaded hearing the door open, sure that Cliff's arrival would bring with it the need to confront this move, the elephant in the room. In the meantime I had contacted the Virginia State Department of Education to see what it would take to become certified to teach in the state. Based on the requirements, I figured I was about two years away from getting a teaching job here. At least I had more information than I had during the last discussion.

Sure enough, the day arrived, as those days of reckoning always do. A Friday. The decision I had been dreading had forced its way with my husband through my lovely green door This time he waited until after dinner and the kids were in bed. I poured myself a glass of white wine whose essence sparkled at me through its delicate goblet. I twirled its stem between my fingers as if it were a crystal ball of sorts. Cliff watched my fingers, waiting for an opening.

"We have to make a decision about the Colorado move. We don't have much time. Pat Gray needs to know by Monday morning."

"We need to make a decision? I thought you had decided for all of us. And why the rush? How about a decision in six months or two years or no decision at all?"

"Director Gray has approved my transfer back to the field if I want it. But, he can't guarantee it will be Denver. The SAC in Denver needs to know if I'm coming as he needs to fill the slot in Glenwood. He can't wait any longer."

"Wait any longer? I didn't know anyone was waiting for anything from us." I looked at the concerned anticipation on my husband's face. "You really believed I would change my mind and say 'let's go?' I can't."

He was prepared for my reaction. "I've thought about this and looked at every angle," he said. I've even created a chart with the pros and cons for staying here or going to Denver. Do you want to see it?"

"No, I don't need your chart to know what I want."

"Listen to me for just a minute. The biggest plus I see is the lifestyle we could have in a small town. We would know everyone; you could have a career if you wanted because we wouldn't be waiting for the next transfer. This would be our final move."

"Final move? You can't be serious. We'll get out to this paradise of a small town and you'll be looking for what's next."

"No, this will be it. I know this is the right decision for us as a family."

"Haven't you been listening, not just to me, but to the kids as well? We don't want to leave here. This is all about you and your whim. Another thing; what do you know about living in a small town that you've never even seen? And what if we get there and we hate it?"

"We won't hate it. Honey, this is going to be great for us. It'll be a new start for you and me. I know it's been rocky."

"It has, and this won't cure our problems. Also, you talk about my career. Say I get a teaching job and you decide it's somewhere else you want to be. What then?" I continued my objections. "Wait—isn't there another problem called Las Vegas, not exactly an ideal place for raising a family." If I lost this fight to stay put, and the assignment were Las Vegas, I would stay here and end this relationship. Oh God, could I really do it?

"That's a risk," he said, "but I really feel it's worth the try."

"Oh, yes, another risk so you can have your way and get to someplace that makes no sense. I'm not going be part of this decision. I've accepted transfer after transfer and made them work because they were just that— transfers. This is a selfish voluntary request."

"So I don't get input and support from you?"

"No. I'm out of input and I'm out of here." I rose from the raggedy brown sofa where Cliff and I used to meet to make decisions and discuss our future. It was tired and almost threadbare in places. This night it looked as forlorn as I felt. In a sweeping sign of victory, capitulation or something else, I knocked the stack of magazines from the table in turn toppling my glass of unfinished wine. Clad in corduroy slacks and warm sweater, I yanked open the sliding door, stepped onto the patio and through the gate out into my neighborhood where I walked and walked and walked, oblivious to direction, down side streets and the country road where the cows lived. I cried from anger, disappointment and the sadness I felt for my children and myself. When I returned home, the door was open and the mess picked up. Cliff was lying on the sofa. I quietly walked past him and up the stairs.

The weekend passed mostly in silence. Sundays were our museum days so we bundled up for the trek to the Smithsonian. As we walked the long exhibits, my thoughts turned to leaving these experiences behind. I would very much miss living here.

Sunday evening Cliff shared his decision with me.

"I've decided I'm going to request the transfer back to the field."

I looked at his assured countenance. He had this passion for his work, his other wife, the one he really listened to. With this decision our relationship had irrevocably changed.

"I hope it works out for you."

"What are you saying? If it comes through, it's going to be wonderful for us. I know it. I love you. You're the most important person in my life. I'd do anything for you."

"Anything other than stay here. My life needs to take a new direction." As these words tumbled from my mouth, a chill spread through my body.

"This'll be a new direction for both of us. Sandy, I'm doing this for us." He moved closer to me on the couch. I stiffened and moved away.

"I'd like to believe that, but this decision of yours has little to do with us. It's about something else." I put up my hand as if to ward him off. "It's not about me; none of this FBI stuff has been about me."

Within a couple of days, Cliff had his answer.

He didn't call me on the phone to give me the news. Instead he caught an early bus. He walked in the kitchen door with a smile on his face and a loving card for me. I knew what the Bureau's answer had been.

"Please don't say anything," I said. I felt a thickness in my throat before the tears rushed down my face. I laid the unopened card on the table and walked into my peaceful living room. My feet curled under me as I leaned against the arm of my favorite reading chair. Sadness enveloped me. After what seemed a long time, I heard Billy and Scott upstairs waking from naps. As I walked up the steps, I noticed things about my pretty house that I had taken for granted: the smooth hardwood steps, the wall colors I had selected, the colorful carpet I'd found for the boys' room. Once again I'd be leaving what I'd created.

Cliff called the SAC in Denver to tell him he had received his transfer to the Denver Field Office and would expect the assignment to Glenwood Springs. Shocked that Cliff had been able to pull this off, the SAC agreed and amended the orders to read "Glenwood Springs Resident Agency." He shouldn't have been surprised. Cliff had managed to pull off "miracles" before.

We told the children it was definite—we were moving west. Big surprise. They had spent their lives moving. When I called Mom I didn't know what her reaction would be as I hadn't shared this possibility with her when she was here for Christmas. Taking a deep breath, I somewhat hesitantly dialed her number.

"Hi, Mom. It's me," I said quietly.

"What's wrong. You never call in the middle of the day; it's too expensive. Are the kids okay?"

"It's not that, Mom. Everyone's in one piece. It's something else."

"At least everyone's okay; that's the main thing." I could hear her relief.

"We're moving."

"Gosh, this is unexpected. Cliff must have gotten an early promotion. Are congratulations in order?" I could feel her smile over the phone line.

"No, Mom, it isn't like that. He hasn't been promoted. In fact, he's decided he doesn't want to be in management. He wants to go back to the field so he's wrangled a transfer to some dinky town in Colorado." I could hear my voice quiver.

"Honey, I don't know what to say. I know you love it in D.C. I guess I thought Cliff did too. When do you leave?" No more smile in her voice.

"February. Mom, the boys are waking up. You can tell Dad, and I'll talk to you both later."

"I just thought of something," she said. "Dad told me on the way back to San Diego that Cliff had told him he was working on something in

Colorado. I guess I wasn't paying attention. Honey, it's going to be okay. I love you."

Cliff didn't tell me he had said anything to Dad. Why not? I placed the receiver back onto the cradle, wiped my eyes, drank a glass of water and headed upstairs.

Call the real estate agent, put the house on the market, begin the sorting and packing, retrieve the boxes from the basement closet, line up a mover and sell things that wouldn't be needed in the new location like my darling new white Ford Pinto. Cliff told me that a Jeep would be more practical in our new home. A Jeep? Where in the hell were we going that we would need a military vehicle?

Our pretty house at 5304 Pomeroy Drive was new and beautifully finished, so it sold the first day on the market. I took the boys to run some errands, and when I came back, there was a note from the Realtor saying she was bringing a contract by later. I would have cried if I could have.

From the basement I carefully retrieved the perfectly stacked boxes just waiting for their orders. This would be the last time I would need to save the cartons for a next move. They were tired and maybe relieved. With each move these brown packages had held the riches of my life, and they had never let me down. Once in this place called Glenwood Springs I would say good-bye to my packing friends as I emptied each repository. They would finally be relieved of their loads.

I looked at the signed contract for the sale of my home, one I had been able to enjoy for such a short time. The price was right; the timing met Cliff's requirements so all was well in the greater plan. I could start again, couldn't I? It was just a move, or was it? No, this time was different. The baggage we carried was heavier; the scars were deeper; the way we worked together had been irreparably compromised.

Part Six

Becoming isn't marked by instant success; it's a series of steps one takes on the road to discovering one's purpose in life.

Glenwood Springs
1973-1984

TWENTY-ONE

You can make me leave, but you can't make me like it

I would soon be a long way from home, wherever that was, headed for a place called No Name, a fitting descriptor for a temporary destination for this our fifth FBI assignment in ten years.

It was a cold, overcast, sniveling kind of February day when everyone who could would be inside savoring the warmth produced by fireplaces and hot chocolate. A handmade quilt, a scintillating novel, and all would be right with the world. On the other hand, my world would be four bored, argumentative children, a cranky husband who was trying to be cheerful and me, an unhappy wife, strapped within the confines of a too-small station wagon for four days as we traveled west from Washington, D.C. to Colorado.

Yes, I knew they were waiting. Cliff had elicited Ray's help in packing the car. Each child had claimed a spot: Tami in the very back of the roomy wagon, Billy next to her, leaving Ray and Scott in the back seat. One vacant seat remained, but I couldn't yet fill it.

"Wait, everybody, I want to be sure we have everything." I could hear the frantic nature of my own voice.

"We've got everything," Cliff said. "You and I've already checked. I want to get out of here. We're already going to hit traffic. We have a long trip ahead of us."

"I know. Two thousand miles."

I moved away from my open car door and walked for the last time to yet another house I was leaving.

I felt the cold, brass door handle against my warm left hand as I depressed the familiar thumb mechanism. I opened my teal green door into the living room now bare except for my lovely formal draperies framing the large bay window. They were perfect for this room and probably wouldn't fit the next house anyway. It was as if I needed to leave a piece of myself, a reminder, if only in my memory, that I had once occupied this space, filling its rooms with cries of joy and excitement that come with a growing family.

The gray February skies, along with the cries from my family to "hurry up," pushed my steps into the dining room almost to ensure my capture of this memory for future reference. In the kitchen I opened each cabinet door, mostly to buy time. Then I walked slowly up the hardwood stairs to the bedrooms where I found one of Scott's bears, the one with the green ribbon, hiding behind the closet door. Would that I could join him. Instead, I picked him up and held him close. What was there about a small stuffed animal that could make one feel just a little safer? I took one last look in the master bedroom before heading down to the family room. This was the space hardest to leave. As I looked at my wall of slightly crooked wall shingles, I stifled a sob against the bear's soft fur. Cliff and I had built this room from scratch, together. A bittersweet memory built just in time to leave it. I snuggled the brown bear to my chin and walked up the stairs. Reaching the front door, I paused yet again, unwilling to close this phase of my life. Head down, tears flowing, still clutching the bear, I made my way that cold winter morning to my place in the wagon heading west.

He waited. He wanted to leave. She wanted to stay.

They left.

Before backing from the driveway, Cliff reached over for my hand whose fingers had curled into a fist.

I took one last look at the house that was no longer mine. For two years it had been nearly perfect.

I had lost the battle to stay in D.C.; but it was also apparent I had lost the war to have an equal say in the direction our lives would take. My heart was heavy; much as I tried to will a smile, my face refused to cooperate.

A smile takes many, many muscles, and mine were tired.

We left the traditional red brick towns of the northeast with their tree lined streets and rolled into the farmlands whose fields were now snow covered rows like marching soldiers waiting for spring orders.

Smokestacks and the noise of industry welcomed us to Indianapolis and St. Louis, sights and sounds reminiscent of my growing up in Lansing where Oldsmobile and its suppliers were its lifeblood. Few of my friends had left Lansing. I had, and here I was.

Miles and miles of no change. How had anyone settled this landscape? I felt connected to pioneer women ripped from their homes, often dying along the trail. It was winter, and the land was dead awaiting some signal to come to life and enrich those who'd been too stubborn to leave. Cold, windy and barren, a metaphor for my outlook.

A sense of anxiety rolled in, unwelcome, through my window. I'd been right; this move was all wrong. To add an exclamation point to that thought, the kids were now bored and arguing over who sits where, how much longer, who's hungry, who has to pee.

"Look, if you don't stop arguing, I'm going to stop this car and paddle everyone," Cliff yelled.

"How about just stopping," I said. "I think we all need to get out for a while."

"If we keep stopping, we'll never get to Colby tonight."

"If we don't stop, we may not get there either. Besides, what's the rush? This whole trip has felt like a forced march. Everyone has to eat at the same time, pee on the same schedule—what is this?"

I turned more squarely to face him, my jaw set against Cliff's demands. He reached across the seat for my hand, "It's just that I want to get to Colorado as quickly as we can. We need to land before we kill one another."

"Well, maybe that's hope on the horizon," I said, pointing to the white peaks in the far distance. There they were, jagged whiteness, the Rocky Mountains, those huge piles of rock for which we had been scouring our non-ending landscape. First, mountains on the horizon then buildings, a cityscape before us.

"We made it, everyone. Finally, we're in Denver." "Looks okay, don't you think?" Cliff looked at me as he spoke as if to remind me he'd been right in making this decision.

"At least it's a city. Could we just stay here?" This place had a name unlike our destination.

"Surely, you're kidding. I asked to go to Glenwood Springs. Besides, wait until you see it! It'll make Denver look dumpy." In our early talks about this move to Glenwood Springs, Cliff had secured magazine articles extolling this small town's beauty and desirability like he was the local Chamber of Commerce representative. And he still hadn't seen the place.

"Please don't decide you aren't going to like it before we even get there," he added. "This move is going to be great for all of us." He always said "all of us" as if we were a package he was delivering to the new destination.

"I'm just suggesting that maybe someone else would like to go to Glenwood, a place that could be great for them."

Our car now resembled an abandoned homeless shelter full of dirty clothes, half-eaten snacks, shoes and socks of every size and shape, not all of them matching, stuffed animals loved a little too much in four days, books, magazines and God knows what else that was now unidentifiable. I looked at the mess and smiled at the comparison to my life.

After checking into our hotel, Cliff took care of whatever business he needed to conduct with the Denver office while the kids and I wandered the nearby streets, taking in the energy of the city. As the five of us wandered the unfamiliar terrain, I was hit by a recurring uneasiness. I didn't want to go to this next place. I hadn't even wanted to come this far.

Wandering each block of Denver's unfamiliar streets reminded me that in this the last of our Bureau destinations, I would need to build a plan, one that held promise in its future. For building blocks I'd need a belief in myself and my ability to become once more a strong partner in a relationship where I'd so far been a 'trailing spouse.'

In the middle of these internal musings Cliff emerged smiling from the FBI building. All was in order. In the morning we would be on our way.

The sun did rise the next morning, and our rambunctious bunch repacked for the final day of our journey. Once again loaded into our trusty wagon, map in hand, we headed out, our last leg of this endless journey. Actually, this whole ten year FBI journey had at times seemed endless. Our map pointed us west, due west. Seemed a pretty straight shot, but I was soon to learn that people didn't go across the mountains; they sort of drove up and around, exiting from these mammoth rock piles somewhere close to one's destination. When I asked Cliff how long it would take to get to Glenwood, he was vague, said it would depend on the weather and how clear the passes were. Why wouldn't they be clear? Surely, this state owned snowplows. The radio soon informed us, however, that this was February following a very snowy January, taxing demands on the plows. Did this mean we would need to stay longer in Denver? Wait for winter to subside like the early travelers west? Reconsider this Glenwood idea and stay in Denver? No, I had already explored that.

Undeterred as a true frontiersman and in somewhat better spirits at the prospect of finally arriving at our destination, Cliff aimed our two-wheel drive station wagon toward the mountains. Denver behind us and with it most traces of civilization, we climbed to such places as Idaho Springs and Silverthorne, which brought to mind movie sets depicting desperadoes and saloon scenes. All that was missing were some horses and perhaps some questionable looking characters in cowboy hats and boots. I had been transported via time travel into a landscape only familiar on film. We couldn't be going to a place that looked like this. No.

The approaching sign directed us to Loveland Pass where a few skiers at the Loveland Ski Area were out for runs on the new snow. We had now climbed almost 5,000 ft. since leaving Denver, and I felt my body tighten and my fists clench as I looked up the road for the first round of switchbacks. New words were entering my vocabulary: passes, switchbacks, altitude, hairpin turns, summit and some silently uttered profanities. Up the incline, turn 180 degrees in the opposite direction, straighten out and then turn again.

Stately green pines lined our roadway, temporarily obscuring our view of what lay beyond and below. We climbed around and up, over and over, like a slow moving top winding down for lack of momentum. Our speed slowed as we rounded another opening some pioneer had forced through this landscape. For some distance my side of the car had faced the granite abutments where I felt secure and protected by the rocks and trees, and then the wind began to blow, lifting the snow from the road onto our windshield, obscuring our vision. I could barely see the tall pine trees lining the road, and where did the side of the road go where shoulders should have been? I looked to my right off the side of the narrow road and saw nothing but an abyss, no guardrails, nothing, giving me an unobstructed view straight down the mountain, which is exactly where I knew we were headed. Was this to be our ending? My hands grasped one another for comfort, and l confirmed all the doors were locked. If we were all to be thrown off the side of this precipice, I wanted us to be together in this car. Thank God there was so much snow piled up along the sides that we would have a momentary buffer before our cascade into the abyss. We continued to climb to the place where there were no trees, only towering granite monoliths in formations, standing alone and sometimes as sentinels to something, their coating of snow softening their imposing jaggedness.

There are adventures, and there are foolish escapades. Shouldn't someone in this party, maybe the driver, have checked the roads and weather before heading west? This was insane. Why was it we were always doing things Cliff's way? Had I been in charge, I would have turned around, driven back to Denver and negotiated with the FBI. But I wasn't in charge of our destiny. I wasn't even in charge of mine. Not yet.

"Hey, everybody, we're at the top of the world. We've crossed the Continental Divide." Cliff had decided we needed a little education about this place from which it was possible we might not return. Until this moment I didn't know what a good driver Cliff was. How had he learned to manipulate our sliding car around these treacherous turns now called switchbacks? Probably when he learned to drive high-speed chases.

"Dad, I'm going to be sick. Stop." Car sickness and altitude had had their way with Tami's stomach.

"I'm sick too, Dad." Billy echoed from the very back. I now had visions of a car full of vomit, wet clothes and a smell we would never get rid of. One cross-country trip, and this nearly new car might not be salvageable.

Cliff barely brought the car to a stop when we all erupted like steam from a belching volcano onto the snow packed lot, an escape from this endless adventure. Tami was throwing up, Ray was throwing snowballs from snow that would barely pack, and Billy and Scott were on the ground making snow angels. I looked at my ragtag family against a panorama stretching before me. They were my reason for picking up the pieces. Close by was a snow sculpture resembling a museum piece, angular and imposing, a picnic table transformed into art. Just beyond, grey clouds blown by the wind teased me with momentary glimpses into what lay beyond: more statuesque rock formations reaching ever higher, snow so airy it felt like a fine ocean spray on my face.

This is what the world looks like with no obstructions, a picket fence of jagged peaks suggesting security within their folds, a place for one to stop even if only for a respite from car sickness. Clouds hanging overhead create a dark grey canopy from which snow freely falls, covering all the blemishes of man and nature. A single, straggly pine firmly entrenched in the rock face struggles to stand upright in hopes of attracting what it needs in this precarious existence. Sounds of wind whistling, perhaps across one of the canyons, then the grunting of the snowplow, and the rattle of the semi's diesel engine disturbs the summit's serenity. All a background for children's squeals as they chase each other with snowballs that won't pack.

I felt my hands growing stiff, clenched in my pockets, the collar of my parka wet against the back of my neck. My blue and yellow moon boots crunched on the newly plowed parking area designed for those just needing to stop and assess the possibilities of this landscape. I smelled clouds and frozen greenery. I smelled my own fear and uncertainty. I tasted remnants of bitterness for being here, a hostage to another's dream, my own thoughts ranging from anger at Cliff for bringing me to this place to resignation then finally to hope for what could arise from this wilderness. As far as my eye could see through the blowing snow and low clouds was a pristine vista of opportunity. It was all here, in these faces, on this landscape, right before me.

My world, a new one from this moment on. I had crossed the divide. I pulled my parka close around me and felt the moisture on my face. I tasted the melting snow on my lips mixing with tears of hope and expectation which kept creeping from that place where they secret themselves. I pulled the glove from my right hand and carefully snow carved my initials into the drift atop the picnic table much as pioneer women must have done to remind future women they had been in this place. Their lives had mattered.

TWENTY-TWO

No Name

Descending Loveland Pass our world was wrapped in white. Small towns looked like picture postcards. Smoke curled from chimneys inviting us to stop. Lunch provided that opportunity. Exiting the car, the smell of burning firewood twinged our nostrils in a homey, woodsy way suggesting I was the last pioneer and this beauty had been saved just for me. It was cold; it was snowy; its pristine ruggedness strengthened me.

"We're almost home," Cliff declared. "One more mountain pass and two more canyons."

Ten Mile Canyon paralleled Ten Mile Creek, seductive in its winter wandering, deceptive in its iciness and enticing in its message of subtle power. I took a deep breath as we prepared for another snowy climb, this time over Vail Pass one lane each direction recently plowed, curving up into another switchback and another and another, almost rhythmic. One more turn and then the next until white knuckled we were down the mountain into Vail where we could see the ski mountain rising in its majesty. Lifts were running, skiers were schussing down the hill toward town, and we all wanted to stop and ski.

"I know you're all sick of being in this car, but we only have about eighty more miles to go. This is our last stop, so if you have to be sick or have to pee, do it now. Once we're living here we can ski anytime. Right now we need to get to Glenwood Springs." The mountain passes had taken the last of his patience.

More surprising to me was the fact that in our five-hour trek from Denver not once had we slid down the steep mountainsides.

One more challenge, Glenwood Canyon, which should be one of the Seven Wonders of the World. I stared in awe as we entered the jaws of the Colorado River, flowing in, around and through its icy patches, reflecting off the sun's rays, creating a white and azure blue watercolor. Sheer red canyon walls embraced the river, promising to protect and revere its banks. Patches of white clung to the austere vertical walls declaring its winter posture. We snaked this narrow winding road slowly, not daring to absorb the beauty surrounding us. Cries of "oh and ah" came from the back of the wagon. "Look at this." "Look at that." "I see a cave." "Maybe a bear lives in there."

Miles passed, tranquilizing my soul with God's canyon architecture. The trip from Denver had been daunting and scary, but when I entered this world of color, contrasts, rock, water and life, I knew this special landscape could be my strength and refuge in my resolve to discover my path.

I can do it one more time. I can make this marriage work. This time is going to be different. It will be my plan, my path.

As with previous transfers, Cliff had once again found a house for us to rent until we located a suitable property to buy. Since Glenwood was such a small town, there weren't many homes available, especially ones large enough to accommodate a family of six. Enter No Name, a small enclave on the Colorado River wedged between steep red canyon walls, a railroad track and the interstate. I thought this an appropriate moniker. We land in a place with no name, and I have no home.

"Look how beautiful this place is, honey." Cliff was exuberant, the children were snow covered, and I was looking for something I could connect with: the river, the mountains, the wailing trains. Maybe that was it, the mournful sound from the track embracing the bank of the Colorado River.

My response to my husband was silence.

"Let's go get the key," he added. "The sooner we can get settled in the better. Just look around. This place is going to be so great."

He still hadn't seen the town. Why hadn't we come out here to look this place over before making this decision? Too far, too much money? So perfect we didn't need to?

We pulled our filthy, stinky wagon from the snow packed driveway onto the recently plowed highway where we immediately noticed a fog, smoke or was it steam ahead?

"Dad, what's that smoke from? It smells funny," Billy asked.

"Oh, that must be the Hot Springs Pool. I saw it advertised in the brochure the city sent us. Yeah, the building looked just like this." I had to admit it was a unique concept with its charming sandstone castle and steam welcoming one to its warmth.

We would soon enough explore this town, its pool and everything else, but right now I wanted out of this car.

Over the Grand Avenue bridge to the real estate office and a late afternoon snapshot of the small Colorado town waiting to become our home. Mis-matched brick 1800s buildings lined the street, some leaning in response to geologic forces of the narrow valley. A few more modern stores were painted with no particular color scheme in mind. Yet, a certain quaintness belied this lack of architectural planning.

Snow had been shoveled in mounds resembling igloos, obscuring views of some of the storefronts. Names like Ben Franklin, Andersons Pants Pocket, Doc Holliday Bar and Bullocks stared back at me. Surely there was a grocery store somewhere in this valley. I took a deep breath.

As I stood outside the slanted red brick real estate office, I watched the trickle of pedestrians wander down the main street and speculated who they might be and where they could be going. Feeling like the lost waif I was, I watched them enter stores thinking, "I don't even have the right clothes for this town. I don't own any jeans or are they called Levis? Do people other than cowboys wear denim? Are these people ranchers and cowboys? No, some dressed in jeans appear to work in the shops." I also noticed lots of boots: snow boots, leather boots, cowboy boots. I had only blue and yellow moon boots for before and after skiing. I had skirts, dresses and casual slacks suitable for life in the city. Okay I'd find my own fashion identity. I didn't have to match everyone, did I?

Cliff snapped me from my reverie, waving our house key in his hand, a big smile on his face. Back in the filthy car with four hungry, fighting kids, we opted for a snack at Ben Franklin's soda fountain, which seemed a better choice than Doc Holliday's bar. In better humor, we settled in for the short drive back to No Name, this time to get an inside glimpse of what would be home for a while.

Since No Name was at the mouth of the Glenwood Canyon, fenced in by the raging Colorado and ominous cliffs, there wasn't room for more than a very small seasonal RV Park and half a dozen houses. Our clapboard duplex backed to a small, ambling creek whose soothing sounds hopefully would heal my weary soul in the coming months. We would live upstairs, directly overhead of the unit occupied by the District Attorney and his wife. My first thought was how this couple would be able to tolerate a family of six living directly over their heads. We weren't exactly quiet.

I stood outside, knee deep in an unplowed snowy walkway, a stranger looking in, trying to picture my little family huddled here temporarily. This time I wouldn't worry about furniture placement, wall colors or even the color for the front door. I was merely a guest seeking my place in this valley.

Trooping through the deep, freshly fallen snow, we approached the overhung entry exposing its status as a vacant property replete with un-shoveled snow, abandoned circulars and expired newspapers. Unlocking the weakly secured door with our only key, we walked into a structure begging for attention. Love had been absent from this home for some time. It would not be my mission to fulfill its needs; I was only a visitor.

"Okay, this is it," I said. "Let's get the bags and the rest of the stuff from the car." I looked at my children taking my orders and swallowed hard to keep the emotions in check. Their faces registered sadness and confusion as they began to realize they were in a very different environment from what they used to call home.

At the moment I wasn't sure if the coldness reflected in my blue fingers was from the low temperatures or from the lack of emotional blood flow.

Looking out my wide front window, I could easily pretend I was on vacation in the Alps. My mountains were tall, red, rugged and snow frosted suggesting I could trust their strength. In a dreamy haze one afternoon, a thunderous roar shook the house. I dropped the laundry I was folding and raced to an image of a snow mountain careening straight down across the railroad track on its ravaging journey to the Colorado River. Snow was billowing before me creating a dense fog as if a cloud had fallen from the sky. Billy and Scott came running, each of us certain our world was crashing in around us. It was.

"Look, Mom, look," Billy said. Another resounding crash shook the windows. "The mountain's falling down into the river. How will the train get through?" His questions begged reassurance.

"It's an avalanche. Boys, look at this. The snow got too thick and heavy at the top so it had to come crashing down. Oh my gosh, this is so amazing. And, you're right, Billy, the train won't be able to get through."

"Can we go closer, Mom," Scott asked.

"Sure, let's get in the car and drive down to where the river makes the bend into town." We couldn't get close enough to see the tracks, but snow from the slide was still blowing from its landing. We had seen the power of nature making a new path.

"Dad, guess what we saw today. An 'abalanche.' A huge snowball roaring down the mountain," Billy explained.

"Did you see it?" he asked, looking at me. "It tore out part of the train tracks so you won't hear any trains for a few days."

"It was stunning. I've never seen nature behave this way. It was so beautiful and so powerful. I'm so glad I was home to see it. How was your day?"

"Well, Dave and I are still trying to put the office together and decide on how best to manage this huge territory."

"What's it looking like? Will you be home at all in this assignment? Remember, this was supposed to be different."

"It's looking like Dave will work Aspen, and I'll have Vail, Steamboat and the northern counties, but I won't have to be in all those places every week."

"So you travel and Dave doesn't?"

"He gets to deal with Aspen, and I don't have to. There's a huge international drug problem there. I'd rather not work that stuff."

"But you'll travel more."

"It's all going to work out. You'll see. I'm going to have time for you and the kids; that's why I came here."

"Is it?"

Settling in is what we needed to do. If I settle in, do I settle for?

We were the FBI family, a moniker we wore like an unwanted badge. Being part of an agency designated to fight crime was initially viewed by many of Glenwood's proud residents as an insult to this small community. At a morning coffee for the Newcomer's Club, I was introduced as Sandy Browning, recently moved here from Washington, D.C. whose husband was part of the new FBI office.

"Why do we need an FBI office here? We don't have any crime," said one attendee whose name I've forgotten.

"We were surprised too that we were coming here," I answered. "It's such a peaceful, lovely town, but the FBI's territory covers much of the western slope: Aspen, Vail, Steamboat, and even up to Rangely. Plus, you've probably heard concerns about the drug trade in some of these areas." I could always blame our presence on what was perceived as going on in Aspen. Finding myself in the role of marketing agent for the FBI, I positioned our presence as positively as possible. Reassuring nods greeted my explanation. Someday I hoped to be known and accepted as Sandy Browning rather than Mrs. FBI.

We had company in this mountain oasis. Dave and Mardell Yates, the other FBI family, was a long-term Bureau family of six like ours except their youngest child was the age of our oldest. They, too, were in a small temporary house awaiting completion of the home they were building up Four Mile Road. Because of Mardell's health problems, they had spent their entire Bureau career in Denver. Thus, their FBI experiences were much different from ours. When I had suffered serious health issues in Florida, Cliff had told me that requesting a medical transfer to a healthier location would be the end of his career. How different our lives might have been with no move to New York. In one sense he was right: we probably wouldn't now be in Glenwood. Which could be construed as positive.

Thinking we needed something fun after our long trek from the east coast, Dave invited us to ski with them the following weekend at Sunlight, the local area, just a few miles from town. They assured us we would love it, and there was even a nursery for Bill and Scott. I needed a diversion; we all did. As a family we hadn't done much playing together lately.

As we approached the mountain from Four Mile Road, Sunlight looked like a picture out of a winter sports magazine; a rustic lodge, where we found great food, a ski rental facility in the basement and a nursery on the upper floor. One main lift terminated at the top to views of Mt. Sopris, almost too beautiful to commit to memory. From the top of Sunlight that first ski morning, I felt a spiritual closeness to this local landmark as if I could reach out and touch its surface and always know its protection. Of all the mountains we skied as a family over the years, Sunlight is where we became skiers, played together and solidified the ties that bound us as a family.

Cliff had steadfastly asserted that "this would be the perfect place for us." Maybe—or maybe not. A breathtaking day on the ski hill would not a relationship repair.

Midweek following our first ski outing, Cliff came home unexpectedly for lunch.

"Hey, anybody home? I'm hungry, and I have a surprise."

"A surprise," we all asked.

"Come on outside."

Billy, Scott and I dutifully followed him out the door to the driveway where a white 4-wheel drive Jeep sat awaiting our inspection. It wasn't new, but it had a cute rag top and seemed to be waiting expectantly for someone's approval, probably mine.

"Is this ours, Dad?" Billy asked. "Can we take it up these mountains?"

"It isn't ours yet. I brought it home to show you and Mom. What do you think, honey? Shall we all go for a ride?"

"Sure. It's kind of cute, and I know how to drive a stick shift. It's not my Pinto, but maybe I won't get stuck in the snow so often."

At least once during the remaining weeks of the season I would bundle Billy and Scott into our gently used Jeep and head for the mountain. Skiing fed my spirit, filling many of the voids with a positive energy. I loved the alone time. From the chair lift I'd look with renewed wonder at the beauty of my surroundings, the roofs of rustic cabins, the lodge decreasing in size as I traveled upward through the trees to the top where I could breathe deeply and almost touch Mt. Sopris to my left. Where to go? Straight down Blue or Sun King, good choices in the morning. I could feel my weightlessness as I traversed the groomed slope hearing only my breathing and the hissing of my skis against the snow. Freedom was my jacket, my armor as I slid ever faster toward midway where I'd catch the chair for the ride back to the top. I was free, unencumbered by rules, expectations, a need to be someone I wasn't. Sliding down the snowy hills on two skinny boards became a metaphor for the quiet serenity I craved.

When the mountain closed for the season, I suggested we get serious about finding a permanent residence. Cliff favored a more rural, mountainous terrain—a rustic he-man environment reminiscent of 1850s Colorado. I only saw long drives into town on bumpy ill-maintained roads, lots of upkeep and no he-man at home to maintain it. I wanted a house in town, close to schools and neighbors with a small yard, which even I could maintain if necessary. I already knew about the "if necessary" part.

Miraculously, 1215 Riverview Drive came on the market, an adequate home on the west side of the Roaring Fork River on a corner lot within walking distance to all necessities. It was not one we designed; not quite big enough, but it would work.

It was time. Time to stop pretending I was on vacation and settle in as part of this community I had not chosen. It was time for me to look at where this life with Cliff had brought me and to decide what I wanted to make of it. Someone far wiser than I had once stated, "build a plan, then work the plan." What was my plan? How did I work something I hadn't yet built?

TWENTY-THREE

Settling In

"Settle" is what we needed to do. In our ten years with the FBI it had been all about the next exciting place to call home, the place where work would provide Cliff what he needed, and we could continue to make adjustments to our relationship. If the current assignment were less than desirable, there was always the next one. This time there wasn't a next one. The future was here whether we liked the assignment or not.

One evening as he pulled himself and his bags from the car. I met my tanned husband in the driveway, more relaxed than I'd seen him in some time. He was smiling that captivating smile suggesting something.

"You must've had a good week." I smiled.

"Ya, it was. How about you?" He waited.

"How about me? I'm settling in."

My focus was connecting with other women new to Glenwood, building a network independent from my husband's FBI life. Like me, a few were looking for a fresh start in an idyllic setting. A popular notion exists that a change of residence will solve relationship problems. I knew otherwise.

What was it I needed? In these reflective moments when the house was tidy and quiet, it was easy to tell myself that I had it pretty good. Just look out the window! Who wouldn't love to have this view every day? Subconsciously, I was hearing my mother saying how lucky I was to have a loving husband and beautiful family. I agreed with her. But…there was always the "but."

And now there was the nagging, the itching to try new things, to see where my ideas might lead, this yearning to grow into Sandy Someone. She was inside me; I could hear her at times nudging me to move forward. With my college degree in hand fourteen years ago, I had planned on a high school teaching career. Is that who I was? Possibly, but could I do it here in this small town? Looking for courses required for state certification to teach might be the place to start. Maybe it wouldn't even be possible here. I might have to leave the valley to get the classes I needed. That would be an out, wouldn't it? Whatever the outcome, I promised myself I'd look.

One morning I dropped the kids off at the pool where Ray and Tami had gotten part-time jobs, and Billy and Scott needed to report for swim lessons. It was one of those indescribably beautiful Colorado mornings when a quick breath of the night cooled air is like tasting that first sip of morning coffee. Colorado Mountain College, located across the street from the pool in the basement of the Hotel Colorado, was my next stop. I hadn't found certification classes in their brochure, but I had found courses in weaving, needlepoint and home decorating. I registered for the needlepoint class, excited about learning something new and meeting other women, women who would know me only as Sandy.

After registering, I looked around the small office hoping to see a brochure for continuing education. Noticing that I wasn't leaving, the tall middle-aged woman who had signed me up for my needlepoint class asked if I were interested in another class. I looked at her tanned face and fit body clad in sensible slacks and shirt and decided to tell her why I had really stopped by. She looked professional; surely she would understand.

"Oh, so you're wanting to go back to school? I'm pretty sure there are some programs here in the valley. My friend is a teacher, and she takes re-certification classes somewhere. Let me check with Elaine. She may know."

I watched her walk into the back office area, the nook where educational information must be stored. I could hear voices before they both came out, Elaine with a piece of paper in her hand. In a friendly but businesslike demeanor, she walked toward the counter where I was standing, waiting for words that would alter my course.

"I have a number for you. This woman teaches classes for Adams State College here in Glenwood. Her name is Neva Daniel, and I know teachers who have taken her classes. I don't know what she has scheduled, but she would be a great starting point. Good luck with this. What did you say your name was again?"

"Sandy Browning. I'm new here, and I'm anxious to get something going professionally." There it was; I had put it on the table.

Elaine nodded her understanding, or was it her approval?

Armed with my new information, and with a lighter step, I walked to my car. I could do this. I could become a teacher with four children in the school system and a mostly absentee husband. Sure. Sure? It would be easier not to do anything, wouldn't it? No.

As I waited beside the pool for swim lessons to end, I practiced my phone conversation with this person called Neva. Once home, I fixed the boys a snack and picked up the phone for the call that could begin the unveiling of who Sandy was and the person she could become. A soft low-pitched voice answered the ring at the other end. I pictured Neva as scholarly: hair in a bun, flowing skirt and maybe a loose shirt, probably blue, and definitely wearing Birkenstocks.

"Neva, this is Sandy Browning. I'm new here, and I'm looking for teacher certification classes. Elaine at Colorado Mountain College gave me your name." I took a deep breath.

"Yes, I teach recertification courses for Adams State, and I often have teachers in my classes. Are you wanting to teach in the state?" Her soft voice encouraged me to go on.

"Yes, high school English. That's what I started out to do when I got my BA. It's been a while since I've taken any college courses so…"

"What is your timeframe? When would you like to have your course work completed?"

"I've looked at the requirements, and it seems I will need maybe three semesters. I'm ready to start right now." Did I sound like I really knew all this?

"Sure. Well, I have a course starting up in a couple of weeks called Literature as Fine Art. It's a three credit graduate class. I think it might be a good starting point for you. It's one night a week for eighteen weeks. We meet at my house. If you like I can send you the registration materials, and you can decide if this looks like something that will work."

What wouldn't work? Neva spoke to me as a professional. I could hear her confidence; she believed I could do this.

I would complete the registration materials, order transcripts from the University of Delaware, drop the class into my home schedule, hire a sitter for the evenings I had class and talk to my family.

It had been a long time since I had been in school. Now here I was about to be taking graduate classes with people who were either fresh from college or currently teaching. I felt a slight tremor, an intellectual apprehension.

Sunday evenings meant Cliff was home. I remembered the time ten years ago in Delaware when Cliff had come home and told me he had written a letter to J. Edgar Hoover regarding a job with the FBI. Now it was my turn. Perhaps a glass of wine was in order.

I poured two glasses and suggested we might enjoy a refresher on our enclosed back porch located off the kitchen and furnished with a large stained picnic table where the kids and I often enjoyed late summer meals. The privacy felt conducive to a conversation.

"A time to talk. This is nice, isn't it? With you on the road all week, we don't get much time like this, and there's something I want to talk to you about."

"You're pretty cagey. What's going on?"

Seated across from one another, we clinked our glasses to health.

"Was moving here a good decision?" He seemed to ask me that often.

"I don't know, but we're all settling in. Tami and Ray made it through seventh and sixth grades so we're over that hurdle. It's been a tough adjustment for them."

Idle chatter is usually a prelude to the meat of a conversation, isn't it?

"The house is looking great, and I know you've made friends here. So what's up?"

"What's up is pretty exciting. Since we aren't going to be moving, I've decided to work on a professional direction." I lifted my glass as a toast to me.

"A direction? What does that mean?" He looked puzzled.

"I'm going to get my Colorado teacher's certificate."

"How are you going to do that? And why would you want to? Why can't you just enjoy this place?" I could see his frown lines deepen.

"Because I need to do this. I've done some checking around, and I can get the classes I need right here through Adams State. A woman named

Neva Daniel teaches English courses for them locally, just what I need. Pretty exciting, huh?"

I looked for a reaction. Nothing came immediately as if he were hearing something unexpected from a person he no longer knew.

"I suppose. I just wasn't anticipating anything like this. Where'd this come from?"

"Cliff, it's not new. I want to become what I started out to be, a high school English teacher."

"Why? You've got enough going on as it is. All these kids and their activities and the other things you like to do?"

"I want my own career. I want to become someone. It's time for me."

"I don't understand this, but go ahead and take the classes if you want to. You know, though, that you probably can't count on me to be home on those nights you have class."

I nodded, knowingly. "Yes, I know about your job."

I slid from the bench and motioned I was going inside to get a sweater. Late summer evenings reminded me fall was approaching. I walked down the hall past Tami and Ray's rooms and into our bedroom as tears began to well. I wanted him to be proud of me, smiling that famous smile of his. I grabbed a Kleenex along with my favorite red sweater, squared my shoulders and walked back to the porch. This was my journey, and I would not cry.

Just as I was walking through the kitchen to the porch, I heard Cliff on the phone, obviously business, as I heard him say "Red." That would be his Florida informant. As I walked onto the porch, he signaled me he would be through in a minute. FBI interruptions were the norm.

"Sorry, I needed to talk to Red about a car ring operating in Vail."

"So how is Red? Is he still in Florida?" I should have asked if he were back in prison.

"Yes, but he has connections to this Vail case. Amazingly, he's just provided the missing link. Back to your classes. Sounds like you've checked these out. What are you planning to do if you get your certification?"

"Not if, when. Look for a teaching job here in the valley but no further south than Basalt. This is a pretty small district, so I don't know what my chances will be. I figure this certification process will take me a year."

"You know you don't need to work."

"I know you say that, but yes, I do need to work. I'm ready for some financial independence. Tami and Ray will be off to college soon and my teaching salary could help, especially since we had to take a pay cut to come here."

I looked into his eyes as he reacted to my statement. I had hit a nerve. He shifted his position at the picnic table and reached for his glass.

"Have you thought about where the money's coming from for these classes?" Was this another roadblock?

"Actually, I have. After looking at the budget, I should be able to shave enough to pay the course fees and buy books. I can make it work."

"I'm puzzled. Has someone put this idea in your head? Why haven't we talked about this before?"

"It never seemed possible before. Now, we're in a different place. For the first time I can plan ahead; I don't have to worry about your next assignment. So I want to challenge myself, find out who I am." I looked for an expression of doubt or approval but saw only questioning.

"Now you're sounding like one of those women's libbers or new agers."

"Maybe I'm becoming one of those too. We haven't agreed on much lately so that would figure."

"Wait a minute. I'm not saying I don't like the idea; I'm just surprised. Go ahead and sign up for the class if you want to."

"I already have."

I straightened my shoulders, placed my laced fingers solidly around my nearly empty glass, and looked directly across the table at my husband. In that moment I knew I was becoming an individual more directed than the nineteen-year-old woman he had married. I wasn't yet sure I understood this evolving woman, but I was already liking her.

TWENTY-FOUR

Journey on Another Level

It was here, and it was time. I dressed with care, not too dressy, not too casual. Passing the mirror for a last look, I nodded my approval. Yes, this was right. My first class, my first toe in the river, feeling the current and allowing myself to lean into its forces, hoping I was going to find a setting where women were on an intellectual plane with men, where smart people conversed on an esoteric level and where I would find a niche. I was hungry.

I backed from the driveway sensing I was not going backward but forward. I turned toward town and drove the mile or so to Neva's house. I pulled off Grand Avenue onto her street, the one with no street sign. Checking for house numbers, I found the right one dangling on an angled post partially obscured by wandering vines. Confident I was in the right place, I parked my car in front of a largely wood and stone house nestled on a hill surrounded by out of control flowers in every shape and color in a landscape design of their own making, an airdrop of wildflower seeds. Not unlike the unsolicited nervous spasms gurgling in my stomach.

I grabbed my course materials, locked the car and climbed the angled, uneven railroad ties intended as steps, leading to the front door that was really on the side of the house. Architecturally, this aberration seemed right. I stood at the top of the steps relishing the randomness of my teacher's out-of-control garden. A magical meadow leading me to a door, slightly ajar, welcomed me to an experience not unlike opening those first pages of a book into an atmosphere Coleridge so aptly described as a "willing suspension of disbelief." *Okay, I'm here; I'm open. I'll walk into your world of mystery and join you on this journey. I'm willing to become whatever is next for me.*

Before I could knock, an older woman, perhaps in her early seventies with an ageless face, dressed in a long blue denim skirt and a loose sweater over a softly flowing shirt, met me at the door. Yes, she was the person I had imagined except for her eyes; they were much bluer than I had envisioned. I admired her long silver hair tied loosely at the collar. Birkenstocks finished the look. Neva Daniel had entered my life.

"You must be Sandy. I'm Neva. I'm so glad you decided to take this class. I know you'll be a great addition. Come in, and I'll introduce you to the others."

I followed Neva through the door into the large family room filled with books from floor to ceiling and stacked on every available table where she invited me to have a cup of coffee or tea and to make myself comfortable. My nervousness had sloughed from my shoulders like an unneeded shawl. This room in its orderly disarray mirrored the outside garden assuring me randomness and calm confidence were not mutually exclusive. I looked around and claimed an end seat on one of the very over-stuffed couches supplied with pillows and throws. This would be my spot.

I placed my new quilted calico day pack on the floor and stood to make my way to the large round oak table hosting coffee, tea and interesting snacks. I poured myself a cup of tea and holding the flowered cup in two hands, my eyes circled the room taking in Neva's decorating scheme. I was standing next to the kitchen which was filled with fresh produce, obviously from her garden, along with jars of jam and jelly, numerous cookbooks and smells one would find in a serious homemaker's kitchen.

Tea in hand, I walked back into the family room to peruse the exhaustive display of reading material. Books, magazines, journals, as well as publications for upcoming events overflowed from shelves and tables onto the floor in a graceful unplanned design. Several windows peeked through openings left by non-matching bookcases. This was a reader's paradise inviting me to make a selection, curl up absorbed in one of the overstuffed chairs with a cup of fragrant herbal tea and lose myself in another writer's world. But, wait, I was here for class.

As I moved from bookshelf to bookshelf, I found myself next to another book browser. Noticing my presence, he introduced himself as

Don, an English teacher in Basalt, and asked how I came to be part of this class.

"I learned about Neva through Colorado Mountain College. I'm really here to get credits for my teaching certification."

There it was, out in the open, my goal. Now two people, other than my family, knew where I was headed.

The other ten or so students arrived. Each seemed to know Neva's routine: select one of the unmatched flowered cups, pour coffee or tea, find your seat, introduce yourself to new people and settle in for the instruction.

Cup in hand, the same columbine cup I would see her use each week, Neva settled herself into her maple rocking chair, her materials overflowing from a small table at her side. In what I came to know as her contemplative manner, she perused the gathering, gazing at each of us, acknowledging our role in this class. Introductions came next; we were asked to share something personal about ourselves. Suspecting this might be coming, I had formulated a safe description of my many moves across the country. I didn't tell them why there were so many moves, just that Glenwood seemed a lovely place to live and I was eager to become part of the community. For the first time I was in a setting where I wasn't someone's mom or wife; I was Sandy Browning, aspiring teacher.

Neva's teaching style was that of mentor, sitting among us in a Socratic manner allowing each of us to feel our contributions were important. So many thoughts, so many interpretations. I had forgotten the enticement of intellectual stimulation. Tonight's discussion was stretching my curiosity, challenging me to look at my world in the context of literature as I hadn't done in a long while.

The three hour class felt like thirty minutes, and I wanted it to go on. At the apex of the discussion, Neva announced we would take up the discourse next week-- a whole week.

I unfolded myself from the couch's cushions which seemed to have enveloped me like a warm coat and shuffled to the kitchen with my empty cup, placed it in the overflowing sink and gathered my belongings for the short trip home. As I approached the door, Neva wished me well in the coming week and extended her arms for a warm hug. Remnants of the thought provoking discussion interrupted my focus as I tripped my way down those same slanted railroad ties serving as steps. My thoughts retreated to the path I had taken to Neva's door. After one class I instinctively knew it was the right course. Forget the certification, I was where I needed to be with the right person to be my guide.

Once inside my car, I leaned my head back against the seat and took in a long breath of the cool, invigorating fall air. I drove the ten minutes home, acutely awake as if I had drunk espresso rather than herbal tea, relishing this natural high, not considering I would eventually need to come down to normal. After all, I had a family to take care of in the morning.

I released the babysitter, checked on the boys and walking past Tami's room I noted her light was still on. I suspected she was through with homework and was now reading. I cracked her door open.

"How was your class, Mom?" She had encouraged me to take this step.

"It was wonderful. Oh my gosh, Tami, there are so many smart people, and Neva is the best! I'm going to learn so much. I'm so glad you told me to go for it."

Thursday morning rolled around as if Wednesday's class hadn't happened except I knew it had; my bag was sitting on the dining room table waiting for me to dive into next week's assignments. My mood felt lighter as I peered out my favorite dining room window framing Mt. Sopris. Like me, it soon would be changing, adding its beautiful white coat to its symmetrical peaks, while my transformation would be slower and more subtle.

The week rolled by with an almost normal schedule of piano lessons, swim practice, school activities and a weekend family outing cutting and gathering wood for our winter warmth. I packed a full hamper of food, and we all donned boots, jeans and flannel shirts, just like mountain people. Yes, I had given in to fashion pressure and put aside my city clothes for jeans. Well, not completely.

The day of the next class arrived, and I was ready. Now I knew the routine, and I found myself beginning to contribute more to the discussion. I had stepped off the shore and into the flow, experiencing that adrenaline rush as its currents took me into unknown territory. Neva taught me that it was okay to think differently and to ask uncomfortable questions, stretching my intellect to a new level. She validated for me that intellectual rigor has its own merits. I rarely use the word "wise" to describe people. Neva was the only truly wise person I had encountered thus far on my life journey.

With the ensuing classes from romanticism to realism to a literary bicentennial celebration to a final course in women's literature, I could feel myself transforming into the person who would become a teacher, not just an ordinary one but one who would challenge her students to achieve at a new level. I read as never before, exploring new genres, questioning what I believed about my world of the socially disruptive 1970s, and allowing myself to address some uncomfortable possibilities.

I finished my certification requirements and applied for my teaching credentials. The paperwork reminded me of Cliff's application for the Bureau: forms, agreements, transcripts, all to certify my qualification to teach in the state of Colorado. Within a week of mailing the packet, I began to watch the return mail for the news.

It came; I was now certified to teach English in the state of Colorado. My authentic certificate along with its support materials found a home in a folder, my first professional folder that would soon house my resume, letters of recommendation and all the materials that might be significant in my job search. A folder, recognizable for its color: a red one nearly the same shade as my New Jersey front door.

The following day, certification in hand, I went to the Roaring Fork School District office and proudly requested they add my name to the substitute teaching list. I told them I would sub for any grade, any subject area. The secretary explained how the calling of substitutes was handled, and I went home to wait for my first call.

But the next call was from Cliff.

"Hi honey, how is everyone?"

"We're fine." I wouldn't have told him otherwise; he was far away and couldn't help, and I had friends and neighbors. "Where are you?"

"Steamboat. You'd really like it here. Maybe we can plan a ski trip up here this winter. Anything new there?" He sounded preoccupied, probably meeting with the Sheriff.

"I took my teaching credentials to the school district today and asked to be placed on the substitute list. I'm new so I probably won't get many days, but that's okay." I spoke quickly, not expecting much in the way of support.

"Is this about finding a job? I thought maybe you'd forget about that."

"Nope. Now I just wait for a call."

I had asked myself for months why Cliff was opposed to my working and could only speculate that he felt he would be losing control over me. For fifteen years I'd been dependent on him financially. Now I was on the verge of becoming the second bread winner.

My first call for a substitute came a couple of weeks later.

"Sandy Browning, this is Cheryl at Basalt High School, and we need a sub for ninth grade English tomorrow. Are you available?"

"Yes." I would make myself available. It was here, my opportunity to put into play what I had dreamed about for the past year. What to wear? Oh, I knew just what the outfit had to be, my favorite skirt and jacket with heeled boots so I'd appear a bit taller.

I took the boys to school and as I traveled east on Highway 82 to my assignment I congratulated myself on having pursued this course. I proudly pulled into the parking lot for faculty, removed my bag containing emergency lesson plans and other things I might need in case the teacher hadn't left directions for the day, locked the car door and stood for just a moment looking at this mountain valley as if for the first time.

The regular teacher had left extensive plans so the students and I managed just fine with me pretending these were my students. I dismissed my students as the final bell rang and looked around the empty classroom dreaming of the day a room like this would be mine.

I didn't have to wait long until a different opportunity presented itself in the form of a call from the district to teach remedial reading at the vocational center. I accepted, knowing this would be an easy assignment as vo-tech classes were always small, and the environment was conducive to learning. On this particular day Gary Fisher, the district vocational director, met me when I checked into his office and told me he had been awarded a grant, providing him money for a reading/writing program for his vocational students who were behind in these skills.

"This award allows me to hire a part-time teacher two days a week. Could this possibly work for you?" He slowly sipped from his cup while observing my reaction.

"This might be perfect." These would be motivated students attending on a voluntary basis, a dream come true for a teacher. It would be perfect.

I struggled to contain my enthusiasm. I had just been offered a job. I thanked my prospective boss and exited the building, barely able to keep my feet on the ground. At that moment I loved life and my new opportunity to participate. I drove the back road home following the Roaring Fork River as it maneuvered its way north toward its destination. I smiled at the synchronicity.

TWENTY-FIVE

False Security

Life in the outside world in the mid 70s swirled around me: Gerald Ford was no longer president so Cliff was no longer on Secret Service duty when Ford vacationed in Vail; Jimmy Carter was president; Saigon had fallen ending the Vietnam War; a man named Clarence Kelley had been named the new FBI Director; Elvis died; New York City endured days of blackout and the first Apple computer hit the market, all of which would impact us now or later. My outside world was Glenwood Springs, where what touched my family mattered most: whether they were safe, whether the fridge was stocked, whether there was enough money in the checking for the next month, whether I was making progress toward getting a job. This was my world.

However hard I tried to think of us as a normal family, I knew it was different for us. Normal families didn't communicate through the dispatcher; normal families didn't worry too much about what they said in public; normal wives didn't shiver when the phone rang, and normal families didn't live with the uncertainty of some insidious event trespassing into their private space.

Cliff had his cases, and I had my classes. We were keeping it together; sometimes it was better, sometimes worse. My heart told me probably neither of us was getting all that we needed, but we were still committed to providing as stable an environment for our children as possible. This was our cliché.

The end of the school year came and after July 1, I would most likely know if a high school English teaching position had opened. Teachers on contract had until June 30 to notify the district if they would not be returning. Since Cliff and I both had some time free, he suggested we take a trip to Ohio to visit his parents whom we hadn't seen since moving to Glenwood. It felt good to be able to carve out this time for a road trip. Ray would be in swim camp at CSU. A trip to Ohio was not on Tami's agenda for this summer, but she was certainly capable of staying by herself. Cliff felt her request to forego this trip was reasonable; we agreed she could stay home.

After all, Glenwood was a safe place. I didn't even lock the doors anymore. Well, maybe I did lock the front door, but the side garage door was a different matter. Whoever wanted something from us, even the raccoons and skunks, could usually waltz right in. I wasn't sure I even knew where the key was. Here, in my mountain oasis there wasn't much to worry about. Just a couple of years ago Glenwood Springs had earned the citation for the "Safest Small Town in America."

Feeling somewhat assured that all was well, Cliff and I loaded up the boys in the trusty station wagon and set off for Toledo. As the mile markers rolled by, I reflected on that February trip west years earlier when I had been years younger with four children facing a move I didn't want to make. Now settled into a new life where I was building a reputation, I waited for a job to open up. Maybe this year.

After two lengthy days, we pulled into the long gravel driveway leading to a relatively new brick and siding one-story ranch house belonging to Cliff's family. We had always lived long distances from them so these family visits were like an interlude in life, a stopping place to renew ourselves and become reacquainted with those who loved us.

Cliff and I had come from very different backgrounds, and both his mom and I had worked to make our relationship meaningful. Goldie, a product of the depression and World War II, had taken on a "Rosie the Riveter" role and gone to work for Libby Owens Ford, a glass supplier for the war effort. There she rose in the union ranks to become a steward. Aside from being her son's wife and her grandchildren's mother, she wasn't sure where I fit into this whole family equation. If she didn't understand me, she didn't understand her son either. He had chosen a profession she considered foreign and dangerous, and for some reason she thought I could control all these moves and this crazy lifestyle.

Teary-eyed, Goldie reached for her son. I could only guess, with Tami and Ray almost ready to leave, how disconnected she must feel from Cliff. He didn't call her very often; visits were rare, and I knew Goldie missed him very much. Late night conversations this visit would be in order as part of catching up. Phone calls, though, could always interrupt.

"Cliff, Dave's on the phone," Goldie said.

Per Bureau vacation policy, Cliff had filed an itinerary with both Dave and the Denver office. Dave would never call unless it were important.

I watched Cliff as he listened, brows furrowed, saying little at the outset, just listening to this one-sided conversation. "Sure. No, that's no problem. I'd rather be hearing from you than the office," Cliff said. "Yeah, I'm aware of the case out of Salt Lake."

A long silence followed as he listened interminably to his partner. Dave was great for detail. My hands fidgeted in the pockets of my shorts as I watched Cliff's face for any clues as to the state of the world in Glenwood. "Listen, keep me informed, Dave. I'm going to call Denver myself and a couple of my contacts in the field to see what I can learn. Will you do me a favor and go to the pool and let Tami know what's going on? I don't want her to hear of this problem from one of her friends."

What problem? I shivered as I stood waiting for him to hang up and explain this call. The words I heard next were mine.

"I knew it. I just knew I should never have agreed to let Tami stay home. What's going on? Why did you ask Dave to go to the pool? What does it have to do with Tami?"

"Wait. I can't tell you anything if you keep talking. Sit down, take a breath and I'll tell you what I know."

I looked at this man whose whole life had been attending to matters such as the one he was about to divulge. I wanted reassurance that whatever was transpiring at home would not affect our daughter.

"Listen, a prisoner has escaped. I want Dave to talk to Tami so she hears from him what's actually going on." His wrinkled forehead told me he was in his Bureau mode. But just another question or two.

"Who escaped? Glenwood never has jail breaks. I thought the only people who were ever there were drunks." A jail break? No, he said an escape. An escape from where? Well, if someone escaped, they could find him, couldn't they? And who was it anyway?

"I don't know if you remember my mentioning a prisoner named Ted Bundy, a murder suspect, who was recently transferred from Salt Lake City to the Garfield County Jail?" I looked at his drawn face, which inspired no confidence this was an ordinary prisoner or an ordinary escape.

"Vaguely. I'm not sure. I guess I wasn't paying attention." I reminded myself that the world had been going on around me while I was focused on myself. *Wake up, Sandy, look around.*

"Well, he's a suspect in a number of other murders across the country. This morning the deputies transported him from the Glenwood jail to the Aspen Court House for a pretrial hearing on a different murder charge. You probably remember the nurse who was murdered in Aspen? Well, this Ted Bundy is a suspect in that murder. Anyway, during this proceeding, Bundy, acting as his own attorney, wasn't shackled or handcuffed."

My jaw went slack in disbelief. A murder suspect in our safe little valley and not even in handcuffs? "I remember this Aspen murder, but I'm not sure I've heard anything about this Bundy guy." As Cliff talked, I felt my sense of complacency about my husband's cases and a false sense of security in my little world may have tripped me up. Time to remove the blinders.

"He's loose? Tami's home alone. My God, we need to get home." My hands were sweating and that sick feeling was rising from the pit of my stomach.

"Maybe." Cliff continued "At the lunch break, Bundy asked to go to the law library on the second floor to do a bit more research. He walked towards an open window when the guard was looking elsewhere and jumped out...."

"Jumped out? Of an open window two stories up? Surely they caught him. Broad daylight and the courthouse in the center of town? Didn't he break a leg or something?"

The incredulity registered on my face must have said everything. This was like a cheap paperback mystery novel where you know the sequence of events couldn't have happened.

"Dave said Bundy may have hurt his ankle, but he walked down the street and disappeared." Cliff's expression and pale color told me he wasn't exaggerating.

"He disappeared in the dinky town of Aspen with a busted ankle? How is that possible?" The visual image of this scene played before me in a sick comic way. I had walked past that courthouse so many times and never once considered the possibility of a body falling from the second story.

"I'm sure they'll catch him. He needs a car and money for starters. Right now I want to get hold of Tami and make sure she isn't alone. This guy targets young women." He didn't need to tell me the latter. I saw his jaw tighten, accenting the tension in his face.

My eyes wide, brimming with tears, sorry about so many things: my daughter home alone, my husband caught up in the criminal world while on vacation, and the boys who would be so disappointed if we had to leave early.

A killer, maybe a serial killer, was walking the streets in my valley, maybe even my town, by now, or maybe he had decided to go for a swim. The one time we leave our child home on her own, a creep breaks out of jail and is now wandering around somewhere in the Roaring Fork Valley. Surely they would find him, wouldn't they? Caution: the very people who were looking for him had let him escape out of a courtroom window.

I nodded as Cliff picked up the phone to make calls to the pool, home and some of Tami's friends, hoping to connect with her. About an hour later she called. Cliff confidently and patiently explained the Bundy situation to her. His directions left no room for guesswork. At that moment I was proud he was a Special Agent. At least, we had inside information on this murderer wandering the streets of our valley.

"Tami, I want you to be very careful. I want you to drive to work, no bike; keep all the doors and windows locked, especially the garage side door; be sure the deadbolt is fastened on the door from the family room into the garage." It was as if Cliff were reading from a list, a safety list.

"Okay, Dad. Does Dave have all this information?"

"Sure, and you can call him anytime. Do you think Dana could stay with you until we get home?"

"Probably."

"Okay, just one more thing. Check in with Joe and Ann when you leave and come home. And call us when you get off work. Oh, your mother wants to say a few words."

Yes, I did, but what could they be? My hands were shaking as I took the phone feeling the tears welling behind my eyes not yet blurring my vision. *Stop.* I told myself. *She's scared and so are you, but you're the mom. You can cry after you hang up, but now you must be strong for her.*

"Hi, honey, are you okay? I know it's frightening. We just want you to be extra careful especially with people at the pool."

"I always am, Mom. We get some creepy people; I'm not sure they're here to swim."

"Are your friends around? I really want you to be with someone every minute you're not working."

"Dana's coming over when I get off work. She'll stay with me until you get home."

"I love you, honey. Call when you get home from work tonight. Stay safe."

Tami's call didn't come until after midnight. I kept looking at my watch, subtracting hours for time difference. *Please call, honey.*

"I'm home, Dad. Dana rode home with me. Have they found him yet?" Cliff's relief at hearing his daughter's voice registered on his face.

"No word yet. Law enforcement from all over the state is working on it. Hopefully, they'll get a break soon." Cliff was walking the line between warning his daughter and bringing her up to date on Bundy's whereabouts. I watched as he tenderly spoke to her, not wanting her to be more afraid than she already was yet cautioning her to be observant and extremely careful.

Cliff and I finally went to bed around 2:00 a.m., but no sleep was forthcoming. Colorado was a long drive from Ohio, and we would be filled with worry until we pulled into our driveway. We still hadn't shared any of this with the boys, and I anticipated their protests. Early the next morning amid a few tears we promised to visit again before so many years had passed. Cliff wanted the first day on the road to be a long one so we could get home early on the second day. Cliff would pick Ray up from swim camp later in the week.

Over the years, I had never been able to decide whether the road seemed longer heading to our destination or returning home. This time each mile felt like an hour as I took turns looking at the map and the clock. We were crawling when we needed to be flying. I had always worried about my husband's safety, not without reason, but that didn't measure up to my level of anxiety about my daughter's safety. He was trained for these kinds of situations, and I had vicariously lived through many of them with him. Now, if I could just be home, all would be well. I could make it better. I would be more diligent; I wouldn't take our safety for granted. I would be a better gatekeeper. I would be everything everybody needed me to be.

After an inane initial conversation, silence settled in, even from the back seat. No one was hungry, and even the boys had stopped arguing. How much did Cliff really know about this Ted Bundy? My husband's frown, tension on the steering wheel, cryptic answers told me he was on edge. I needed to worry.

Just as I had on that wintry February day a few years back, traveling across the plains, I set my sights on the horizon straight ahead so as to connect with the earliest indication of the Rocky Mountains. Closer, we were ever closer. Denver was on the horizon. Over the mountains and through the Glenwood Canyon, off the exit and over the one-lane bridge. Our haven, only recently invaded by some lunatic who specialized in leaping from courthouse windows.

We found our daughter safe, a bit rattled and a little less trusting. And Ted Bundy was still walking around somewhere, with reported sightings in Carbondale, Telluride, the Maroon Bells, Marble and Redstone, but no capture until one day when a local police officer noticed a suspicious car weaving down the street. Bundy, dirty and limping from his dive out the window, was placed back in the Garfield County Jail, hopefully under more watchful eyes.

My daily drives into town meant I usually passed the courthouse where Bundy now resided. I shuddered each time I passed the stone structure. This time would local law enforcement keep us safe from a man who was suspected of killing up to thirty women? I had doubts and rightly so.

On December 30, 1977, Bundy escaped again, this time by using a hacksaw he had gotten from another prisoner to create a passageway overhead in his cell through the heating duct to a loose light fixture in the chief jailer's apartment. In six months he had accumulated nearly $500, mostly through the mail from an ex-girlfriend. Perhaps more importantly, he had lost nearly forty pounds so he was slim enough to fit into the ceiling passageway, slide down into the empty apartment, dress himself in the jailer's clothes and walk out the front door. His escape was not discovered for seventeen hours. His destination: Florida where he would commit many more murders.

TWENTY-SIX

Steps to Becoming

I was looking forward to a couple more months of Colorado summer, my second favorite season behind autumn. No teaching, no classes, just family stuff and time walking the local trails outside my back door. My time to explore Red Mountain and the overgrown ski runs that whispered of adventure where Billy, Scott and I one morning walked the trails and surprised a rusting single chair leaning from its cable, calling to me to claim this piece of history that dated back to 1942 when Red Mountain Ski Area was built by the Conservation Corps. Now thirty-four years later I stood reveling in its history, wondering who the persons were who had slid down this mountain relishing the magnificent views, spying on the bathing tourists in the pool, then leaving me this single chair to claim.

"You want to do what?" Cliff asked.

"I want you to help me bring down an old ski chair the boys and I found on Red Mountain. Someone told me there used to be a ski area there, so we decided to check it out."

"So, what about this chair?" I looked at him to note he was only half paying attention which might mean he wouldn't come up with objections like "no place to put it," "it isn't ours," and other inconsequential questions.

"It's tired and worn, and it needs a home," I continued. "Can you help us? It's too heavy for us to manage, but if we could get it down the mountain and into the station wagon, we could get it home." I was hoping my enthusiasm was contagious.

"What are you thinking? We can't just go up there and take it," Cliff offered. "It belongs to someone. All I need in this small town is to be accused of theft." Well, that was a consideration so I agreed he should check it out.

It had all seemed simple to me. "Finders, keepers." But I was married to a lawman who needed to investigate who owned the chair and what the process would be for claiming it. Like any other investigative matter, my husband was on top of it, and we were soon legally the proud owners of one old, faded orange single ski chair. Since the garage was filled to capacity with other treasures, my ski chair moved to the back porch. Actually, it looked pretty cute propped against the white cement block enclosure. It made me smile each time I went out there. I joked that it made one more seat at the picnic table.

In the cool of the summer mornings as I wrote in my journal, read my books, drank my coffee and reflected on where I was in the execution of my plan, I had plenty of opportunity to enjoy my latest acquisition. Yes, its orange paint could use a touch-up, but it appeared happy to recline in my space. At times I thought my chair was beckoning me to try out its seat as if a new place on the porch could provide me with a different perspective.

In my conversations with myself earlier that spring I had posed, "What if I don't ever get a job here? Is my husband's job going to be a hindrance to my obtaining a position?" This was the mid-seventies, and the negative bias against the federal government was still alive.

Just as I poured myself a second cup of coffee to accompany my list-making for the week's duties, the phone rang. Maybe I could complete some of these errands before I had to pick up Billy and Scott at the pool. Preoccupied is what I was. Another phone call. Right now, an interruption, not yet a surprise.

"Sandy Browning? This is Janice from the RE-1 School District. The superintendent asked me to call to see if you would be able to come in for an interview for an open English teaching position at Glenwood Springs High School." My senses awakened sharply. Was I hearing correctly? A position had opened?

"Certainly. What would fit Mr. Mathews's schedule?"

"Perhaps either 10:00 a.m. or 1:00 p.m. on Wednesday?"

Being first might be an advantage so I took the ten o'clock slot. She went on to say that normally the principal did the interviewing for his building openings, but Bob O'Neil was currently out of town.

I had a job interview! Just what I had been hoping for and in just the building I wanted. Momentarily, I wondered who had left. Only momentarily. It was my opportunity to shine, to show Mr. Mathews that I would be the perfect hire for this position. I wanted this job.

I broached this second surprise of the summer as we gathered on the back porch for dinner.

"Hey, everybody. I've got news." I looked around the table to see frowns, suspicious stares and even a wrinkled brow on Cliff's face. I smiled.

"News?" Cliff asked.

"What's this about, Mom? Tami and I are going out tonight," Ray said. It wasn't often I could get my family together like this. Tami and Ray had time for their teenage lives but not much for where my life was headed. This was as it should be.

"I know. I'll be short. You know, I've been looking for a teaching job in the district."

Oh, no, their faces read. Not more about her school stuff.

"Well, an opening has come up at the high school here, and I've applied. Today I was called for an interview." I had caught my family's attention.

"Well, that's what you've been hoping for, isn't it?" Cliff said.

The children had been looking to their dad for his response. If he gave his blessing, it would probably be okay.

"Mom, I think it's great. We've seen you in the building when you've subbed anyway." Tami was pretty confident about the situation.

"As long as I don't have to take you for a class," Ray said jokingly.

For Billy and Scott there would be less impact. I would drop them off at school in the morning, and they would walk to the high school to meet me after classes.

Tami and Ray looked at me. I met their gazes trying not to impose any influence. Finally Tami said, "You should do it if you get the chance, Mom."

"Yeah, Mom, but no classes with you." Ray's response was a statement, not a question, but I thought I glimpsed pride in his expression. I knew if I wanted this job, it would be okay for him.

I still had the interview to go. The job wasn't yet a given, but it now opened a long overdue dialogue with Cliff about my professional direction.

"Honey, I know you really think you want this job, but are you sure you know what you're taking on? Just going to the building and teaching isn't all of it. There will be days when you get tied up after school. You know I'm not much help."

"No, you're not." I looked at him across the table which the children had now vacated.

"How can I be sure if it's too much until I have a chance to try. I want this job so badly I don't know what I'll do if I don't get it. Besides the personal reasons, I want to make a financial contribution. I want to have my own income."

"But I don't want you to feel you have to work. We can make it on my salary," Cliff said.

"It's not just the money."

First I had to get the job.

Interview morning. First consideration—what to wear? Something professional like my black and white jacket dress, which would go well with my new white summer sandals. Twenty minutes ahead of time, I took one last look in the mirror and proclaimed myself ready to become a teacher for Roaring Fork District RE-1.

Janice offered me coffee which I declined. I didn't need anything to exacerbate my nervousness. Mr. Mathews immediately put me at ease with his questions about my substitute teaching experiences and my success with the reading program at the vocational center. From there he posed classroom management scenarios. I assured him I had experienced plenty of classroom management challenges in my two years of substitute teaching: situations without lesson plans, and classes totally out of my discipline like band and math. I also told him I knew the English curriculum would be up for review soon and felt confident I could contribute to that conversation.

"Once Bob O'Neil and I have discussed each candidate, I will call and notify each of you of our decision by Friday."

I thanked him, and with knees only slightly shaking, I left his office.

I couldn't just go home. I needed a little time to let the experience permeate below skin level. Before I faced my family, before I stopped for groceries, I needed to stop, do a reality check and reconnect. Just a little time by myself would do it. Not certain where I was going, my car instinctively took me down Grand Avenue onto the highway and out to

No Name, the place where it had all begun, where in my disappointment of having to leave D.C. I had experienced the strength of its red mountain walls carved by the currents of the Colorado River. Embraced by the strength of its natural beauty the seeds of my plan had been sown.

I pulled off the highway, drove past the RV park and our first residence, stopping next to the river where it negotiated a sharp bend, gaining momentum as it glided like a ribbon into town. I got out of the car and walked to a large fallen boulder providing me a familiar seat. I had found this spot on a walk in those early months here. Now, yes now, I could quietly replay the interview scene. What was he looking for, and had he found it in me?

The rhythms of the water, knowing where they were going, served as confirmation of my own direction and a reminder of the river's lessons. I marveled at the power before me yet how effortlessly it moved through its terrain, knowing its destination, confident in its purpose. With this job possibility before me, I knew I would take the position if it were offered.

Friday, when Mr. Mathews's phone call came, I had already mentally practiced how I would respond. He offered me the position and a contract. I told him I would call him Monday morning with my decision. My decision.

Since this was a day Cliff was in the office, I called him and asked if we could meet for lunch. This was an unusual gesture on my part as I almost never called his office. I didn't want to tell him over the phone about my offer, nor did I want to wait until he got home. I wanted to read his face when I told him my news.

"Sure. I haven't had such a good offer in a while. I'll meet you at that new restaurant across from the high school about 12:30. Okay? What's up?"

"I just thought lunch today would be nice." I didn't want to show my excitement just yet.

I dropped the kids off at the pool and went to meet their dad. Cliff was waiting as I arrived. He waved from a table, appointed with a checkered tablecloth and napkins, a nice touch for our little town. We could use a few more restaurants like this.

Instead of appearing in my shorts and top as I normally would have for a summer lunch date, I decided my favorite pink sleeveless dress fit my new status a bit better. When I accepted this job, I would, from this day on, be seen as a Glenwood Springs High School teacher. Starting today I needed to look like one.

"Hi hon. You look nice. You're pretty dressed up. What's happening?" Well, he had noticed. Was my new stature already showing?

"What's happening? Well, it's like this…." I wanted to appear casual and business-like about this job offer. It wasn't every day I'd been offered a job. I looked across the table and smiled. "I received a phone call from the school district this morning."

"Oh, yeah, I forgot you were going to hear something today."

How could he forget? I'd talked of practically nothing else.

"And?" His question had a smile attached to it. I think he was actually proud of me.

"Yep, I've been offered the English position." I again checked his expression, hoping for the elation I felt. His smile was broad.

"Congratulations! You've worked hard for this. What did you tell them?"

"I said I would let them know Monday. This has to be right for all of us: you, me and the kids."

Cliff reached across the table and took my hand in a familiar gesture.

"I think you should do it. I know you've wanted this opportunity, and I support it. It's time you got your turn. The kids and I will probably need to make some adjustments, but those shouldn't be too hard."

"I'm going to accept."

This was a celebration luncheon, hopefully one of many in the future. I remembered fondly another celebratory lunch when he gave me his anniversary pin for ten hard years with the FBI, a pin he said I'd earned. Now he was supporting me. Had we made the turn into the place where we were both getting to do what we wanted professionally?

TWENTY-SEVEN

Ready

Pinch myself, temper the broad grin, slow down. No, go to the grocery store for something special for dinner. A celebration's in order. Maybe something on the grill with a salad, corn on the cob, and my famous potato salad. I could even spring for a bottle of wine. I could. I had a job.

I had a job, a real job with a paycheck and real benefits. This was my "just in case" plan realized. I shivered with excitement as I carried the groceries up the stairs to the kitchen. Oh my gosh. How could I be so happy? I changed my clothes and looked in the mirror. How could I still look the same when inside I felt all different? I felt taller, stronger.

I needed a walk, a river walk along the Roaring Fork. It wasn't roaring today, just gurgling along in a peaceful, inviting way that had become seasonally familiar. I gazed down the bank, observing changes in the route the translucent blue water was taking. As always, its sounds and flexibility as it rounded fallen boulders, assured me that my life would continue to flow in the right direction. Up to this point I had searched hard for this direction. Now it was before me.

I rose from my perch on a medium sized boulder, stretched my arms and fixed my eyes and ears on the energy surrounding me. Reaching the comfort of my back porch, my summer haven, I settled into my favorite spot.

"Hey kids, I'm on the porch. Grab something to drink and come on out." Hair wet and messy from the pool, they all tumbled through the kitchen door and to the clothesline to hang their suits and towels. I was shivering with excitement to spill my news.

"Hey, I heard from the district today."

"Mom, you got the job!" Tami squealed as the Billy and Scott clapped.

I wanted, most of all, for them to be proud of me. I would make sure they were.

By the time Cliff got home, my new job was old news although my enthusiasm bubbled out in the form of smiles and hand claps. Should I really be this excited? After all, people got jobs every day. But they weren't me.

My meeting with Bob O'Neil confirmed I would be teaching two classes of freshman English, two classes of sophomore English, and one class of junior high home-ec. The home-ec was a surprise, but if I could run a household, maybe, just maybe, I could teach eighth graders to cook and sew.

Bob handed me my keys, and I walked proudly to Room 1 where I could see the river and my house framed by my beautiful red mountains.

Summer ended all too soon, bringing with it a serious case of the jitters. Within days I would be welcoming my students just as many years ago my favorite teachers had welcomed me.

I remembered my first day of kindergarten when fear walked with me up the steps to the Lake Lansing Elementary School on the arm of my mother with my little sister trailing behind. This was my big day; I was five and ready for school. Mom and I walked through the red double doors, my brand new shoes noisily tapping their way down the tan marble floors shined to a luster suggesting this was a very important place. Down the green painted hallway past rooms filled with big kids onto the last room on the right where we paused before a doorway framing a grandmotherly looking woman, much older than my mother, dressed in a long blue printed dress with a jacket that didn't see fit to button. Sturdy lace-up black shoes that looked like they could withstand any abuse, peeked beneath the hem of her dress. Standing before her, gripping my mother's hand just a bit tighter and shaking beneath my first new school dress, I looked up to determine what kind of face was attached to this large blue dress. Slowly, I raised my eyes as her face leaned forward to fit into my line of sight. First, I saw a smile, not a make believe smile that sometimes people put on when they have to talk to children. No, not that kind, but rather a wide, lip parting smile that comes from deep inside. I stopped shaking, moving my eyes upward to look into her whole face, a face whose memory has accompanied me over the years, a radiant face whose eyes told me she was going to be an important person in my life.

"You must be Sandy. I'm so glad you're in my class. Would you like to come in and choose a desk?"

I released my mother's hand and followed Mrs. Adams inside where I timidly chose a small desk at the front of the room near her large desk. She was my teacher, and I already felt special.

Now, as I prepared for my own classroom, I carried that secret with me. No matter how scared and lacking in confidence my freshmen might be, my job was to convince them they were safe with me and would learn something important each day they came to class. How that would happen in Room 1, I didn't yet know. What I did know is that remarkable teachers made things happen for students, and I intended to replicate Mrs. Adams in this small Colorado high school.

Lesson plans were ready, and posters hanging on my walls left no doubt this was an English classroom. Poets and dramatists were part of the population. Once more I arranged and rearranged the desks and then moved them again. I changed the back of the room to the front, and Bob agreed to have the chalkboards moved. This way the students would face me, and my whole room would be before me as I taught.

I was ready. The day before students were to report I drove to the high school, parked in the faculty parking lot, opened the outside door with my own key, walked down the polished tile hallway and stopped before my classroom as if I were a student and asked myself, "Well, what do you think? Will it work the way you've envisioned it? Will great things happen here for kids?"

Before I got too emotional, I closed the door, locked it and walked back to my car. Tomorrow would be a special day. I would make it one I could look back on with pride.

TWENTY-EIGHT

Day One - Year One

I smelled the coffee before the alarm rang. In fact, there had been no need for the alarm. Even after all the years of practice, I never slept very well when Cliff was away so I couldn't blame the sleeplessness entirely on my apprehension for the first day of school. I slipped on my summery robe, followed my nose to the kitchen, and filled my favorite mug before stepping out onto the back porch. An early fall coolness bathed my face in contrast to the coffee's warmth encircling my hands. I smiled as I greeted my orange ski chair, looking lonely in the morning darkness. Sunshine would find its way to this spot much later in the morning.

This morning, before sunrise, I sought a few moments with my thoughts. Not worrisome thoughts, no what-if's, just quiet enfolding me in preparation for this next chapter in my life. Since moving to Glenwood, an intense need for independence had steadily moved me forward. My rivers and my mountains had been patient teachers, nudging me, for some time, to go with my own internal current.

Here on my sheltered porch in its soothing darkness, I was alone but not afraid. For the past five years I had planned and worked for this moment when I could be confident that no matter how the cards played, I would be able to financially and emotionally support my family. This change in direction from dependent FBI wife to a 70s woman stepping out to execute her own direction was upon me. In just a matter of hours I would be Mrs. Browning, high school English teacher.

Okay, one more cup of coffee, then off to the shower. Today was about me. I was ready. For the past five weeks I had read, worried, and planned my way to this moment. I was sad Cliff was away for this my teaching debut. As if reading my needs before he left the house yesterday, he had taken me by the shoulders, stared at me with those penetrating brown eyes, and smiled, communicating a message of confidence, and wishing me well on my first day. As I stood with his arms around me, I recalled how excited he had been on the day he left for training to become a Special Agent with the FBI. I, on the other hand, had been apprehensive about this law enforcement adventure and its possible dangers. I remember putting on a proud front, waving him off, then wrapping myself around my two children and hugging them tightly. Now, as he left for his territory each week would he be uneasy about changes in our household and our relationship as a result of my new role? Unlike many instances when I didn't feel he really heard me, this time I sensed he knew our life together was going to be different.

Fired up and ready to go, we loaded ourselves in two cars. Tami and Ray often had after-school activities so they went in one car. Billy, Scott and I headed out in the other car. This would be our routine. I drove the few blocks to the high school and pulled into the empty faculty parking lot. Not surprising, I was early by design. I needed to take one more look at my day's plan before my students arrived.

I walked to my classroom aware of my journey. There would never again be a first day of teaching for me. Key in hand, I unlocked the door, turned on the lights, and without yet breathing, walked to my desk where my plans for the first period of the first day lay open. I deposited my bag on my chair, my purse in the file drawer and my lunch in the faculty room refrigerator.

I wrote my name on the chalkboard along with first period's agenda. Then I walked to the back of the room to take one more look. Okay. It looked fine. Posters alive with color promised their literary messages against a backdrop of institutional green walls.

I watched as student cars pulled into the parking lot and voices in the hall got louder. Here they come! I walked to my door at the back of my classroom ready to greet the students arriving for my class—just as Mrs. Adams had welcomed me as a kindergartner.

My first class of ninth graders filed into the room searching about for just the right seat. Not surprisingly, the back rows filled up first. They couldn't yet know that in my class the room configuration could change with activity: an all class discussion might find us in a large circle, peer writing might dictate small groups, and at other times it would look like it did today.

I looked across the rows at their anxious faces. It was their first high school class, and their nervousness showed. The girls were giggling while a few boys were attempting to act cool. I remembered this stage of awkwardness. In fact, in college when I decided to go into teaching I told my roommate I wanted to be a high school teacher because I remembered how painful it was being a teenager, whether you were popular or not. If I could help even a few get through this uncomfortable period in their lives, I would have achieved a whole lot.

"First things first, let's get acquainted. I see you each have a seat. If you like the one you're sitting in, you may keep it. If not, you may move to one you like better or one closer to your friend."

This was their class. I wanted them to experience both their freedom and responsibility. I looked around at these faces, and I was struck by how very young they looked. A junior and a senior lived in my house, and I had already forgotten how they had looked at this age.

"When you've settled in, I'll assign books and tell you what's going to happen in this class and what I expect of you. Any questions?" I looked around expectantly, knowing someone was curious about something.

"Are you Tami and Ray's mom?"

Sure, they would want to know. This was a small school and a small town where connections were well known. After confirming that they were my children, I took a few moments to give them some information about myself: where I had grown up, gone to college, cities I had lived in, why I had decided to become a teacher and nothing about the FBI. Either they knew that part or they didn't, and I was pretty sure they wouldn't ask.

Almost too soon, the bell rang. My first class was over. In the five-minute break between classes I laid out my materials for my second period sophomore class which pretty much followed the first period plan. Tomorrow we would begin a short story unit. Third period was my planning period, giving me time to regroup for my next three classes.

My room's west facing windows were welcoming the afternoon sun's warmth as I ended the day. I loved that feeling on my skin of being caressed by the rays streaming across the desk filled room. It smelled warm, a toasty odor rather than a sweaty one. Back at my home base. I straightened the desks, re-anchored a couple of the posters and sat down at my desk to look at my plans for my second day.

Billy and Scott arrived on schedule. I so wanted this to be a special year for them. Right now it looked like it was off to a promising start. When I asked them how their day had gone, they chorused "okay," a pretty normal response for two little guys. I could go home, get into my shorts and flip-flops, put my feet up and enjoy a few moments before feeding my family. A reasonable routine.

All in all, it had been a good day, a nice start to the year. This was where I belonged; I knew it.

As the days progressed into weeks and on into months, it became apparent that I needed more help from my family. I couldn't be super-teacher, super-mom, and super-wife. Or how about super anything? While I had initially thought I could be all of those things, I soon realized that the effort I was expending was not infinite. By Friday I was tired and already feeling behind for the upcoming week. My frustration finally peaked. Five other people lived in this house; surely they could do more.

One Saturday after the holidays, as I prepared the shopping list, I looked around my disheveled house. The laundry had piled up in the bathrooms, trash bins were overflowing, recycling needed to be delivered, the furniture and carpets were dusty to say nothing of everybody's junk lying all over the place. And it wasn't just the house, I still had groceries to get for the coming week, laundry to manage and, oh yes, papers to grade. I walked into the bathroom and looked in the mirror. I didn't just look; I inspected the face staring back at me. Just as I suspected, a very tired person. I was in charge of this mess so I was the person to initiate changes.

I dressed for this meeting with myself in my favorite jeans and sweater and sat down at my planning desk where I took out my choice pen and a yellow legal pad from the drawer. First things first. Make a list of all the duties and drudgery required for this family to enjoy some level of orderliness. I needed the list; I'm not sure anyone else cared unless they were running out of clothes. I just hoped Cliff wouldn't greet my observations with an "I told you so" attitude. I had been idealistic about my super capabilities; I didn't have to be reminded.

I took my newly developed list of weekly tasks and began assigning names. With each task I estimated the amount of time to complete just as a production line manager would do. It wasn't perfect, but it was a start.

Cliff came in the door from the recycling plant looking for me. "What's going on? I thought you'd be at the store." It occurred to me that I wasn't the only one who could do the grocery shopping, but maybe that was a different discussion.

"I've made a decision. I have to take control of running this household. Everything seems to be falling in my lap." I looked up to see if he were smiling or frowning.

"Aren't the kids helping? Look, let's have a family meeting and lay the law down."

"Before we do that you and I should talk. I've been working on a task schedule; I'd like you to look at it and tell me what you think." I went to Tami's room and got her desk chair so he would have a place to sit. I didn't want to have him walking around or wandering off. I had to take advantage of this moment.

"I'm sure it's just fine." This was plainly not how he wished to spend his Saturday.

"No, your name is on this list, too. There are things I need your help with."

"Well, you know I'm hardly ever here…." There it was again, the same old line.

"Believe me, I know that, but I'm sure there are some things you can handle. And, if I'm making a task chart, I think all of our names should be on it." I had to hurry. So I decided to dive into what was my biggest concern.

"Here's the big issue for me; you and I need to deal with the finances together. We have more income to manage now and more decisions to make on how the money is spent. I'd like us to sit down each month to make decisions on the budget, savings, and even vacations.

"This finance meeting seems okay, and you're probably right; I do need to know. Anything else? I was afraid managing all of this was going to be an issue when you took this job."

"Well, maybe you were right. It can't be the way it always was; things have to be run differently." This was a start. I was never very good at asking for help, but that was going to change too.

My classes continued to go well. Each year my scared freshmen were still scared, and the girls still found the senior boys interesting, much to the ninth grade boys' dismay. My sophomores were delighted they were no longer on the bottom rung. And after my first year, I no longer taught home-ec.

My presence in the building was prominent. When you teach 150 kids a day out of 450, students know you. Also, because my room was close to the office, it became a stopping off point for many students including Tami and Ray who appeared to be adjusting to my presence in their building. I worked hard to give them space. I grew year by year. I could feel it. I wasn't taller although I felt a stronger presence. I was emerging as a confident educator, and I was growing in even more areas as a person.

Each year as the last day of school arrived, I met it with it a degree of sadness I hadn't expected. Students often walked in with gifts. Others cheered the end of their academic year. Whatever their reaction, I saw older, more confident students than had walked into Room 1 in September. I smiled at them with pride as they chided, "I bet you're going to be glad you don't have to put up with us anymore." I cautioned them that we might be learning together again down the road.

The halls now nearly empty, I went next door to wish my colleague a happy summer. Several staff members were going for Happy Hour, but I declined. I would normally have jumped at the opportunity for socializing, but melancholy had drifted in requiring inner quiet as I dismantled my classroom. Packing up had always been therapeutic, and here I was again re-packaging my latest year of teaching. Boxes, a reminder of a significant part of my life as we traveled around the country, were now housing a different treasure: my academic life, my books, plans, tests, my teaching lifeblood.

I stacked my boxes on the dolly and paused one more time to reflect on the past nine months.

I loved teaching even more than I thought I could.

TWENTY-NINE

Drama

Drama happens when you least expect it. Another school year behind me. Summer was before me and with it a reunion with Tami and Ray coming home from CSU for the summer. I moved toward my car with my final load of class projects I intended to take on over the vacation.

"Hey, Sandy, wait up. We're going up to Grizzly Creek for a little end of school year celebration. Meet us up there and bring Cliff if you'd like." Don was one of my closest friends on the faculty, one I frequently teamed with and the one who helped me write the curriculum for the new gifted program.

"I might do that. I'll stop by Cliff's office and see if he wants to come. What do I need to bring?"

"Nothing. Jenny and I'll pick up some snacks. Just park in the parking area and start up the trail. You'll probably hear us before you see us. See ya up there."

He was right; it would be nice to have a celebration. I drove the few blocks to Cliff's office to see if he wanted to join me; usually he declined. An unwritten truce had entered our relationship: he took care of Bureau stuff, and I took care of school obligations. For whatever reason, this time he agreed to the Grizzly Creek expedition.

"Okay, where are we going?" He always preferred to drive.

"Just park at the pull-off for Grizzly, and we'll walk up the trail. Don and Jenny shouldn't be hard to find."

"Who's going to be here?" he asked. "I guess I'll know most everyone."

"Just a few teachers. It's not a school activity, just a few friends."

We pulled into the make-shift parking area where I revisited with awe the grandeur of the canyon. I hadn't been to this spot for a while, and I was once again energized by its unleashed power. In a couple of months Grizzly would be tame, welcoming its over-heated, sweaty hikers to enjoy a toe dip into its ambling icy waters. I stepped closer to the stream, feeling the soft spray of its gyrations on my warm face. Yes, this was right. I should be celebrating. I was now tenured and experienced. Here I could loudly proclaim with friends how happy I felt, how complete, how satisfied.

"Come on, let's go find the party," I said. "We won't stay long." Cliff and I walked single file up the trail with the sounds of the river our companion. I could feel a wide smile across my face.

"I hear voices," Cliff said. "Must be your group."

"Hey guys, it's us," I called out.

Just then, Cliff stopped at the side of the trail, held up his hand and softly said, "Do you smell that?"

"What? Fish? I smell the river."

"No, it's not the river I smell. I'd know this smell anywhere." He stopped and looked around.

I sniffed the air, and my elation ended. I, too, recognized the odor. Within a few steps we came upon my friends, and the origin of the smell became clear. They were celebrating with a little pot. I dismissed it, but for Cliff it smelled of a set up and betrayal.

"Hi guys," I said. "Beautiful, huh? I love this place." When in doubt, say something. I would have talked forever if it would make this scene go away. Don got up and walked toward us. He had met Cliff once or twice at school functions, but he probably wouldn't have recognized him unless he saw us together.

"Hi, Cliff, it's good to see you. We're just celebrating the end of another successful school year." Then he noticed the icy expression on Cliff's face.

"Look, I know you're Sandy's friends," Cliff said without extending his hand for a shake. "But I can't be party to this kind of behavior. What you're doing is illegal."

"Gosh, I'm sorry. I certainly didn't mean to create a problem." For most of our friends in the valley smoking a little weed wasn't a problem, at least not one Don considered socially acceptable.

"Well, you did. I arrest people for this stuff, and you invite me and my wife to be part of this?" He turned his back as if he didn't know me and began walking back down the trail.

"I'm so sorry, everyone. I guess we can't stay." Embarrassed, I raised my hands in resignation and headed down the trail like an obedient wife, angry with myself and feeling sorry for everyone playing out a role in this drama.

"Don't ever invite me to one of your parties again," Cliff said. "You work with nothing but a bunch of druggies."

I was sure my friends overheard his comment. I stepped up my pace, nearly running back to the car as if to escape the situation and Cliff's anger. I got in the car and slammed the door. "Cliff, aren't you overreacting? I don't say anything when you come home smelling to high heaven of smoke, booze and probably pot. Gosh, we're with pot smokers every time we ski. Why is this so different? Is it because they're my friends?" It was my turn to be angry.

"Look. You don't get it, do you? My job is to enforce the law and smoking pot on a public trail is a crime."

"Maybe it shouldn't be a crime. If it doesn't look like a crime or feel like a crime, is it? I don't care who's smoking what. These are my friends." We drove back to Cliff's office in silence.

"I'll see you at home," I said as I slid into the driver's seat. I pulled out of the parking lot saddened by my celebration experience. I blamed myself for inviting Cliff at all. It really was better if we kept our professional lives separate. For sure, I wouldn't make this mistake again.

The boys were at the pool so I decided to join them rather than dwell on this embarrassing experience. How would I ever explain Cliff's reaction to my colleagues? I would need to go in repair mode in the fall, but at this moment I didn't know how much damage had been done. Would Cliff tell the kids and make a big deal out of it?

Several months ago when Tami and Ray were home for the holidays, we were talking in the living room when the discussion escalated to drug and alcohol use. Cliff had confronted Ray saying, "I suppose you've used marijuana."

"No, but I know plenty of people who do. You probably know a lot of them, too, right here in this perfect little town."

I had suggested that we change the subject before one or both of them began screaming.

Following the debacle at Grizzly Creek, I wasn't looking forward to seeing Cliff so I decided to take Billy and Scott to Charburger, which had just opened for the summer. We drove up, placed our order, parked and sat at one of the two picnic tables. They were excited for swim team and were looking forward to having Tami and Ray home from college for the summer.

Cliff's car was in the driveway; he was on the back porch.

"Hi. We brought you a hamburger from Charburger. I didn't feel like fixing dinner tonight. When did you get here?"

"Just a few minutes ago. I had a stop to make." His tone of voice told Billy and Scott this wasn't going to be a pleasant conversation so they fled to the TV. It told me his stop wasn't any ordinary errand.

"I still can't believe you'd put me in a compromising situation like you did with your friends," he said. "I've worked so hard in this small town to create a pristine reputation. I thought you cared about the values we've lived by." He shook his head in disbelief. I'd committed some mortal sin by inviting him to a casual party.

"I'm sorry. It wasn't my intent to put you in a difficult situation; I should have asked more questions before inviting you. I never gave it a thought there would be drugs. Maybe we were early and they weren't expecting us yet. They wouldn't intentionally embarrass us. They know you work for the FBI."

"I suppose you'd have gone anyway. Even if you'd known there was going to be pot there?" His frown lines grew deeper.

"I don't know. Probably. They're my friends. Besides, we've talked about how many of our friends have used pot. It just isn't a big deal to me. Anyway, it's not for me to judge." I looked at him and shrugged, trying to minimize the issue.

"God, you sound like one of those hippie liberals."

"Do I? I sort of think that's a compliment; at least they think for themselves."

Cliff began walking around the porch, a sign that there was more to come.

"You're going to get a call, so I may as well tell you."

"What are you talking about? Is this more about this afternoon at Grizzly?"

"After you dropped me off at the office I went to see your principal. I told him what we'd experienced with your friends and his teachers and asked him to take action for their illegal behavior. I told him if he didn't handle this, I'd escalate it to the police and make it a law enforcement matter. I know he'll be talking to you." He folded his arms across his chest, a sign that he meant every word he'd just uttered.

I stared at him. I couldn't answer. My mouth was filled with an offensive taste, which clung to the roof of my mouth and tongue. I tried to swallow, but there was nothing there. I rose from my seat on the bench, grabbed his hamburger and threw it across the porch landing it in the crevice of the cinder block wall. Words erupted from the vileness.

"You had no right to do that. You didn't even talk to me. Once again you sneak behind my back. I work in that building with those teachers. That's my world, my territory. You had no right. How would you like it if I tramped into the inner sanctum of the Denver FBI and told the SAC I didn't appreciate the type of people you were working with, that I wanted him to demand you sever your relationships with your beloved informants? But, no, I have enough respect for your work to stay out of the way. Obviously, you don't respect me or the people I work with. With your actions you've compromised me with my colleagues; you've sculpted a person I'm not, one who judges anyone and everyone with impunity. I'm not that person. But I am the one who will do whatever is necessary to repair my relationship with my colleagues.

"I don't understand why you had those people for friends in the first place—a bunch of hippies."

"I don't expect you to understand anything about me or my job, but it's mine to build, not yours. Look, stick with your own druggies, your felons, your rapists, spies and all the rest, and I'll stick with my talented teachers who may once in a while enjoy a joint."

I slammed the door and walked down to the river, walking further than normal, propelled by anger. I thought about how sad I was for all of us. I liked these people. Bob would call me, probably either tonight or in the morning. I'd talk to him. I'd reassure him it was all an innocent mistake and that perhaps Cliff overreacted because of his line of work. But

Cliff was the FBI, and Bob would be fearful of the town gossip about his teachers. And, here I was again the damn FBI agent's wife.

I would profess my allegiance to the school and its staff. I would apologize. This would probably mitigate the situation with Bob. But what about my friends?

My conversation with Bob went as planned. He just wanted it over; he wasn't into unpleasantness or confrontation. As for Don and Jenny, I didn't see them over the summer. When the faculty assembled for a series of meetings before students reported, I determined to clear the air with Don. I went up to his room where he was putting up some posters. He turned as I entered. A hug would have normally followed and something like, "Here we go again. What are we going to do together this year?" Don and I had created some great team teaching pairing social studies with literature.

I walked up to him. No hug. I extended my hand.

"Please, Don, I'm so sorry about what happened. It was an honest mistake; I never should have asked Cliff to join us. It was terrible for all of us. Please accept my apology."

"It was rough. You know the parents here as well as the administration find me a bit too liberal. I really think they'd like me to be gone. This incident surely didn't help."

"Don, I told Bob it was all innocent, that no harm was done and that it all should be kept quiet. There's another thing you need to know. Whether I like it or not, I live in two worlds: this one here at school, and Cliff's FBI world at home. Sometimes the two are alien to one another."

"Bob was pretty hard on us, especially me, and I still don't know how long I'll have a job here."

"Okay then, let's dream up some truly great things to do for the kids this year. Then, there'll be no grounds. Please, Don. I like you a lot. I want our professional relationship to be like it was."

He put down the poster he was about to hang and walked toward me. No hug—not yet.

"Okay, let's do it. We'll figure out the 'it' as we go along."

I smiled. I knew it would take time to rebuild a level of trust, but it would happen.

THIRTY

It's a Matter of Economics

I could feel fall's approach. The night air was a few degrees cooler, and I convinced myself my backyard mountain with its aspens, sage and wildflowers was already beginning to sport its vibrant colors.

In my own tradition of enjoying my first cup of coffee on the porch in those early morning hours, that tranquil part of my day, my solitude was broken by Cliff's voice.

"Nice out here, huh?"

"Hmmm. I love this time of day. It's funny, I wake up around 4:00 with ideas for my classes. When I start a new school year I always have so many thoughts and ideas. Then I can't go back to sleep."

"I guess I can understand that. It's been a long time since I've taught although I was recently approached to teach at Quantico. I'm not sure if I told you. By the way, I was talking to my friend, Glenn, yesterday in LA. Remember him from Jacksonville? Anyway, he's in California now. He loves the work there; big office, lots of activity, high profile." I shook my head, waiting for where this discussion was going.

"I remember Glenn. That's good. What else? Is he still married to Sharon?"

"I didn't ask him about his personal life. We just talked work. Anyway, he told me they're looking for experienced agents to work some classified cases out of the L.A office."

Okay. Now I knew where this was going.

"I'm sure those big offices are always looking for experienced agents. Who wants that life? Surely you're not interested; you've already done the big office thing."

"I thought California might be attractive to you since it's close to your parents." He extended his hands palms up across the table suggesting a possibility? The expression on my face must have told him my answer. I folded my hands around my coffee mug, stretched out my legs and stared blankly at my husband.

"Look, Cliff, those days are over. We have four kids, and I have a career I've waited for way too long. The answer is 'no'. I'm not interested in going anywhere, not even to be near my parents." The promise I had made to myself on Loveland Pass was a serious one, one I was in the process of fulfilling.

Shortly after taking my job, he had brought up the possibility of returning to the D.C. area, possibly to Quantico. Saying no to these possibilities didn't make me feel controlling or powerful, just confident in finally being able to look out for myself and my children.

Discussion over. On to fall and football and plans for skiing. Not quite so fast. There was another idea brewing.

"I think I'm ready for something new," Cliff said. "The one huge disadvantage here is the size of my territory. I'm tired of driving hundreds of miles every week, mostly on two lane roads. There's always some obstruction: a wreck, rocks on the road, a wandering elk, or cattle crossing to seasonal pasture."

"Dave's retiring, isn't he, and then you can take the Aspen territory and won't have the driving issue at all."

"He's going to retire, but it won't be for another year or so. Besides, I don't want the Aspen assignment. But I think I've come up with a solution."

Oh no, not moving. That cow had died. Curious would describe my expression.

"You do? A new territory? Get another agent to handle the far north? Convince Dave to retire earlier than planned?" Those were my immediate reactions.

"No, I don't think any of those ideas would fly with the Bureau, but maybe I could convince them that having a trained mountain pilot would be to their advantage."

"A trained what?"

"You know, I've always wanted to fly." He actually looked serious.

I laughed.

"No, I didn't know that. Is that the same as always wanting to be an FBI agent? Where is this coming from?"

"Well, I've done some calculating, and I could save the Bureau a lot of money by flying my territory instead of driving. It could be a huge savings." He had a piece of paper in his hand that was now waving. "Wait, just listen. I couldn't fly for the military because my vision wasn't good enough …."

"No, you wait. What are you saying, that you now want to become a pilot for the FBI? Do they even have pilots?" My incredulous expression was causing him to smile.

"They do have a few; in fact, they have one in Denver. His name is Bill Smithson."

"And I suppose you've talked to him about all this." Just when I thought my life was stabilizing and our lifestyle was resembling that of normal people, a new idea flew into the conversation, probably one that had been germinating until just this moment.

"You actually think the Bureau is going to pay you to fly your territory? Is that where this is going?" Nothing this man came up with really shocked me, but his ability to pull it off did, and I had often envied him this uncanny ability to manipulate his career direction.

"I believe there's a case to be made. I've worked the numbers, and they look good both in terms of money and my time. It now takes me hours to get from Glenwood to Steamboat; whereas, if I flew I could get there in an hour or so and have the whole day to work my contacts." He was trying his logic out on me.

"Okay, tell me how you get to this point of savings. You aren't currently a pilot. Surely, you need a license to fly one of these things. Who pays for this license? And how long will this take?" Learning to fly would involve time he already didn't have with us. Wrinkling my forehead and shaking my head, I retreated to the kitchen for a coffee refill.

"I've worked out some of the details, and I've a solid idea how much this will cost. Actually, as I get started, it looks like it would be cost effective to buy a plane, then sell it when I'm licensed. That way I wouldn't have to pay plane rental for lessons or practice."

This wasn't a new idea. He'd been working on it for some time, probably since I took my job. Our bi-level communication was back.

"You know the budget; we don't have spare money for flying lessons. So where's this money coming from? We have four children to educate, and with my job we're just beginning to feel a little relief from living paycheck to paycheck." I glanced at the charts outlining instructor costs, plane rental costs, insurance, fuel costs and more.

"Cliff, I don't want to own a plane, and I think your idea of becoming a pilot is pure folly." I looked squarely into his eyes. I would not flinch from this latest notion. "There's another thing. It's not enough for me to worry about you driving your territory; now I get to worry about your flying over these mountains? These small planes go down all the time."

"There you go again with that worry stuff. Besides the driving benefit, there are personal benefits to my getting my pilot's license. We could fly to California to see your folks...."

"No, we couldn't. I won't get into one of those dinky things. I can barely stand to fly commercial."

"You'll see. First of all, it's safer than driving a car." He was smiling.

"Cliff, look at me. Count me out on this one. I won't fly with you. No trips in a small plane. Plus, you must be kidding if you think the Bureau is going to buy any of this plan."

"Actually, my timing may be just right. I've been checking around, and it seems the Bureau is informally putting together a cadre of pilots primarily for surveillances. The Soviets are using our national parks as places for intelligence drops so air surveillance is perfect for this kind of work. Bill thinks the office might go for a proposal where I would fly my territory and also fly these surveillances."

"I see the same glitch. You aren't a pilot."

"I've been working on that too. There's a very good instructor here in Glenwood."

"I didn't even know we had an airport. There's some place to land between these mountains?"

"Yup. It's perfect for mountain training. According to Bill, the Denver office wants a mountain pilot. If I can sell the Bureau on my plan, they'll cover most of my training and expenses for the plane. I've started working

on the proposal; it will save the FBI money, and it will give them a pilot."
And give me tremors.

He began to pull some papers from his briefcase. "I've made some schedules and looked at costs. Here, let me show you."

I stared at him and wondered if I had somehow landed in a looney bin with a person I'd never seen before.

"This has gone from a positive discussion of our careers here to buying an airplane. Either you've lost your reasoning or I have for sitting here listening to this. What are you thinking?" I was married to a madman.

The first of these impossible schemes was the one where he was accepted into the FBI. He was sure he wouldn't make it, but he did. Then, there was the interview with Hoover for the supervisory promotion to D.C. It probably wouldn't happen, but it did. Most recently, there was the transfer to Glenwood, thanks to Director Gray. Now, he was going to try this?

"I'm just going to say I hope the Bureau doesn't approve your plan but, knowing you, they probably will." The whole thought of his flying around in these mountains in a small plane was terrifying. For him, it was another challenge, another way to set himself apart. From what? Me?

His plan unfolded. He found a used blue and white Piper Tripacer for his training; he hired the local instructor, and he flew every available minute. The savings went down as did his time with us. Throughout his enthusiasm was unbridled, announcing to Bill and Scott that soon he would be able to take them for a ride over the town, over the valley and even over some of the lower peaks. I listened and shook my head. It was one thing for him to be in this flimsy flying thing, but I didn't want any of the kids with him. And I certainly wasn't going up.

He soloed, then got his license, bought another larger plane and then started working on his instructor's license, his instrument and commercial ratings and God knows what else. Like all the previous impossibles, the FBI bought his proposal. They would pay all costs associated with flying his territory and for other flying assignments as well.

Our conversations became multi-level. For him, it was all about flying: how many hours he had, how close he was to certifications. For me, it was about the kids and my job. And in this division there was a new comfort.

THIRTY-ONE

An Unplanned Pause

How high can you pile your responsibilities before they begin to list on the plate requiring adjustments that create another imbalance?

My teaching job was a joy and stretched my imagination and creativity. I found myself writing new curriculum, inventing multi-disciplinary course work for creative students and presenting new, interesting possibilities to the school board. All was well. Except it wasn't. I was sacrificing time for my family and myself, often teaching five different courses in a day, coaching drill team and cheerleading and taking graduate courses for my own professional development. The women's movement had told me I could have it all. They failed to mention the cost.

When you are a couple marching out of step and the only connection is your children, you take a deep breath and hope the connection holds. He talks about flying—you think about a commercial flight to a romantic vacation spot. He wants to buy a new plane and does. He loves the freedom he finds in the air. You love a romantic dinner on the water in some exotic place. You are both lonely even when together.

Cliff was happier than I had seen him since his early FBI days: he was chasing fugitives and flying the mountains. I was currently seduced by what's next. Would it be a Master's, an administrative position?

On Wednesday before Thanksgiving break, 1982, I stood before my fourth period class leading them in discussion of a literary piece. As I looked out over the class, the faces before me blurred, and I felt myself lean into the front row, grasping the closest desk, holding on until the room's movement stopped. I moved cautiously around my desk to my rolling chair. The faces before me were a little clearer so I spoke to them from behind my desk.

"There's only a few minutes of class. You may work on your assignment or visit until the bell. Have a wonderful Thanksgiving holiday." I rested my forehead on my hands feeling a warm moistness emanating from my forehead like the onset of the flu. *Not now. I can't get sick now just when I'll have everyone home for the holiday.*

Morning came; I wasn't better. Nor was I better in the mornings to follow. New symptoms like chest congestion, fever of 104, and terrible chest pain. Cliff and Tami managed the turkey and its trimmings with my guidance from the bedroom while at the same time suggesting I check in with the emergency room.

Surely, a few days, and I would feel better. Not to be. By Sunday I knew I had pneumonia and most likely pleurisy, judging from the pain in my chest and back. Monday morning I called in sick and checked in at the hospital. I was burning up again. I threw off the sheets covering me on the gurney.

Shortly after settling in, Dr. Kelly came in.

"Sandy, I've looked at the x-rays and other tests. You have lobar pneumonia as well as pleurisy. It's very serious. Listen to me, people die from this."

I nodded with tears running down my face. I was sad for myself, my family and my students. Why hadn't I slowed down? I must have done something to cause this.

My nurse came in with needles and liquids. She asked me to sit up and told me in seconds I would feel no pain. She was right. She shook the needle and inserted it into the IV port. I took a breath as I felt the warm liquid move from my wrist, up my arm across my chest and into the other arm. Soothing, heavenly warmth flooded my body. I had experienced the miracle of morphine. I lay back down and immediately slept pain free.

As I began to recover, I forced myself to think about my professional future and the possible correlation between the way I pushed myself professionally and this physical breakdown. Maybe I needed to back off, way off. Defeated, I wrote Nick Mathews, my mentor, a letter of resignation telling him I didn't want to quit, but I had to get well, and that was going to take time, perhaps as long as six months. I assured him I would call him for an appointment when I was released. No need for an appointment. The next morning he stood by my bed holding my folded up letter in his hand. He waved it toward me.

"Sandy, I never got this letter, and you never wrote it. Do we agree?"

I nodded, and he pulled a chair up next to me.

"You're very sick, and I have no intention of losing you. Your students and the district need you to be in your classroom, but first you have to get well. How about this: you go on sick leave second semester; we'll get a long-term sub, and next fall you'll continue right where you left off." He nodded with a smile.

I smiled back.

And so it went. I got better, slowly.

A second miracle hit. She was an English teacher named Julie Andersen who had been subbing in the district for a couple of years. I knew I had to turn my students over to my replacement, and I had to do it unselfishly, which would be hard for me. Once I began to regain my strength, I worked through my second semester class files, arranging plans in order of importance so as to assist Julie. When she came by the house to pick up the plans, I knew my students were going to be in excellent hands.

Early spring, I received a phone call from Gil Reese, our new principal who had replaced Bob O'Neil.

"Sandy, I wanted to talk to you about something pretty special. The senior class has come to me with a request that you present the commencement address at graduation. We all hope you'll say yes." Did he hear me take that breath?

"I'm speechless. This is a wonderful honor. Please convey my acceptance and appreciation."

I hung up the phone and wrapped my arms around myself in glee. This particular graduation class had been difficult from ninth grade onward, and I had worked hard with many of them. Now we had all made it.

As my health improved I began to think more seriously about what my future professional life might look like. I loved being in the classroom, but …. maybe counseling would be a good next step.

I ran the counseling direction by Nick, my mentor. "It may be a fit, but it won't accomplish what I'm hearing. If you want to effect change in education, you need to be in administration. That's where you have the responsibility and authority to make a difference. As a principal you could have a whole building working on your ideas." He opened his palms face up to indicate the possibilities in what he said.

"I don't know. That would put me at a distance from the kids. I don't know if I'd like it, but I'll certainly think about your suggestion."

I left his office feeling flattered and somewhat confirmed. I had time. I would do some research.

I'd been talking to Cliff on a limited basis about this graduate school idea of mine, but he was busy with his own professional plan. Dave had recently retired, and Cliff as the senior agent had reluctantly agreed to take over the Aspen territory. The office was already short of manpower so the Bureau authorized a third agent for the Glenwood office. While he wasn't driving as much, his flying requirements had expanded to include the continental U.S. and Puerto Rico.

One spring afternoon, Cliff came home for a late lunch.

"It's nice to have you home in the middle of the day," I said. "I haven't seen much of you lately."

"Yeah, it's been busy. The Hostage Negotiator training at Quantico was the best. I hope I'll get called to use the training. They're putting together a SWAT team too."

"Things are changing in the Bureau, aren't they? Women agents, pilots, a new director."

"Speaking of the Director, William Webster likes to vacation in Aspen. I've already talked to him about places to stay. My guess is we'll get to meet him this summer."

"That's interesting. You always seem to connect with these directors."

"What's going on with you now that you're feeling better?" he asked.

"Remember when I told you I was thinking about getting my Master's and Type D so I could be a building principal? Do you think I look like a principal?"

He smiled that beguiling smile, "I suppose so. Would you like all the discipline though?"

"I'm not sure, but I've been contacting schools, and CSU has a program that looks like it might fit with my timeframe. For any program I'll need to take the GRE so I've scheduled that for Grand Junction in a couple of weeks." As I talked, I looked at him, and he appeared preoccupied. That was okay for now.

I met with Dr. Jarvis from CSU to plan my program, which would require me to be on campus for two summers. This would mean I would have completed my Master's and Type D by the end of summer 1984.

I left the meeting exhilarated. I could do this. My Master's would mean a nice pay increase. And if I were successful down the road in landing an administrative job, it would mean a larger pay increase, finally making me financially independent.

When I outlined my final plan to Cliff, he had reservations other than the familiar one about not being available.

"I didn't think you were this serious about school. I don't know how we're going to pull this off."

"Look, take some vacation time. You owe this to me. It's your turn for a change." My firmness surprised even me.

"I know you've sacrificed a lot for my job, but the boys are off in the summer and…"

"And there will always be something," I said. "Look, I believe I've figured out this summer. It may sound kind of kinky, but I can rent an apartment in married housing. Ray can stay with me, which means we won't have his rent. Bill and Scott can go to swim camp at CSU and live with me as well. It probably won't be an ideal study environment, but I can make it work."

"You're right, it is kind of different."

"The second summer, though, I need to be there longer so I'll live in the graduate dorm. This most likely means you'll need to take some vacation time. I'm telling you early so it won't come as a surprise. Look, I want to do this, and I know I can. I just need some support from you."

My confused looking husband nodded in agreement, probably hoping none of this would happen. But it did.

THIRTY-TWO

How Can You Know When It's Right?

Special events often transpire as surprises. Such was the case late one afternoon following my first summer in graduate school. It was nice to be home, back in my own valley with my family.

"Hi. How about a date? Want to go to Aspen for dinner?"

"Now? Tonight? What's the occasion?"

"No occasion. Just thought it'd be nice to have dinner with you. Now that I'm working in Aspen, I know more places."

"Sure. Let me change."

"You don't have to dress up. We won't go real fancy."

"Yes, I do. I have a date, remember?"

It was a date. Sort of. We drove Highway 82, the beautiful scenic two-lane road into the iconic ski town. I hadn't been to this part of the valley in a while so it was a stunning reminder of the rugged beauty surrounding this former mining town. Cliff negotiated the narrow streets expertly to our dining spot where the host ushered us to a private table.

"This is pretty special. I love times like this. I'm so glad you're working in Aspen. Maybe there can be many more of these dates."

"I know you like it here. Remember when we came to Colorado and looked at a house in Aspen? You really liked it then. We could have made a lot of money if we had bought that house."

"Yup. But we didn't, and Glenwood has been okay," I said. "How are you liking working here in Aspen?"

"It's not my first choice, but as long as I get to fly as the other part of my job, I'm okay. Speaking of my job, I have to ask you something," he said. "While we're here would you mind if we surveilled a couple of properties? We have our personal car, and you're with me so no one will suspect it's the FBI. I'm working a couple of new cases here that I'm sure are laundry operations; in fact, I've been going through their trash." He looked at me expectantly.

"I'm a decoy, is that it? Is this the reason for the dinner?" My shattered expression must have been evident. Why? Why did he do this to me? Set me up and then ruin it all?

"Don't be silly. I thought this would be a nice date. It was, wasn't it?"

I shook my head and turned away revealing my disappointment. Nothing had changed: Bureau first, everyone else last.

Soon, we would celebrate twenty-five years together. We once loved each other, and maybe there was still some left. Or maybe it was called something else like two people living together with separate lives, two individuals hungry for something more but not knowing what. We followed convention and celebrated our anniversary in Hawaii. We swam, sunbathed, drank mai tais and reminisced about our life together.

"You know, honey, this has really been an exciting adventure with you. You've been my right hand in this FBI journey. I can say I've loved every minute of it."

"I know you have. It's been different for me: lonely and scary mostly. I married you because I wanted to be with you. But you haven't been around much. I find it very sad how little you know about your children or about me for that matter." I twisted the stem of my glass looking for answers.

"No, I haven't been around much. It's not that I didn't want to be. And now that I'm in Aspen, close to home, I can have more time with the family."

"That would be nice but Tami and Ray are gone, and you scarcely know Bill and Scott."

A vacation does not a relationship make, but it could be a beginning, another ragged start. Thousands of miles from the FBI it could feel renewed.

Tanned, rested and after vacationing and a semester off teaching, I was ready to finish graduate school. Dorm life took me back to my days as a freshman coed. It was me and five weeks of study, a thesis and orals to complete. Once home, I wouldn't have much of a break before school began, but I was curious to begin a preliminary job search. I had made many good contacts at CSU and now wanted to be sure they didn't forget me.

Seated in my favorite spot, I looked out my dining room window framing my view of Mt. Sopris, reminding me how much I had missed my valley these past two summers. I looked at her and marveled at her snowy field reflected in pinks and purples by the sun. As the afternoon faded, I wistfully watched clouds descend over her twin peaks blanketing her for the night's rest. I was reassured by her presence. What limitations could there be in my life with such inspiration?

"Cliff, do you have any need to go to Denver this week?"

"No, I don't think so. Why?"

"Remember my telling you about the principal from Bear Creek that I met at CSU? Well, he called and would like me to interview with him this week. I just need to tell him the day."

"Is this a for real interview? Are you telling me you're thinking about taking a job in Denver? I don't know if the Bureau would move me there."

"I'm not really interested in this particular position because I don't think moving to Denver would be good for Bill and Scott. The interview practice could be helpful though. Also, it's a real compliment."

I made the drive to Denver alone and left the interview feeling someday there might be an opportunity there, sometime in the future but not now.

Shortly after the Denver interview, a new contact I'd made at CSU called to tell me a position had opened at one of Grand Junction's high schools. Would I be interested? I scheduled an interview but upon meeting the principal I knew I would not be a fit in that particular building. Maybe next year a position would open in my own district. I drove home thinking the job search was over for the current year.

Within days, another high school principal from grad school, called to tell me a different Grand Junction position was opening, this one at Fruita Junior High. The principal was looking for an assistant principal who would administer an independent seventh grade building. I waited for a call from personnel and scheduled an interview. I liked the principal, I liked his educational philosophy and I especially liked the idea of having my own building: twelve teachers, two hundred seventy students. Perfect.

While this new job direction was as yet a fantasy, it might materialize. If the job were right, could I make the move—how selfish was I to consider it? Would Bill and Scott be truthful with me about leaving their friends and school? And Cliff? How would he take this decision? Well, it wasn't mine to make yet.

On the eighty-mile drive home from my third interview in two weeks, I mulled the pros and cons and how to approach my family. If this job were offered, I wanted to accept, but I knew if the boys had objections, I wouldn't do it. I rationalized Cliff's position by telling myself he only had two more years to retirement. Besides, he might be able to get a transfer to Grand Junction.

"Yeah, it's the right job," I said. "I'd have my own building, my own staff, my own students and a secretary." I looked at my family sitting across from me at the picnic table.

"It sounds good. I can probably get a transfer to Junction since I fly out of there more often than not," Cliff said. He actually looked optimistic.

"Bill, Scott, what do you think? They haven't offered me the job yet, but I really want to know how you feel." I looked at each one waiting for the other to answer.

"You don't have the job yet, Mom," Bill said. "It might be okay."

"I guess we need to know more about it, Mom," Scott said.

"Well, you'd know the swim team guys, and there is a high school team. They'd sure like to have you swimming for them. And since the high schools are bigger, you'd have more courses to choose from." I told myself I'd better slow down.

Cliff and I had a decent discussion later that evening, and his response was favorable. We decided if I felt good about the interview and if the job were offered, I should take it. This time I was making the career decision. But it wasn't just a career decision; it was a life adjustment, a 180 degree turn away from what was familiar but confining toward a liberated state, one where I assumed responsibility for my own happiness. My arms goosebumped themselves with the thought, the excitement of this new venture, my statement about myself.

Two days later I was offered the job. By this time we were approaching the start of school. Many years later as I try to recall our discussion, much of what transpired around this decision is mushy. Was Cliff sincerely supportive? Did the boys really want to move? Or did I tell myself this? How guilty was I going to feel if this didn't turn out well?

Decisions had to be made quickly. We needed a place to live. I needed to resign one position and accept another. Cliff and I decided that the boys and I would take an apartment and be in Junction during the week and in Glenwood on the weekends. With a few days left of the summer break, I found an apartment, moved us in, registered Bill and Scott and reported to my new position.

Another new community; this time it was my idea. It had been eleven years since our last move, but I hadn't forgotten how to make even temporary quarters a home. I did question whether Grand Junction could ever be home. Or would we always have one foot in Glenwood where we had planted strong roots.

Glenwood would hold us for now because the Bureau turned down Cliff's request for a transfer to Junction even though there was a vacancy, even though he flew out of the Junction airport and could still cover his territory from there. Why? Because they were the Bureau and they could. When Cliff got the notice declining his transfer, I had accepted the position, and the boys were already settled into school. We would need to make it work even in the short term. Besides, in two years at age fifty Cliff could retire and live where he wanted. That's what we told ourselves.

My plan was in action. I told myself on a daily basis that this relocation would prove to be a positive move for the three of us. From the perspective of time, I believe accepting the position was my declaration of independence. I no longer needed to ask anyone for permission regarding the life changes I saw fit to make.

September, October, November came and went with a frenzy of activity. Cliff was with us as much as he could be and was supportive of our move. He liked Grand Junction and flew from the airport at least once or twice a week.

I loved my new job, especially working with my teachers to come up with creative ways to deliver instruction. It was everything I had hoped it would be.

Before long, the holidays were upon us, and because we had moved into a larger townhome, we decided to have Thanksgiving in Junction. Tami and Ray would not be joining us this year.

Traditionally, Cliff and I spent the Friday following Thanksgiving doing our Christmas shopping. This year would be no exception. We saw the boys off to Glenwood for skiing before heading out to breakfast and shopping. As we moved from store to store, we were attacked by cold and a few flurries. Skies were gray threatening even more snow. A good day for shopping even though that wasn't Cliff's favorite activity. We finished with all of our purchases around 4:00 p.m. and settled in for coffee before heading home.

In the coziness of the café, I looked across the table into my husband's dark brown eyes. He was staring intently at me. He smiled.

"I love you," he said. "This has been a really nice day. I don't even like shopping, but this was nice."

"It was, and now we're ready for Christmas. I'm so excited to have everybody home for the holidays."

"Can we make it? Our relationship, I mean?" he asked.

"We have a lot of baggage, and it's not all pretty."

"Post retirement, I'll have a new lease on life. I'm looking forward to doing something new."

"Some sane job where you're home?" I smiled.

We finished our coffee in silence and walked out to the car carrying our remaining packages. Once inside, behind the wheel, Cliff reached for my hand in his familiar way.

"I'm so lucky," he said. "My life has been so full and complete. Only two years left in this career. It's been good to us though. And, you know, I've done everything in life I've ever wanted to do. I don't think many people can say that." He looked at me questioningly.

"I can't. There is so much more I want to try and places I want to see. I could still make a very long list."

"I have a beautiful family, a job I love, flying, travel. What more could there be? I've accomplished everything I've set out to do." He clasped his hands in the space between us like an exclamation point.

I felt a little mystified by his statements. Was he saying he had nothing left to live for? Was he through at 48? No. Surely, he was just reflecting on his life as he saw it that afternoon.

Part Seven

From there to here is rarely a straight line in living one's journey

Grand Junction
1984

THIRTY-THREE

Missing

On this particular Saturday morning when the light teased me with a new day of possibilities, stillness accompanied me as I padded around the kitchen enjoying my domain, all by myself, a time just for me. I stared out my kitchen window and waited for the coffee maker to complete its gurgling, already savoring its thick warmth. I filled my cup and stood watching the light grow brighter on the eastern horizon. It was nice to be able to see a sunrise once again; that was something I had missed in Glenwood. Moving to my favorite kitchen chair, I warmed my hands around my much loved mug, the one whose tumble from the kitchen counter had resulted in a painful gap in its once perfect rim.

So far the decision to move to Grand Junction had been a good one. My job was going well; I was learning and had already been able to implement some programs to help kids. One of those was the formation of a team to help students in a crisis. I had invited people from throughout the district to participate. Now it was being discussed as a possibility in other buildings.

As a family we were feeling our way although, surprisingly, Cliff spent more time with us in Grand Junction than we did with him in Glenwood. That might change once we were into ski season. Thoughts rambled through my head only to be interrupted by the ringing phone, as if it were announcing something pressing. It would have to be important at this hour. I grabbed for the receiver before it woke the rest of the family. Cliff had already heard it and assumed it would be for him. Only the Bureau called at this hour.

"Sure," I heard him say. "No problem. I know this case has been developing. I'm pretty sure the plane's available. I'll need to check weather as well. I'll get back to you."

"What's the assignment this time?" I asked. Can I fix you some breakfast? Coffee, toast?" I looked at him wistfully, really wanting him to be home with us this weekend.

"Maybe a quick cup of coffee. The office needs me to fly to Laramie to provide air surveillance for a ground investigation of the Order, a group of white supremacists. Denver's thinking it might not take all day so I should be back home late afternoon." He sounded like he was reading from a teletype.

"I don't suppose you could suggest that someone in the Denver office fly this one. I was hoping we would have this weekend together."

"Hey, I'm sorry, but the office wouldn't have called if they thought someone else could handle this. Since I should be home early, how about a date?"

"Sure. The district Christmas party's tonight, or we could do something else."

Methodically, Cliff gathered his necessities: holster, gun, credentials, and wallet.

"You know it won't always be like this." his voice softening. "Hang in there a little longer."

"I'll miss you. Stay safe, please."

As he leaned to kiss me, I felt more melancholy than usual. I returned to my chair thinking of the many tasks on my list. This might be a good day to get a start on them.

"Hi, Mom, where's Dad? Did I just hear him leave?" Scott asked.

"Yup, the office called early, and he's on his way to Laramie. Should be home this afternoon though. What are you up to today?"

"If Bill will drive me up to Powderhorn, I'd like to try out the ski area here."

"Maybe he'll ski with you."

"No, I don't want to ski," Bill said as he walked down the stairs, "but I'll drive him up there."

Scott would be skiing, Cliff would be flying, and I would be marking items off my proverbial list. As the afternoon approached, skies darkened, threatening snow.

Perhaps Cliff would be staying in Laramie.

No, mid-afternoon he called with an update.

"Hi, hon, well, this was a bummer and a complete waste. I got up here, and they cancelled the surveillance. Good thing is I'll be leaving here shortly. Should be home in a few hours." His voice barely disguised his irritation.

"That's great," I said. "So maybe we can have that date. Scott went skiing, and Bill is going to pick him up. Call me if your plans change. Stay safe." I worried a little less when he flew during daylight.

"I will. Love you." His reassuring voice soothed any apprehensions.

Shortly before 4:00 p.m., Bill came into the kitchen where I was working. "Mom, wanna ride up to the ski area with me to pick up Scott?"

"Sure. I'm tired of working on this stuff. Besides I've never been to Powderhorn." I welcomed a reason to leave the house. With a bit of luck, their dad would be home by the time we got down from the mountain.

As Bill maneuvered our 4-wheel drive up the mountain two-lane road, I felt my spirits lifted somewhat by the stark whiteness of the softly falling flurries. Evergreen trees hugging one another for warmth stood as sentries as we wound our way to the resort. Scott flashed us a grin as we approached the lodge entrance as if to say, "You guys missed a great day!" Five inches of new snow had provided the perfect base for his fast, new skis, an early Christmas present. The sun had even broken through the cloud cover at the top. It had been one of those perfect days when God's landscape was painted faultlessly.

Descending the curvy, narrow road toward home was a bit more worrisome than the drive up, but Bill mastered the turns like a pro. A few miles into the curving descent, I felt an uneasiness not affiliated with the road conditions. I adjusted my position in the back seat to shake off the discomfort. It wasn't that I felt sick; it was a more troubling, disquieting sensation. I looked at my watch to confirm it was not yet evening. Its face read 5:43 p.m. Cliff would be home soon; he might already be there.

Not to be. Once home, I checked the answering machine: no messages. Not even Cliff's voice to say he was leaving Laramie or that he had arrived in Junction. A little unusual, but perhaps he had been in a hurry to head home. Someone would call soon.

There wasn't a call. Only a knock on the door around midnight.

From my bedroom I had heard the car pull into our cul de sac. I walked to the window where, through the darkness, I saw a car, a sedan, not Cliff's car. I saw two men in suits exit the vehicle and walk to my door. *They're agents; I'd recognize them anywhere*, I told myself. *Why are they here? They didn't have to come out in the snow.*

As their gloved hands made contact with the oak door, I quietly descended the stairs. I opened the door to a familiar movie script: Frank, Cliff's partner, and another FBI agent wearing dark suits and even darker expressions,

"Sandy, this is John from the Grand Junction office. We're sorry to be here at this hour, but we need to talk to you about Cliff's surveillance flight today." Frank's words came slowly from his downturned mouth. This tall, slim man had a sincerity and soft-spoken demeanor that would never cause him to be identified as an agent.

John and Frank entered, shaking the newly fallen snow from their shoes, which at the moment seemed incongruous. At a time like this, what did I care about snow sliding from their boots onto the cheap entryway tile?

"I thought about calling you, Frank. I haven't heard from Cliff, which is a little unusual although sometimes the dispatcher isn't real good at contacting me. When Cliff called this afternoon, he told me he'd be home late afternoon/early evening. I'm thinking he must have decided to stay over."

"Please sit down," I said. "Would you like some coffee? I can make some," I pleaded for a diversion. Tears began to build beneath my lashes for what I didn't know.

"Frank, I don't think your news is good. Something's wrong, or you wouldn't be here." If I kept talking I wouldn't have to hear what these two men had to say. Nothing is scarier than silence unless it's what you fear most.

"Sandy, just before we came here we received information from the FAA stating that Cliff left Laramie late this afternoon headed for Grand

Junction." He looked at me, allowing me painful seconds to process the message. I could feel my body collapsing from inside out.

"How late?" I whispered. "I had a call from him about 3:00 this afternoon saying the surveillance had been cancelled and he'd be leaving for home earlier than he'd thought. So where is he?" I struggled to stuff the rising panic from erupting.

"The FAA said he filed a flight plan with Denver before he left Laramie; however, since leaving the Laramie Airport there's been no radio contact. That was around 5:15."

"What time did he leave? Sometime between 3:00 when I talked to him and 5:00 when the radio contact ceased? Why didn't anyone call me when the radio contact stopped? That was seven hours ago, Frank, and the Bureau in its infinite wisdom just got around to asking someone to contact me?"

"No, listen to me, Sandy. Air traffic control has made numerous attempts to contact him. Right now his plane is considered missing. Not down, missing. The authorities have drawn no other conclusions. He could just be somewhere out of radio contact." Frank's voice pleaded with me to understand.

Didn't I know missing wasn't the same as dead? But it could be.

"No, please stop, Frank, give me a minute. Once again, the Bureau leaves the agent's wife and family alone, knowing nothing." I meant my words to be weapons.

"Sandy. I've known you and Cliff for a long time, and this was the last role I ever wanted to play. Even without much information, we're pretty sure we'll find him somewhere in the wilderness area near Meeker."

Frank had been Cliff's partner for over five years, working difficult Bureau cases together. In addition, Frank had lost his seven-year-old son to the Roaring Fork River in a kayaking accident. That had been two years ago, and neither he nor those closest to him had recovered. Frank was a man who knew loss. I looked into his icy blue eyes and saw the tragedy all over again.

Frank continued, "Denver has a ground search party with air support organized for daybreak. We plan to meet at John's house here in Junction around 5:00 a.m. as part of a ground search and rescue party. We'll caravan to Meeker. If you could bring blankets, warm clothes and some snacks, that would be helpful. We want you and the kids to be with us, Sandy."

"Yes, of course. I'll need to call Tami and Ray so they can get on their way from Ft. Collins and Colorado Springs. Waiting is the hardest part, isn't it? The not knowing makes every possibility real." Frank shook his head sadly in the affirmative.

So logical, so planned, like a raid, like a military maneuver. Hearing this conversation I reminded myself this was my husband we were discussing.

Feeling uncomfortable about having so little to tell me, the two agents proceeded to phone patch me through to Bill Gavit, Denver's Special Agent in Charge.

In his official government voice Bill stated his case. "Just let me say the Bureau is going to find Cliff. I have ordered all of our Denver resources directed to this search. Unfortunately, we can't do much until morning...." It was as if he were dictating some mundane memo. I was the wife of a veteran agent. I deserved better than this.

"Wait before you say anything further, Bill. I may be a widow as we speak. As far as I can tell the Bureau hasn't done anything since 5:15, and you want me to listen to some bureaucratic plan you have?"

"I understand, Sandy...." His voice less bureaucratic.

"Hardly. You sent him on this mission, and he went like he always does. Now what I've feared for twenty-one years is becoming a reality just when his career with this self-centered organization is almost over."

"Sandy, Cliff is our best mountain pilot; I believe we're going to find that he put the plane down in a remote valley somewhere near Meeker so that's where we'll start the search in the morning. I'm so sorry. We're going to find Cliff." Bill was firm in his conviction.

"I'm sure you are sorry, Bill. As sorry as you'd be if some faithful piece of equipment died." I needed to direct blame somewhere.

It was true, Cliff, being who he was, would never turn down an assignment even if offered the opportunity. His job was not work; it was his life's passion. I often wondered how our lives would have been different outside of the FBI. Was it the job or his passion for it?

Tragedy is defined as "an event causing great suffering, destruction and distress, such as a serious accident...."

At 12:55 a.m., Sunday, December 9, the Denver SAC sent a teletype to all FBI offices.

> *On 12/8/84, at approximately 5:45 p.m. MST, a light aircraft piloted by SA Browning vanished from FAA tracking radar in the vicinity of Meeker, Colorado.*
>
> *SA Browning was en route to Grand Junction, Colorado, from Laramie, Wyoming, where he had been assigned duties in connection with the Aryan Nation Special.*
>
> *SA Browning, a Bureau designated PIC (Pilot in Charge), was the sole occupant in the Cessna 212 aircraft. From his last recorded radio transmissions, apparently he had encountered bad weather and indicated his instruments were failing....*

Finally ushering John and Frank from my living room, I made the difficult calls to Tami and Ray. After hearing what little information I had, Ray and Tami decided they would rendezvous in Denver and drive overnight to Grand Junction to meet up with us to take part in the search effort the following morning.

In the midst of this chaos and sadness, I cautiously approached Bill and Scott's closed bedroom doors. My knock on their doors would change their lives forever.

"Bill, Scott, please wake up. I have to talk to you." My voice left no doubt the situation was grave.

Awakened, they stumbled downstairs behind me to the living room. I looked at their sleepy faces, and they looked at my pale tear stained cheeks. My words were going to turn their world upside down.

"You know your dad flew to Laramie today to fly a surveillance. Well, he left there this afternoon, and his plane has disappeared from radar. The FAA thinks the last transmission came in the vicinity of the Meeker wilderness. All we know..."

"Wait just one goddamn minute. Are you telling us the Bureau doesn't know where he is? That figures. I want to talk to Bill Gavit..." Bill's rage had found a target.

"Wait is right," spouted Scott. "Dad's a great pilot. He probably had a problem and put the plane down somewhere. Has anyone thought of that? Jesus, now what do we do?"

"Wait!" I shouted. "It's my turn. The Bureau is organizing a search party, leaving here for Meeker in a few hours. We'll need to put some supplies together. Tami and Ray are on the road and will meet us here. We need to work on getting ready for the search."

Bill, practicing his adulthood, ordered, "Okay, dammit, we have to get the supplies and shit ready for the search. Scott, get the camping stuff and survival gear out of the storage closet. Let's see, we need snow shoes, cross country skis, supplies and food at the very least. Mom, you need to get blankets and figure out what food we'll need. We don't know how long we'll be gone." His assurance that Dad would need us to find him lent urgency to preparing for the morning's search. Scurrying around gathering provisions gave us much needed direction for the daunting task before us.

Scott was confident his dad would come through. He always had. In his mind his dad was strong, bright and an excellent pilot who had promised him he would soon teach him to fly. His father didn't renege on his promises, and this would be no exception. His dad was still alive until we learned otherwise.

Secretly, I feared the worst. Perhaps Cliff had taken an unnecessary chance in bad weather trying to get home. No, he didn't take those kinds of chances. Other possibilities: someone had tampered with the plane's instruments. Homicide? Suicide? He seemed healthy emotionally, but he was approaching the end of a long, fulfilling career. At 48, retirement was optional in two years and mandatory in seven years at age 55. Was the future weighing on his mind? No, he didn't think like that.

In this black moment I recalled a recent recurring dream, more disturbing now.... Cliff and I were driving into Three Mile Canyon near Glenwood, carefully observing the narrowness of the canyon, and he was estimating a flight pattern in order to see a possible drug operation, hidden from roadside view. Together, we determined that he would need to fly slightly inside a narrow canyon to the west of Mt. Sopris. He said he wasn't sure he'd have time or space to maneuver back out from the narrow, box canyon walls. I encouraged him; he refigured, and we concurred that he could be successful. He went to the plane while I stayed put where I could watch. I saw the plane take off, circle over Sunlight ski area, fly across the valley, enter the canyon and disappear. Why now had I recalled this nightmare?

Shortly before sunrise, Tami and Ray arrived after a caffeine-induced, sleepless drive from Denver over the passes. I gave them what little information we had while Ray called the SAC in Denver to hear the report himself. He blamed the Bureau for taking so much of his father's time and now, perhaps, his life.

Without sleep, our ragtag, distraught family, loaded with survival gear, joined the Grand Junction rescue team at John's house before sunrise to convoy to Meeker where the search would be staged. As the kids and I now loaded blankets, water, food, skis and Cliff's pair of 30-year-old leather and cat-gut snowshoes, we burst out laughing. Cliff had been very proud of these antiquated winter shoes and defended them each time one of us pointed out their idiosyncrasies. He had the last laugh as now one of us would don these contraptions in our search to find him.

Snow flurries were scattered, but the roads were clear. No severe weather was forecast for Sunday, December 9. As our saddened convoy rolled along the deserted highway, our driver's static laden radio updated us on the details of the search: where the planes were, specifics on the ground search and everyone's ETA into Meeker.

The Colorado River, accented by distant mountain peaks, lured us easterly toward the Rifle turnoff then north toward Meeker. No greenery, only brown barrenness, left to give us hope in life's renewal, After reaching the junction of Highway 13 and turning north toward the probable crash site, snow flurries began to adhere to the landscape covering some of the bleakness. If Cliff had crashed into one of these snow covered mountains, he could possibly have skidded on the new snow to a safe landing. Going north, cedar and pinion encircled the vacant two-lane blacktop road. Occasionally, an abandoned one-room cabin would appear. Did life exist in this landscape? Did my husband?

Returning from a swim meet in Craig two summers ago, we had driven along this same two-lane road when providence had introduced us first hand to life's fragile nature. The nearly new blue pick-up traveling in front of us in our lane suddenly veered from the right lane, across the left lane, ascended airborne, and rolled multiple times before coming to a stop on its top in the green field blooming with life. In a split second all three passengers had flown from the vehicle. We all screamed hysterically as Cliff pulled onto the shoulder of the road. I was afraid to look. One moment they were alive and probably laughing inside the comfort of their truck. The next moment, three men were dead, scattered across the field. A fickle twist of fate for these three doomed men. A shocking reality for our little family returning from a fun filled day at the pool.

Would I once again encounter death on this road?

Suddenly, a terrible thought pierced my being. The worst possible scenario would be that Cliff and his plane wouldn't be found, leaving us with an open, ulcerated wound of the unknown. Or what if he were found alive but with a body so damaged as not to be able to function. Or worse yet, what if the team found him dead in the wreckage. *Please God, let them find him!* I screamed within myself.

Five dark vehicles, each with precious family members, moved steadily, silently like a military convoy north along the dreary highway. I turned to look forward then behind us to confirm my children and I were part of a mission where life or death would be the outcome. Snowflakes were swirling a bit more densely now as if to urge this patrol forward ever faster. From above, what did we look like? A motley, desperate team looking for its leader.

"Keep looking for any signs of the plane as we really don't know where we'll find it," John, our driver, directed us.

"Do you actually think it will be down this low? I thought the search was going to be concentrated on the mountain side. Do you have any idea where my dad is? This looks like another Bureau screw up." Ray's impatience was once again apparent.

An endless drive in cold silence terminated at the Rio Blanco County Courthouse, a three story red sandstone building situated importantly in the center of Meeker's Town Square. We pulled in behind the building, parked in the nearly empty gravel lot behind the jail, and marched like a procession of deadened spirits to the upstairs offices. Entering the heavy dark brown door, the atmosphere inside was as cold and lifeless as the stony chilliness of the outside walls.

The Denver search team, along with two planes, was already out. Dim morning light barely penetrated the dark grey haze. Deep snow covered the mountains and mesas where it was supposed he had landed. A soft blanket for landing, a cover for warmth or a comforting shroud.

De-briefing us on the progress of the search didn't take long. In tense life situations, details are often used to mask a situation and soften its piercing terror. If one focuses on the minutia, the problem will seem more manageable. Scanning the room's interior, I asked myself why government buildings are so bleak; always painted institutional green, like hospitals or other unpleasant places. Maybe its intent is to block out any feeling or emotion. Green is said to be soothing. On this day I would have preferred a different color.

Cardboard coffee cups served as something to wrap our hands around, something to grasp.

"Okay," Ray, said. "We've heard your report. Let's go. Dad made sure we were all trained in search and rescue, so we're ready. Frank, do you have our assignments? We brought plenty of gear." His statements were met with questioning looks as if someone there should have some answers.

"Actually, I don't want any of you to go on this search," I said. "Your dad is already missing; I don't need to be worrying about you and your brothers wandering around in this wilderness. The Bureau is conducting the search; they're responsible for this problem."

Ray loudly countered, "Look, I'm trained in survival techniques, and this is my dad. I have a right to be part of this search. The Bureau probably wouldn't know how to find him anyway. I'm going, like it or not, Mom."

"Scott and I agree with Ray, Mom," Bill said. "If anyone's going to find Dad, it should be us."

"I know you want to do this, but let's give this Bureau search party a chance. Ray, Bill and Scott—I need you here with me." They stayed.

Most importantly, I could not bear to have my sons find their dad in any condition other than alive and healthy. And that might not be their finding.

As I sat waiting for life or death news, it was hard to concentrate on words that were rolling from the Sheriff's mouth. Much like a caricature, I looked at him, saw his mouth moving, saw some expression in his eyes, but nothing registered. He was a mime in a room full of expressionless faces. We waited tirelessly, ignoring fatigue and jumping at every ring of the telephone. *Please let us hear news. Tell us something. Surely, you can find him, can't you?* I questioned silently.

After what seemed like days rather than hours, the Sheriff returned from his latest office phone call plodding, head down, into the room, as if to leave no footprint for fear some ancient spirits might be disturbed. Bending over, as he reached my chair, my husband's friend placed his roughened hands next to mine on the table. He took my hand; our eyes met.

"The search team has located the crash site, Sandy." I barely heard his words. My heart raced. He was no longer missing.

"Thank God!" I exploded. "Where did they find him?"

"The plane's wreckage is in a remote area off the mesa. It's very rugged terrain."

Tami and her brothers cheered. "Yea, they've found Dad's plane. See, we knew they'd find him."

I looked up. Why wasn't the Sherriff smiling? They had found Cliff. For me that was everything.

"How are you planning to bring him down?" I asked. "Have the medical crews been notified? How about hypothermia? It was terribly cold last night. And his injuries?"

I rattled on in my relief at the news of the successful search. "Oh, thank God, he's been found. At least, even if he's injured, we've found him. Now, we can do what's next which will probably be air transport to one of the Denver hospitals. When will you have him transported?" So many questions. So much to do. I lifted my eyes, searching the room's sorrowful faces.

"Sandy, look at me. There are no survivors. The Search Team has made it to the crash site, and Cliff's body has been identified." I continued to search his teary eyes for reassurance this wasn't so. No reassurance came. Only his sad bowed head.

The tragic message slowly seeped into my wrenching soul reminding me of the unfairness of life. I pounded the table over and over and over again wanting to feel the pain in my hands rather than my heart. "No, no, no! It can't be! Oh, God, no. It can't be." Anguish washed over me in a flood. Someone's muffled screams rebounded from the walls and ceiling, encircling me. I was right before. There is no God! Otherwise He would have been with my husband last night.

It couldn't be true. In a few minutes I would know that I had misunderstood the message. The Sheriff hadn't finished telling me what they had found. I had read Cliff's death into the message. Surely, that was not the case. I scanned the faces around me, all strong men with tears streaming down their chiseled faces. No, I hadn't misunderstood. This old building with that musty odor of dried glue, wood and newspapers now harbored a smell of death.

I forced my eyes upward to see my three fatherless sons standing close to each other, each of them crying and trying to hang on. Scanning the room, I found my beautiful daughter kneeling on the floor beside me just rubbing my arm. Ray fled the building, pounding his fists into the walls as he left. Bill, now a manly 16, was fighting the tears, recognizing his new role in this family. Scott stood stoically, ostensibly afraid to let the emotions surface for fear they could never again be controlled.

In all those years of worry about the possibility of this moment, I could never have known the devastation this piece of news would bring. My partner was gone, taking part of me with him. And we were a fractured family.

After what seemed to be hours but was probably closer to minutes, I rose teetering and hanging onto my chair. "I'm ready to go to the crash site," I said. Silence followed my request as I stood looking from uniformed persons to FBI Agents.

Finally, Frank spoke. "You can't go up there; the ground is unstable; in fact, the search team could barely make it." His voice lacked conviction.

"But I have to go. How will I ever know this really happened? How do I know it's him? Maybe that isn't his plane or maybe there is no plane up there. And if there is, is Cliff in it?" I looked around. "So who's going to take me to the site? You got up there once; you can go again. I'm not leaving here until I see the crash site."

Frank responded more firmly this time, "I was on the team that located the plane, and it's too dangerous. Any movement could trigger a slide. We must get the wreckage and Cliff out of there before there's more snow. It's not safe for you to go." I looked at my husband's best friend and partner and saw only sorrowful resignation.

"The Bureau took him away most of the time he was alive; now he's dead. Just once, can't this agency do the right thing for one of its own families?"

Other voices joined Frank's, begging me to understand the danger in revisiting the crash scene. They suggested I focus on memories instead of the death scene. Memories? What did these people know? As law enforcement officers, I saw them as part of the problem. Most were married to their careers just like Cliff and had no families left to build memories with.

As if to read my mind, search team members handed me some of Cliff's personal effects brought down from the crash scene: his flight Log Book, wallet, FBI credentials and his twisted, distorted wedding band. Its brokenness called to mind his broken body and my shattered spirit.

THIRTY-FOUR

And Then There Were Five

Alone and torn, my husband's body lay unattended on the side of the mountain while I sought assurance he would be transported that same afternoon to the mortuary in Glenwood. Seeming to read my mind, Frank reassured me, "We're going to treat him with the utmost respect, Sandy, just the way he would have treated us. The mortuary will contact you regarding final arrangements once they've received Cliff's body." Not Cliff, but his empty body.

"Final arrangements? Frank, I haven't seen him yet; I'm not sure that's my husband on that mountain. I don't believe it's Cliff up there. He wouldn't have taken a chance like that with the weather." I had no more to say. It was time to go.

Numbly rising from my seat on shaky posts that served as my legs, we moved as a family wounded and angry in our grief shuffling ourselves reluctantly down the stairs single file and into the waiting cars leaving Meeker and Cliff behind.

Sitting in the back seat of the Bureau car moving toward Junction, questions flooded my mind. Would things have turned out differently if I hadn't moved? What if Cliff had never learned to fly? Perhaps if we had been in Glenwood yesterday, the Denver office may not have called him. Possibly, they would have sent the Denver pilots to Laramie; Denver was closer. Glenwood Springs Airport was small and dangerous on approach; thus, he may have been spared. No, he always flew from the Junction airport.

271

In the face of tragedy the pangs of guilt began to surface. I shouldn't have taken this stupid Grand Junction job. I should have waited until Cliff retired and the boys had graduated. What was the rush? I'd already waited nearly twenty years. Being hired for a job I'd aspired to was a heady experience. I liked the feeling of being successful, of being chosen. My ego temporarily assuaged, pangs of guilt now percolated in my midsection. I had rationalized my decision to accept the job and move to Junction, thinking the Bureau would reassign him from Glenwood. Did I really believe they would do that for us?

At forty-six I now looked through the window to my own mortality. Cliff wasn't supposed to die at forty-eight. He was a man who had worked tirelessly for what he believed. He was honest, loving, faithful, law abiding. So where was the justice? If a person believes that God decides who dies and when, then what sense did this selection make? No answers came for the pain and turmoil working overtime to generate the constant stream of tears down my weary face.

Mile by gut-wrenching mile back Glenwood, I watched the vastness of the west reflected through my back seat window. Even the Colorado River paralleling the highway displayed a dullness rather than the crystal clarity she usually emitted. Traveling around the South Canyon bend, caressed by majestic snow dusted mountains, I experienced my fondness for Glenwood, the small town I had made my home and where I had raised my children.

We pulled the car off the interstate at the Glenwood Springs exit, passing by the Hot Springs Pool where we had spent so many hours, summer and winter. The diving platforms today were empty revealing to me only memories of father and daughter on those boards working together on the latest dive for her competition. Except in my mind, I would not see him there again. I was already looking through a window of past memories.

Our journey's miles were reduced to city blocks as we traversed the Colorado River over the Main Street bridge, down two blocks, turn right, go over the one lane bridge, turn left at the park, bear right, go straight to 1215 Riverview Drive. I could drive this route in my sleep. This little town had been my world, and I knew its every glimmer and blemish. Still, today I was fearful, fearful of going home, alone. An emptiness I had never before experienced crept into the security of our car.

As we neared the house I saw familiar and unfamiliar cars in the driveway and along the street. They knew. My friends knew. The city knew. Everyone knew something terrible had happened. I looked out the car window to see my friend, Julie, coming out the front door, one of the persons I most needed to see. As she patted my back, she uttered soft undecipherable words. I felt her reach for one of the boys. I needed her to love us through this terrible time.

That Sunday afternoon the house with the teal green door, a hue I had chosen so carefully, welcomed our small tightly knit sorrowing community. Their support poured in: food, flowers, snow shoveling, rooms in their homes for guests, trips to the Denver airport to pick up out-of-town family and friends, offers to do anything and everything. I had often speculated that we lived in a special place and that our family had connected with this unique mountain community, but until now I'd never realized how much we meant to so many people and how much they would mean to us.

Numbness is a welcome relief from having to face the reality of tragedy. It's a part of the shock, they say. I looked around the open kitchen of my house now filled with faces. I saw Mom and Dad standing in the dining room before the window framing Mt. Sopris. They stood stoically watching in shock. I remember asking them if they needed anything as if they were here for a dinner party.

These people in my kitchen were crying. Was I supposed to feed them or something? Oh yes, I remember now; there had been an accident. I remembered screaming in the Meeker Sheriff's office. Oh yes, they said they had found the plane, and I wanted to go to the site. Why didn't I go? Someone told me I couldn't. If I could have made the trek to the crash site, I could have comforted my husband and promised him that everything would be better from now on. I would offer to quit my new job in Junction and return home to Glenwood. After the Bureau we would have a life.

I would need to stay strong for everyone. The children and these nameless faces were counting on me. Maybe they still believed we were looking for him and wanted me to organize a search from Glenwood. I couldn't really tell.

These strange thoughts continued to flood my mind, fragments of trivia and meaningless drivel. I paused to look at my surroundings. What was familiar in the past now seemed foreign. But this is my house. I recognize the furniture and the brown flocked wallpaper going up the stairway. Oh—I remember, I think. We were in Meeker looking for Cliff's plane. It must have gone off course in the snowstorm. Yes, that's it. The goddamn Bureau should never have sent him to Laramie! One more screw-up. Bill and Scott said their dad always came through, and up to now, they'd been right whether it was a wreck on the ski slopes, wiping out the timing mechanism in a ski race, surviving being shot at, taking a second story fall, he always came through.

In the past he had.

Now I was home, and my house was filled with people. Nameless, faceless skeletons with rivers running down their faces. Silently, individually, they moved toward me, arms reaching to enfold me in their comforting embrace. I think they had this backward; I should be embracing them.

But my face is wet from a never ending fountain of tears. What has caused these, and why haven't they frozen to my face?

Hesitantly, I plodded to the master bathroom where the mirror reflected a face I would never have called mine. Eyes blank and swollen, red rimmed lids peering into nothingness. Skin pale and grey emphasizing fine lines around a mouth pursed in disbelief. Who was this person invading my personal space?

I looked around this small bath carved from a corner of our bedroom, surprisingly finding it as I had left it last week. My cosmetics were aligned in my medicine cabinet, and without looking I knew Cliff's shaving gear, after shave, deodorant and hair brush would be neatly settled on his side. Had no one told me they would no longer be needed? Or would they? This could be a huge mistake.

In a tragedy, everyone plays a role. For many victims it's helpful to be busy, and we were no exception, grateful for any diversion. Tami's mission was to call her dad's friends and relatives to inform them of his death and give them details of his memorial service, which we had sadly decided would be Wednesday, December 12, Ray's twenty-third birthday. She, along with Dave Yates, worked non-stop finding numbers for people who had meant so much to us in the past. People from the east coast would need time to make travel arrangements so she contacted them first. Dave coordinated all the Bureau details, taking care of the FBI contacts as well as the paperwork involved in an agent killed in the line of duty. Endless mounds of paper required to finalize the end of a life.

Ray helped to coordinate the people traveling into Denver and on to Glenwood, arranging accommodations and transportation. Bill organized everything he could organize. Scott manned the door and the phone, almost a full time job. Sleep, even with sedatives, was absent in this household as if giving in to slumber would accentuate the shock of waking up to our loss.

Because it was an accidental death, an autopsy was required. Its timing was important for me; I wanted it completed before the memorial service. The children and I needed closure. I called and requested one of our very good friends, Dr. Ben, to be present at the procedure to be sure it was carried out respectfully and to also validate for me that Cliff was the person brought down from the mountain in a body bag. I knew this was going to be devastating for him to see his friend sliced open. He later confirmed Cliff's identity and that the autopsy had been conducted reverently. I thanked him for doing something I knew was so difficult.

Amidst the chaos and planning, after the autopsy, but shortly before the cremation, the mortician called regarding my request to see the body.

"Sandy, this is Dr. Jamison. I've been speaking with Dave Yates, and he said you would like time with your husband's body. I can appreciate that request; not unusual for survivors." His even, consoling voice satisfied me that my request would be treated sensitively.

"Dr. Jamison, I hope you understand. I must see him. I have to know he's dead because I don't think I believe that yet. It could be just you and me. Just tell me what time, and I'll be there." I could hear my own begging.

"I wish I could do that, but I couldn't possibly put you through that. I can assure you he has passed, Sandy. He did not survive the crash. He died instantly with no pain."

"Fine for you, but I need to see for myself that he, not someone else, is in the body bag."

"No, that's not possible. You must trust me." His voice was now compassionate but firm.

"I don't trust anyone at this moment."

"Here's what I can do. I can arrange time for you to spend time with your husband's body in the body bag. I'll arrange the small conference room in an intimate fashion. You and your children can come in and spend time with him."

"So that's it?"

"Yes," he somberly stated.

On that snowy evening we snugly loaded ourselves into the Jeep wagon and drove silently to the mortuary. Kindly, the staff had arranged our viewing to occur after hours. We walked up the side stairs into the warmly lit building.

"Please come in," Dr. Jamison said. "I know how difficult this is for you. Please let me know if there is anything you need. And feel free to stay as long as you like." He had done this before.

Somewhat assured by the strength of his presence, we walked single-file into the viewing room where in this case there would be no actual viewing, just a sense of my husband's presence emanating from the carefully sealed body bag on a pristine white table with flowers discerningly arranged to give the appearance of a garden. The warmth of the room permeated my bones as I edged close to the sealed bag containing my husband's broken body. I bowed my head and cried. I wanted to unzip the bag; I wanted to see and touch my husband's face and feel his hand in mine.

As a Special Agent, Cliff was required to do a yearly update of his Last Will and Testament so I knew exactly how Cliff wanted his final arrangements to be carried out. He would be cremated, and his ashes would be scattered over Mt. Sopris, the imposing snow covered perfectly shaped mountain we loved. It was right for his final resting place.

On December 12, 1984, it was as if God had wiped out all the ugliness with His snowy paintbrush. A bright sun broke through turning these snowflakes to diamonds. Over 3,000 people arrived in a foot of new snow to attend the memorial service. The church was filled to overflowing, and the service was even broadcast outside to the overflow in the glittering snow. Law enforcement officers in respective uniforms and FBI agents from across the country encircled the sanctuary's seated congregation. Bill Baker, Associate Director of the FBI and Cliff's close friend, provided the eulogy, using Antoine du St. Exupery's *Wind, Sand and Stars* as the launch for his message. The formality and somberness fortified my inner strength.

Although this tragic event brought Cliff's closest friends together, the most touching moment came when Tami read a letter she had written to her dad immediately following his death. Sobs were heard from within the pews as she spoke.

Rising from my seat in the front row of the 1st Methodist Church to offer my raspy, broken voice in prayer and song, I grasped the hands of my two oldest children seated on either side of me. My four children were my reason for living. I needed them.

As I felt my children's strength, I recalled that day in 1963 when I had watched Jackie Kennedy standing with her two small children, alone against the world. At the time I had asked myself how she was able to be this model of strength. When all about her had crumbled, she had found the might to stand. She was doing what was expected and thus setting the standard for how a person conducts herself in the public face of tragedy. It must also have been important for her as a mother to demonstrate to her children her inner strength.

I had looked inside myself at that moment in 1963 and placing myself in her stead queried whether Cliff's position in the FBI would put me where she had stood. My concern was answered twenty-one years later.

Slowly, the saddened friends and family departed. The experts tell us we have funeral services, wakes, and memorial services for those of us left behind trying to make sense of a life no longer with us.

Christmas was upon us. As fate would have it, Cliff and I had done all of our shopping for the children on that memorable Thanksgiving weekend, so their presents were wrapped and stowed away in Glenwood where we would observe the holidays. While the children and I all agreed we would like to skip the pain of Christmas, I gently reminded them that we were still a family and needed to go through the motions; we couldn't quit! If we started down that path now, we might find ourselves disabled by life. Cliff and I had a rule that if you started something, you finished it. We now needed to celebrate a holiday we'd always celebrated.

"Maybe it's best if we follow some of our strongest traditions this year. Doing what we've always done won't take away the pain, but it may help us." I offered tenderly.

"Mom, we don't want to do that. We don't want to have Christmas at all." Bill forcefully opined.

"Yeah, what's there to celebrate? And I don't want any stupid presents," Scott's downcast teary face said everything.

"Look, we have to find some things to celebrate. Do you really think your dad would like what I see in this living room?" My voice was now above a whisper. We all knew the answer to my question. He would think we were wimps wallowing in our despair.

"Okay," Tami offered, "but could we do something different?"

"Like what? How about like not going to church on Christmas Eve? I'd go for that," Ray said hopefully.

We had been in church a lot lately for the wrong reasons.

"How about still having eggnog and cookies and the opening of one gift. Just like we've done in the past?" I asked.

The faces surrounding me on the living room floor said this was my preference, not theirs.

"Okay, I see it in your eyes. This isn't your idea of Christmas this year."

"No, Mom, it probably isn't. I don't even think this is the right time to discuss it. It hurts too much," Tami's words labored with pain.

"She's right, Mom. I don't want to think about this dumb holiday. I have another question. What should we do with the gifts we bought Dad?" Ray's response was angry, and his question poignant.

"Donate them to charity—we don't even have to open them, do we?" Tami's suggestion got unanimous approval. We had arrived at consensus on our first issue without our family head. In the middle of our tense Christmas discussion, close friends surprised us with a Christmas tree, put it up for us and poured eggnog in the spirit of loving friends. Christmas would never be the same for us, but my children would move on, have their own families and eventually would establish their own traditions for their loved ones. Did that mean this pain would go away? No.

Christmas evening, after an afternoon of skiing and a modified Christmas dinner, I walked down the hall to our bedroom to get a prescription pill from the bathroom. It was time for a new infusion of pain numbing drugs. Looking into the bathroom mirror I saw a haggard face and sad eyes. This face looked like the one I had seen in this same mirror a few days earlier. *Oh God, No!* I screamed in a muffled voice. Cliff's red terry cloth bathrobe, like an apparition, was hanging on the hook of the door staring into the mirror as a background for my shattered face. I grabbed his robe, one that Tami had made for him and one that he loved. I could smell my husband and feel him in the fiber of the cloth. I clutched the garment in its entirety, pulling it from the hook, wrapping my arms and shoulders in its red cocoon. Sinking to the floor, wrapped shroud like, my racking grief swelled to overflowing.

I lay there for some time, feeling sorrow and anger. *Even if things weren't always so right for us, why did you have to leave? Why did you abandon us? You always told me you would die young; did you really know that? I've spent so many years blaming the Bureau for your absences. Now, they've finally won. It doesn't seem fair to be angry with you—angry with a dead person? But I am.*

What to do with the robe? I would know when it was right to let it go.

THIRTY-FIVE

From There to Here

Just because the calendar said January didn't mean the grieving was over or that it had even begun. I flipped the calendar page to January 1985, and the 8th stared at me, the one month anniversary of the "accident," a euphemism for telling myself Cliff had not died. In talking to myself, I carefully chose my words as if to mitigate the stabbing pain associated with the truth of my new status: not single, not married, not divorced but widowed. Each month I'd dread the 8th, each season I'd dread the holidays, each birthday would be sad. Each piece of mail addressed to Cliff would confirm my December tragedy.

The calendar, my enemy, stared back at me, a reminder that school would soon be resuming. I had put off the decision to return to Grand Junction as long as possible, undecided if I should move back "home" to Glenwood Springs where my friends argued that my support lay in this special valley I'd called home for eleven years. I listened. In many ways it would be easier to give in and move back to my old life, familiar and comforting. I hadn't yet discussed this possibility with Bill and Scott because it had to be my decision. What would I be telling them if I resigned? That it was okay to quit if things got rough? That I could walk out and leave people in the lurch because something bad had occurred in my life?

The Grand Junction school district had been patient. I couldn't hold them off forever. If I weren't coming back, they would need to hire my replacement. It was timely when Jim, my principal, called to ask if he could come over for lunch. We agreed to meet at Penelope's, the new restaurant on the bluff overlooking the Roaring Fork River. As we took our seats next to the window, Jim pointed to the sky behind me where a beautiful bald eagle soared, his elegance a statement about the beauty of life in the midst of tragedy. Wordless, I acknowledged the sight. We made small talk about the holidays, and he filled me in on what he had planned for second semester.

"Sandy, I haven't come over here to badger you about returning to the building. Take as much time as you need. You just need to know we want you to stay with us: the building staff, students, parents and the district. But we also understand that you've suffered a terrible loss. When you've decided, let me know. I'll support you either way."

"Thanks, Jim for your support and for coming over today. This is a difficult decision. I've lived here a long time, and I know my friends expect me to come back."

"They do want you back. I talked to your superintendent, and he said he would make a job for you here."

"Nick's a wonderful man. He's the one responsible for my going into administration. Jim, give me the rest of the week, and I'll call you with my plans."

What was I going to do? Before my Glenwood friends started asking me questions, I had assumed I'd return to my Junction job. I'd made a commitment to them for the school year, and I wasn't big on backing out of obligations. And it wasn't just the job, it was Bill and Scott, my teachers, and my students. I had wanted this job, and I had accepted it with pride. Wasn't all that worth something?

After discussions with my children, I decided the right decision was to move forward. I had made a career decision, and I would stick with it. We packed up the Christmas presents. I drove one car, listening to Neal Diamond's emotional songs, and Bill drove the other with Scott. I was now alone, not just in this car on this journey but perhaps forever. God knows, I'd had plenty of practice going solo, but this was different. Crossing those whitewashed hills surrounded by snow packed mountains, I questioned my strength. Would I really be able to do this? Would I? Could I?

Wait, what choice did I have? I had to make it for Bill and Scott. Tami and Ray were living independently, but my two youngest needed a parent, at least one. So I would have to dig deep for the strength to see that all three of us made it.

Closing in on Grand Junction in the Sunday night darkness, dread began to creep upward into my throat choking my earlier resolve. *This was a mistake wasn't it? I should return to Glenwood Springs. I know almost no one in Junction. Here I'm alone, really alone. Who am I kidding that I can be this super mom, this super educator, this super woman?*

In the darkness we pulled up to our rented townhome, grabbed bags from the cars, put the key in the lock, turned on the lights, and watched the whole place come alive with flowers, candles, candies, a refrigerator full of food, all the laundry done, beds changed, new towels and other beautiful touches. I stood there, open mouthed, as tears began their familiar trip down my weary face. Who was responsible for this? I scarcely knew anyone in this community. Then I found on my bed a huge black and white stuffed panda bear wearing a bright red ribbon with a large, beautiful card attached, signed by all the teachers in my building. Angels, I was surrounded by angels. I buried my face in the soft fur of my now most favorite bear. How did they know what it would be like for me to come back to this empty house? They knew because they cared.

Sitting before the mountains of paperwork strewn before me on the kitchen table in our small Grand Junction townhome, I perused the wrinkled, redundant piles before me. Death certificates, bank statements, insurance queries, checks, condolence letters and just plain junk mail demanding my attention. Put off too long, what had once been carefully sorted stacks were now disheveled mountains of tasks, which could no longer be ignored. Their black and white carefully worded messages were now demands.

My husband's death had generated huge volumes of paper, each day a mill grinding out yet another ream of forms. Everyone wanted confirmation of his death along with confirmation that I was both the survivor and still living. Often I questioned the latter. Numerous forms relevant to our individual status needed to be completed by the survivor, me. Each laborious detail commanded my attention, bringing back to mind the life Cliff and I had shared for twenty-six years. Not only did they demand information about him, they wanted every detail of my life with him and since his death. Our lives had been reduced to answers contained on these mundane questionnaires.

On this particular Saturday morning, I had declared to Bill and Scott that this was the day I would enter this unpleasant world of bureaucratic forms. They took off for Glenwood, avoiding what sounded like a dreadful task.

Rearranging the stacks before me, I was reminded of the application form I had completed for Cliff's entry into the Bureau in 1963. That, too, was endless, asking question upon question about him, his family, his friends, job history, education and on and on. That process signaled the beginning of his life as an FBI agent. What lay strewn before me marked the end of my husband's life in the Bureau. I had come full circle.

I had been less than enthusiastic about Cliff's decision to pursue an FBI career. I feared the danger inherent in law enforcement work and what this life would mean for me and for our two small children. Cliff's reassurances were distinct and many. Despite my reservations, we had moved forward with the application process.

There is no villain in this story although I thought the FBI was when I began this account, but the Bureau was only the jet fuel propelling us forward, the bureaucracy in which we lived as we moved around the country conforming to its dictates. Now I know we all live within the confines of something: our job, church, family, neighborhood or community conventions. We belong sometimes more comfortably than at other times.

And then our world splits open, demanding realignment. My husband is dead; suddenly I don't belong to a marriage, not to a community of couples or traditional families. My life can never be the same. Can it be better? I don't know. Will it be different? Yes, I know it will.

If there is a positive side, I've had training for my new status. I learned how to fix most things like flat tires and flat hair, leaky faucets and leaky scabs on scraped up knees, broken lawn chairs and broken hearts, formal dinner and formal dresses.

Now my practice was luring me forward into new rivers swirling with life where I would continue to be mesmerized by their deep blue clarity of purpose. I would sit and listen for reassurance as I moved forward to claim my place in a new world I would create. In using my experience as an FBI wife, I would look with new insight at my life's trajectory.

Acceptance comes slowly to those who grieve, and it doesn't come consistently. One day you're almost there; the next you're back inside that black cloud. One day your life feels almost normal; you schedule lunch, go shopping, return home and then out of the blue you pick up the mail to see most of it addressed to Clifton Browning.

Six months after Cliff's death I sat alone in my pretty white sundress on the cruise ship deck absorbing the sun's rays into my thirsty skin while listening to the yearnings inside myself. I wanted to live. I wanted a second chance at life. In time I would want to share my life with another man. It wasn't a thought; it was a knowing.

And I did.

Acknowledgments

There are people in one's life for whom words of thanks are so understated to be almost trite. My husband, Ray Windsor, falls into that category. Throughout this project, he has been my first read and my stalwart supporter, sitting up with me at night as I dredged memories I wanted hidden. During those times he listened as only a person can who truly loves another. This book could not have happened without him. Next to him are my four children who encouraged me to go for it, to plow through the hard stuff and finish it. My deepest gratitude. Then, there is Lighthouse Writers Workshop and all the tremendously talented people who assisted me with the craft side, not to mention my mentor, William H. Henderson who coached me for almost a year, encouraging me, calling me on issues that kept re-appearing. And to my writing partners, Sylvia and Arlene, who wouldn't allow me to quit and called me on issues when I didn't want to go deep enough into the story, my thanks. To all of these people along with so many students and friends like Lori Ella Miller, Sherri Loys, Julie Andersen, Shirley Cannon, Shana Kelly and Laura Lee who kept me on tract over the nine year period, my humble gratitude.

Printed in the United States
By Bookmasters